T0329944

International Comparative Employee Relations

To our wives, Ann and Tiziana

International Comparative Employee Relations
The Role of Culture and Language

Edited by

Karl Koch

Emeritus Professor of Modern Languages, Business School, London South Bank University, UK and Visiting Professor, China Three Gorges University, Yichang, China

Pietro Manzella

Senior Research Fellow, Association for International and Comparative Studies in the field of Labour Law and Industrial Relations (ADAPT, www.adapt.it), Italy

Edward Elgar PUBLISHING

Cheltenham, UK • Northampton, MA, USA

Published by
Edward Elgar Publishing Limited
The Lypiatts
15 Lansdown Road
Cheltenham
Glos GL50 2JA
UK

Edward Elgar Publishing, Inc.
William Pratt House
9 Dewey Court
Northampton
Massachusetts 01060
USA

A catalogue record for this book
is available from the British Library

Library of Congress Control Number: 2019951018

This book is available electronically in the **Elgar**online
Business subject collection
DOI 10.4337/9781788973229

ISBN 978 1 78897 321 2 (cased)
ISBN 978 1 78897 322 9 (eBook)

Typeset by Servis Filmsetting Ltd, Stockport, Cheshire

Printed and bound by CPI Group (UK) Ltd, Croydon, CR0 4YY

Contents

Figures

Tables

Contributors

Chris Brewster had substantial industrial experience and received his doctorate from the London School of Economics before becoming an academic. He is now a part-time Professor of International Human Resource Management at Henley Business School, University of Reading, UK, specializing in international and comparative HRM. He has been involved as author or editor in the publication of more than 30 books, more than 100 chapters in other books and well over 200 articles.

Richard Hyman has been one of the most prominent figures in British and European employment relations research for most of the past four decades, and is Emeritus Professor of Industrial Relations at the London School of Economics and founding editor of the *European Journal of Industrial Relations*. He has written extensively on the themes of industrial relations, trade unionism, industrial conflict and labour market policy, and is author of a dozen books as well as some two hundred journal articles and book chapters. His comparative study *Understanding European Trade Unionism: Between Market, Class and Society* (Sage, 2001) is widely cited by scholars working in this field. His latest book, *Trade Unions in Western Europe: Hard Times, Hard Choices* (with Rebecca Gumbrell-McCormick), was published by Oxford University Press in 2013 and reprinted in a revised edition in 2018.

Karl Koch is Emeritus Professor of Modern Languages at the Business School, London South Bank University and Visiting Professor at China Three Gorges University, Yichang. He has published widely on German Area Studies, German Industrial Relations, and Comparative International Industrial Relations. His current research focuses on cultural diversity in international management and European models of employee participation.

Pietro Manzella is a Senior Research Fellow at the Association for International and Comparative Studies in the Field of Labour

Law and Industrial Relations (www.adapt.it). He received a PhD in Labour Relations from the University of Modena and Reggio Emilia and was a Visiting Fellow at Cornell University (USA) and the LSE (UK). He is currently pursuing research in the role of language in the disciplines of Labour Law and Industrial Relations. Translation and terminology issues in comparing and contrasting different labour practices and institutions are the main focus of his research, in addition to the role of English as a lingua franca.

Peter Norlander, PhD, is an Assistant Professor of Human Resources and Employment Relations at Loyola University Chicago Quinlan School of Business. He received his doctorate from UCLA Anderson School of Management. His research on outsourcing, guest workers, and human resources practices have been published in journals including the *Thunderbird International Business Review*, *Journal of Population Economics*, *Migration Letters* and *E-Journal of International and Comparative Labour Studies*.

John Opute, PhD, has a diverse educational and working background from Nigeria, USA, Canada and Europe. He has held several senior Human Resource and Management positions spanning over 20 years in various multinational corporations. He is Senior Lecturer and Course Director, Post Graduate Human Resource programmes at London South Bank University, London and his research interest is in Comparative International Human Resource Management and Employee Participation.

Valentina Paolucci is Assistant Professor of Human Resource Management and Employment Relations at the School of Business, University College Dublin. She obtained a PhD in Comparative Employment Relations from Warwick Business School (IRRU). She held visiting fellowships at the Centre for Sociological Research (KU Leuven) and at the Employment Relations Research Centre (University of Copenhagen). Her paper, 'The role of collective bargaining in addressing flexibility and security', published in the *European Journal of Industrial Relations* received the International Labour and Employment Relations Association (ILERA) 2016 Best Paper Prize.

Susanne Tietze is Professor of Multilingual Management at Sheffield Business School, Sheffield Hallam University. In recent years she has researched the impact of the English language on the production of management knowledge and also the more 'hidden' role of translation as a communicative means to both share and transform knowledge. The role of language agents in multilingual work communities is a related stream of research and she is Principal Investigator of a UK Research Council grant which focuses on exploring individual and collective agency of situated para-professional translators and interpreters.

Aurora Trif is an Associate Professor in International Employment Relations and HRM at Dublin City University Business School. She holds a PhD in Industrial Relations from London South Bank University. She was a Postdoctoral Researcher at the Max Planck Institute for the Study of Societies in Cologne. Her research interests include comparative employment relations, precarious work, collective bargaining and trade unions in Eastern Europe. Aurora was the Principal Investigator for the EU-funded PRECARIR project focused on the strategies of social partners to address precarious work in nine Central-Eastern European countries and Greece (2014–2016). She has published in leading academic journals such as the *British Journal of Industrial Relations* and the *European Journal of Industrial Relations*.

Rainer Trinczek is currently Dean of the Faculty of Humanities, Social Sciences, and Theology at Friedrich-Alexander-Universität Erlangen-Nürnberg, Germany. Professor Trinczek is a highly respected expert in German co-determination, the sociology of work and organizations, management sociology, working-time practices and demographics. A former president of the German Industrial Relations Association he has written widely on the changing nature of German industrial relations.

Michael Whittall is a Research Fellow at Friedrich-Alexander-Universität Erlangen-Nürnberg, Germany and Nottingham Trent University, UK. He is renowned for his work on the sociology of work and industrial relations. His research interests include the future of work in a digital age, transnational employment representation, in particular European Works Councils, the challenge of multilingualism for employee representatives, globalization, German co-determination and life-long learning, he continues to publish widely as well as teach in all these areas.

Jing Xi is an Associate Professor of Foreign Languages and International Management at China Three Gorges University

(CTGU). He is also the executive director of CTGU Research Institute for Cross-Cultural Studies and Employment Relations. With a great interest in cross-cultural communications, he has focused on economic transitions in China, and the employment relations of China's multinational and joint-venture companies from a cross-cultural perspective. He is a frequent contributor to national journals relating to cultural encounters, translation practice and industrial relations and has over a dozen published papers.

Foreword

Richard Hyman

To a high degree – many would say, primarily – the character of national systems of industrial or employment relations is the outcome of material forces such as economic structure, the state of the labour market, or the socio-legal framework defining the rights and obligations of the different actors. But such influences are mediated by subjective factors: the material context shapes constraints and opportunities, but these are set to work according to the beliefs, objectives, traditions and understandings of those involved. To an important extent, the constellation of these subjective factors (or 'culture', in the familiar shorthand) is nationally specific. As the contributions which follow make clear, this specificity is reinforced by the idiosyncrasies of language.

The term 'industrial relations', still widely used in the English-speaking world, has a literal equivalent in few other languages: in most countries, scholars address the employment relationship in different terms. More fundamentally, how the industrial relations 'actors' identify themselves and their interrelationships varies linguistically. In northern Europe, the nomenclature for employers and employees translates, literally, as 'work-givers' and 'work-takers'. Of course, in everyday life this need not mean that employment is perceived as a 'gift relationship' between employer and employee. Nevertheless, it is hard to imagine that the words have no effect whatsoever on perceptions. To refer to employers as 'bosses', one may safely assume, encourages a very different mind-set and consequent differences in behaviour.

In much of Europe, trade unions and employers' organisations are routinely described as the 'social partners'. To the native English speaker, until very recently at least, the phrase has appeared bizarre. For many British trade union militants, the phrase was enough to confirm their prejudices that their continental counterparts were not 'real' trade unionists but were bent on class collaboration. Similar perplexity is caused by the notion of 'social dialogue', which is central to the industrial relations project of the European Union. Yet words – particularly when they undergo translation – are not always what they seem. We may note, for example, that in many European languages 'social affairs' is the closest available equivalent to 'industrial relations'. The idea of 'social partnership' has many available meanings, some more 'collaborationist' than others. One relatively prosaic reading is that trade unions are embedded in a host society, have a recognised status within it and also possess the capacity to shape its development. This, one may note, has made the notion of unions as social partners suspect to many on the right as well as to those on the left. And indeed, it may go against the grain of culturally embedded assumptions for governments to embrace explicitly anti-union policies similar to those pursued by Margaret Thatcher in Britain if trade unions' status is legitimated by the discourse of social partnership.

It is interesting to note that though this discourse has been embraced by the EU for almost half a century, before enlargement in 2004 the term 'social partners' appeared in literal translation in only a minority of community languages. Certainly *Sozialpartner* is used in the German texts, *partenaires sociaux* in French, *sociale partner* in Dutch. But Italian has *parti sociali* and Spanish *interlocutores sociales*. In the Scandinavian languages, the equivalent term translates as 'labour market parties'; English uses the prosaic 'management and labour'. What difference does this make for industrial relations practice? In France, the term *partenaires sociaux* seems to have been invented by employers and modernising politicians in the aftermath of the explosion of militancy in 1968. The literal equivalents are used in Greek and Portuguese, and in the languages of the new member states of the enlarged EU, but have no obvious bearing to actual industrial relations practice. But where a particular discourse is more firmly embedded, we can reasonably expect that aspirations, actions and vocabularies of motive will be shaped accordingly.

Much more generally, we may note that identical words in different languages may have different meanings. Can we assume that the French *syndicat* means the same as the English 'trade union'? In Britain, most union members are essentially passive; membership is a reflection of social custom, or a form of insurance against the risks of the employment relationship. In France, traditionally, to become a paid-up member has been an act of commitment, often indicating a willingness to devote time and energy to the work of the collective. This helps explain why French unions, internally divided and with the lowest membership density in western Europe, nevertheless often seem to punch above their weight. We assume at our peril that the meaning of union membership is the same cross-nationally.

Many of the concepts we use, moreover, are simply untranslatable. There is no accurate French translation of the English 'shop steward', for there is no equivalent French reality: a trade union representative, selected (often informally) by the members in the workplace, and recognised as an important bargaining agent by the employer. Neither *délégué syndical* nor *délégué du personnel* is appropriate: both terms denote completely different types of representative, neither of which has an analogous negotiating role. For the same reason it is quite wrong to translate the German term *Vertrauensleute* – though this is often done – as shop stewards. Likewise, there is no real English term for cadre or *prud'homme*, for the structuring of the technical-managerial workforce, and the adjudication of employment griev-ances, follow very different lines in Britain from those in France. In the reverse direction, to a French or German writer unfamiliar with Anglo-American practice it might seem obvious how to translate *plan social* or *Sozialplan*; but unfortunately the phrase 'social plan' would be meaningless to an English reader who did not already understand the French and German institutional reality. (The Eurofound glossary suggests 'redundancy programme', which is clearly more accurate though not elegantly literal.)

Analogous translation issues bedevil any use of survey data for comparative analysis. Within the EU, 'benchmarking' through the 'open method of coordination' – a term which until very recently was meaningless in any language – rests firmly on the questionable construction of labour market variables. The assumption is that every national labour market or industrial relations system consists of bundles of identical building blocks. Yet we cannot reasonably assume that such terms as 'social inclusion' have the same meaning in different national contexts and languages. The OECD measures of the interaction between employment protection and 'labour market performance' tend similarly to rest on definition by fiat. The consequence for much variable-based cross-national comparison is technical sophistication used to regress the most dubious of 'variables': 'garbage in, garbage out'. Cynics might argue that in policy-oriented research, the definition of comparative indicators is deliberately conditioned to the desired findings.

Ever since Hofstede's seminal work, many of those who adopt cultural perspectives on the world of work tend to assume that national cultures are stable and homogeneous. The opposite is commonly the case. National cultures are typically internally contradictory and contested, and struggles to (re)define their meaning are a source of constant dynamics.

Die Grenzen meiner Sprache bedeuten die Grenzen meiner Welt, wrote Wittgenstein: the boundaries of my language mean the boundaries of my world. The causalities are reciprocal: we cannot usually articulate what we do not perceive, yet if we lack the language to articulate our social world then we do not fully understand it. Let me add that language (like culture) is constantly changing, in ways that sometimes enrich but often impoverish it. For example, think only of the restricted compass of 'international English', the working language of many international organisations.

Linguistic change is often a manifestation of power, a reflection of the capacity of those with economic resources or political dominance to shape our perceptions of the social world. Take the case of 'flexicurity', a concept originally invented to denote specific national regimes (as, for example, in Denmark) where statutory limitations on individual dismissals are relatively weak but where compensatory systems of generous unemployment benefits and active labour market policy provide alternative supports for employment and income security. The term was enthusiastically embraced by EU policymakers at the turn of the century as a rationale for removing labour market 'rigidities' (in other words, weakening workers' employment rights) without compensating measures to sustain security. As many studies have documented, the strategic intervention of employer representatives and neoliberal politicians at both national and EU levels achieved a dramatic transformation in the discourse of labour market policy, so that a Google search for 'flexicurity' will today yield some two million results. Such coercive internationalisation of the language of industrial relations has very obvious material results.

The complex interplay between beliefs, concepts, rhetoric and the social realities of work is a seriously under-researched area of industrial relations. Karl Koch and Pietro Manzella have performed a great service in compiling this wide-ranging survey of the issues involved. The contributing authors provide a rich survey of the ways in which words and social relationships interconnect, and the pitfalls that confront any unwary investigator into cross-national similarities and differences. This book will help us all reduce the risks of becoming lost in translation.

Acknowledgements

This edited book is the result of the shared curiosity and interest of the two editors, Karl Koch and Pietro Manzella, in finding a new approach to understanding the language and culture underlying the similarities and differences in the international area of comparative employee relations. The book has benefitted enormously from the expertise and enthusiasm of the contributors who confronted the challenges of this task; we would like to warmly thank all of those that accepted our invitation to contribute.

Appreciation and thanks are due to the Business School, London South Bank University, which provided generous support enabling the researchers to actively engage in the production of the book.

Also, many thanks to the Association for International and Comparative Studies in the field of Labour Law and Industrial Relations (www.adapt.it), the research of which in this field has constituted the basis for the present volume.

Numerous colleagues, from Asia, Europe, North America, and Africa have enriched our perception through their comments and dialogue. Thank you to Sasha Koch for her assistance in the visual realization, Figures 3.1 and 3.2, of the conceptual model presented in Chapter 3.

Introduction: The Language and Culture Perspective in Employee Relations

Karl Koch and Pietro Manzella

The book provides an insight into the deeper structures underlying the similarities and differences in Employee Relations Systems by synthesis of cultural, language and specific employee relations factors. Enabling the understanding of those involved in international and comparative employee relations matters in a more insightful way than current approaches. It also intends to facilitate a holistic approach to translations, and understanding, of employee relations-focused texts. One of the central issues is that translations, understandings, in specific contexts, such as labor law, employee relevant technical matters, in areas as, for example, collective bargaining and arbitration processes, achieve clarity through the inclusion of cultural characteristics.

The book, therefore, includes an in-depth explanation and analysis of specific and general concepts of employee relations within this contextual field. It identifies examples of how cultural identification shapes, directs and influences distinctive systems of employee relations—moving toward a translation objective which is anchored in a holistic approach providing a deeper understanding of the subject matter.

Employee Relations have been subject to enormous changes over the last decades with the impact of globalization, in terms of trade agreements, the creation of economic and socio-economic blocs, geopolitical constellations and the emergence of developing economies.

The development has generated an essential need for both comprehending and transmitting employee relations issues within the international, as well as the national, context. Although cultural perspectives have been considered as a variable in understanding different national employee systems, particularly in the significant field embracing management studies, there have been no recent publications focusing specifically on language and culture. There is, of course, an increasing necessity for this perspective as the interconnectivity of economies, driven by globalization, demands an understanding of comparative employee systems based on a more in-depth analysis encompassing both language and culture. It is posited that the central mechanism for this is a holistic understanding which requires an intimate link between language and culture.

International impact, which has been a driving force on institutions, employee relations actors, ideologies and the broader socio-economic frameworks, such as corporatism and varieties of capitalism, for example, has created the dynamism for change. In this respect, the book provides an insight into the dynamics of shifting cultural and translation factors, the former adapting and the following expanding concepts and terminologies.

The book ascertains the language and cultural characteristics contributing to an understanding of translation issues in international comparative employee relations. To facilitate this in a conceptual model, for comprehension and pragmatic application in the broad area of comparative employee relations, this is synthesized from selected existing conceptual models. Allowing both discussion and explanation of language and cultural factors, as related to employee relations in the international context, and consequently provide the basis of more in-depth analysis and interpretation of employee relations in different national contexts.

LANGUAGE AND CULTURE IN THE INTERNATIONAL CONTEXT

The globalized world with its diversity of multilingual societies has stimulated recent research interest focused on the relationship and efficacy of language and culture. There has, of course, always been recognition and understanding of the intimate link between language and culture and this connection has been investigated from many disciplinary perspectives. Recent research, however, has increasingly had its genesis in multi- and interdisciplinary approaches, creating conceptual research models on which methodological strategies can be evolved.

The significance of language and culture has accelerated during the last decades as a consequence of globalization and in particular the demands of the broad areas of economics and finance, business, management, innovation and technology for the internalization of mutual communication and understanding. Globalization in the broadest sense is, of course, nothing new. What is new is the rate of acceleration of the factors impacting on the phenomenon of globalization: the shifting boundaries of politics, of global institutions, economic connectivity, the definitions of internationalism and global relations, and the overarching issues of resources and environmentalism.

The mechanisms facilitating the complex intercourse of these relationships are numerous but two factors are critical: First, the continuous technological advancement of the Internet and associated communication developments and, second, the medium of communication, language. The latter has two aspects. First, the phenomenon of English as a global language and, second, the essential connection this has to other languages. It is paramount that language and culture are not viewed as separate entities but as a mutual dependent unit of analysis which is defined by the specific register under investigation.

Placing this understanding in the international context demonstrates that language and culture are essential components of nation-states' international competitiveness and, therefore, the comprehension of correct technical terminology across and in between languages has to be viewed from a broad perspective.

Further evidence for these perspectives can be derived from the data used by the World Economic Forum (2018) to construct an international comparative index measuring the performance of individual nation states in the global economic environment. The Global Competitiveness Index 4.0 2018 is based on a substantial number of performance criteria for each country or economic region, inclusive of cultural determinants predetermined in areas such as education and ability to innovate. It, therefore, integrates macroeconomic and micro business aspects, the latter including public and private institutions, health and infrastructure. The result engenders one index which reflects the competitiveness, and the productivity and efficiency, of the region or country. The index provides a useful tool for identifying critical variables in the economic and social matrix of nation states.

This analysis allows deductions on what particular combinations of variables add to incremental international competitive advantages

Table I.1   The Global Competitive Index 4.0 2018 rankings

Economy	Rank	Score, Scale: 0–100
United States	1	85.6
Singapore	2	83.5
Germany	3	82.8
Switzerland	4	82.6
Japan	5	82.5
Netherlands	6	82.4
Hong Kong SAR	7	82.3
United Kingdom	8	82.0
Sweden	9	81.7
Denmark	10	80.6
Australia	14	78.9
China	28	72.6
Italy	31	70.8
Nigeria	115	47.5

Note: Covering 140 economies, the Global Competitive Index 4.0 measures national competitiveness—defined as the set of institutions, policies, and factors that determine the level of productivity.

Source: Data adapted and taken from *The Global Competitive Report 2018* (World Economic Forum, 2018).

of countries. Table I.1, for example, reveals the concentration of countries in the top of the table, with multilingual societies with educational policies encouraging and nurturing the acquisition of foreign languages, which contribute to their international competitiveness. A closer analysis of the factors used in the Index 4.0 2018 construction also points to the linkages of technology and innovation, for instance, to effective predilections from behavioral attitudes.

Understanding languages is, therefore, indispensable in a comprehensive understanding of contrasting and comparing employee relations within the current international framework. It also raises the question of which languages are predominant in the interconnected global world, a question closely linked to the power languages can exercise. A useful indication is provided by the Power Language Index (PLI), an index constructed from 20 indicators with the aim of measuring the influence of language.

Table I.2 reveals that the top six languages are also the official

Table I.2   Power Language Index (PLI) ranking for top 10 languages

Language	Rank	Score	Native
English	1	0.889	446.0
Mandarin	2	0.411	960.0
French	3	0.337	80.0
Spanish	4	0.329	470.0
Arabic	5	0.273	295.0
Russian	6	0.244	150.0
German	7	0.191	92.5
Japanese	8	0.133	125.0
Portuguese	9	0.119	215.0
Hindi	10	0.117	310.0

Source: Data adapted from World Economic Forum (2018).

languages of the United Nations. The ranking order of Table I.2 also confirms that English is the most powerful language using the PLI indicators; this is reflected by the fact that of the G7 nations, three, namely the USA, UK and Canada, belong to this category. It furthermore is strengthened by the historical distribution and use of English as the global lingua franca. The interpretation of employee relations terminology in the 'global' English context is highly dependent on the cultural linkage of the specific region, country or specific setting of usage.

Cultural factors can, therefore, be viewed as complex aggregates adding to the broader economic effects of countries, and a specific understanding of these factors provide an incremental international competitive advantage.

EMPLOYEE RELATIONS AND CULTURE IN THE INTERNATIONAL CONTEXT

The distinctive relationship between culture and global economic developments and trends can be identified, the nation states' economic efficacy gains from an understanding of this and contributes to national wealth.

Specific studies have analyzed aspects of national economic

Table I.3   Business systems and matching clusters of selected countries

Cluster 1	Cluster 2	Cluster 3	Cluster 4
Canada	Germany	Greece	Finland
UK	Austria	Turkey	Denmark
Australia	Belgium	Portugal	Sweden
Switzerland	Ireland	Spain	
USA	Netherlands	Hungary	
New Zealand		Slovakia	

Source: Data taken and adapted from Hotho (2014).

systems which include cultural characteristics. Thus, for example, Hotho (2014) collected a list of nine variables which included institutional data but also evaluation of 'behavioral' characteristics, such as trust and paternalism, determinants of cultural traits, and applied these to business systems.

Despite the limitations of the number of factors Hotho used as variables, clusters could be constructed which emphasized simple groups of countries sharing arrays of common cultural attributes which distinctly, and significantly, impact on employee relations.

Thus Table I.3 demonstrates that over and above economic organization, institutional arrangements, the predispositions stemming from industrialization processes and socio-political variables, there are differences and similarities in cultural characteristics shaping countries. The significance of the cultural input, focusing, for example, on skills, trust and authority, is illustrated by the following comment on Hotho's findings: '. . .the ways that skills are developed, certified and controlled exert significant influence on prevalent employment relations and work systems, as do the dominant norms governing trust and authority relationships' (Sorge et al., 2015).

A fundamental need to include cultural factors for a full understanding of employee relations is substantiated from the above analysis. However, the identification and definitions used for interpreting cultural characteristics, particularly when translating these between languages, is highly dependent on the specific context, in this case the precise area of employee relations. Importantly, for this book the two main conceptual approaches for the study of culture, the emic and the etic, is not a central issue. Emic analysis assumes that each culture is a distinctive entity that can only be studied from inside that culture, whereas etic analysis assumes that there are cultural universals, and consequently cultural characteristics which can be categorized, as illustrated in Table I.3, across different cultures. What is suggested here is a holistic approach where the etic and emic methods, as described by Lu (2012), are synthesized, allowing language, culture and translation concepts and practices to be viewed within one conceptual framework.

LANGUAGE AND CULTURE AND THE TRANSLATION FOCUS

The pragmatic application of language and cultural perceptions are particularly significant and intimately linked to the process of translation. In the case of employee relations, this is implicitly understood but not always subject to analysis. Blanpain and Blake correctly identified that this is linked to the specific understanding of realities: 'one of the main difficulties, which presents a real pitfall for the comparative scholar, is the fact that identical words in different languages might have different meanings, while the corresponding terms may embrace wholly different realities' (Blanpain and Blake, 2010: 16).

Language does indeed have much bearing on comparative research, for contrasting highly differentiated notions entails knowledge of both the systems under scrutiny and the language of the countries covered. This holds even truer in the domains referred to above, where most terminology identifying practices and institutions is frequently crafted out of negotiation processes. After all, the battle of ideas is often carried out through a battle of words (Hyman, 2007) instantiated in collective bargaining, social dialogue, and concertation; this might lead one to assume that linguistic problems in comparative analysis bear relevance only at the highest levels of abstraction.

Yet this is far from the case, especially in today's labor market, where massive changes in global migration patterns have generated a growing multilingual and multicultural workforce. Misinterpretations of rules and practices cross-linguistically might give rise to ambiguities and confusion as regards workers' union rights, health and safety, and working conditions. One might argue that the use of English as a lingua franca might facilitate understanding when comparing and contrasting national institutions cross-linguistically. Yet this is far from the case, even when comparative analysis of industrial relations practices involves countries making use of the same language (Hyman, 2005: 204). More generally, 'linguistic standardization due to the universal use of English is not always matched by a similarity of structures and functions' (Tiraboschi, 2003: 192).

Accordingly, language plays a major role at the time of contrasting industrial relations and labor law notions cross-nationally. For this reason, Hyman and Gumbrell-McCormick warn us that 'serious comparative research requires the capacity at least to read the languages of the countries covered' (Hyman and Gumbrell-McCormick, 2013: viii). While this is certainly true, it is likewise important to understand how and what to compare. Blanpain and Blake stated clearly 'in order to compare what is, in fact, comparable; one needs to compare the functions institutions perform rather than institutions themselves' (Blanpain and Blake, 2010: 16).

A number of scholars from different disciplines (social sciences, translation studies, industrial relations) have closely examined the problems resulting from transposing concepts and institutions in different languages. Barring a few exceptions (Bromwich, 2006; Manzella, 2015), scant consideration has been given to language-related issues in IR and, specifically, to translation issues arising at the time of comparing and contrasting different IR practices. This might be due, at least in part, to the fact that IR terminology is often regarded as being part of the legal discourse. While this might be true, the terminology that is peculiar to this domain is frequently the result of interactions in collective bargaining and talks between actors involved in negotiations, to the extent that 'the subject has developed its own language' (Green, 1994: 2), leading one to speak of a discursive genre per se, which deserves further analysis. The relevance of the cultural dimension at the time of comparing industrial relations practices cross-linguistically has also been neglected. Meardi speaks of 'the neglect of culture by comparative industrial relations . . . Culture has left aside, as a convenient "emergency" variable, to account for the "unexplained residua"' (Meardi, 2011: 336). Recently, Manzella and Koch (2017) have made an attempt in stressing the significance of culture, and its close relationship with language, in understanding context-bound meanings and national labor relations practices.

Failing to consider the cultural dimension in translating employee relations practices might result in misleading interpretations of industrial relations concepts when transposing institutions from one language into the other.

The book is thus an attempt to integrate the cultural and translation factors to enable those involved with international dimensions of employee relations to be aware of system differentials at a deeper level of understanding. Specifically, the book addresses 'interlingual translation', which according to Pym is concerned with the 'rewording between languages' (Pym, 2014) and with how culture affects comprehension of industrial relations concepts and institutions in this transposition process.

THE STRUCTURE OF THE BOOK

The book is divided into two parts, the first offering an overview of employee relations in the global context and providing a conceptual structure for the language and culture aspect; a central focus for the chapters in the book. The second part provides an analysis, from a selected number of countries, where aspects of language and cultural perspectives are included. Given the diversity of the latter aspects, the book provided guidelines for the individual chapters but did not posit a prescribed framework; particularly in part II, the approach for the selected countries was left to the authors.

Part I: Comparative Employee Relations in Context

Underlying any discussion concentrating on the international dimension of employee relations is the phenomenon of globalization. The concept of globalization encompasses a multitude of processes but at the core is the increasing, and convoluted, integration between nation states, cooperative economic areas, and identifiable geopolitical regions. Employee relations are affected both by the macro level of development where economic consequences have an impact, and the micro level where international enterprise strategies are formulated.

Chapter 1 is a critical examination of how recent global developments have influenced employee relations; market forces and institutions have, in the interconnectivity of the global economy, led to dramatic changes. The chapter draws on original research to emphasize the changes and challenges that employee relations are subjected to, referring to selected countries, Denmark for example, as well as individual businesses, such a Ryanair and Google.

Chapter 2 has a specific focus on contextual differences between employee relations in different countries and reflects on the changing nature of work, which is undergoing extraordinary transformations and reshaping global employment relations. A central theme of the chapter is the role language plays in identifying how individual countries have a symbiotic relationship between language use in employee relations and practice.

To accommodate the cultural and language elements in describing and understanding these multifaceted features in an international comparative context requires a conceptual model.

Chapter 3 proposes that central to such a model is the relationship between culture and language. The role of culture, in particular, is examined and adapted to incorporate the specific semantic field of employee relations, but also to be aware of the broader related aspects of the economy, management, and business. In this respect, Chapter 3 proposes a dynamic model, expanding current theories underlying the analysis of cross-cultural research, and suggesting that a new approach, reciprocal augmentation between culture and language, can construct a bridge across the language and cultural differences between countries. In practice, the mutual enrichment of culture and language provides a holistic dimension to the process of translation which is essential for a more profound analysis and understanding of employee relations in the international context.

Part II: Employee Relations in the National Context

Part II includes the analysis of a number of countries and their employee relations systems, pointing out cases where cultural and linguistic aspects have a bearing in the conception and understanding of employee relations practices and ideologies. Chapter 4 starts with an examination of China's case, where difficulties arise when conveying the very concept of employee relations, with the local culture that has contributed to the creation of specific employee relation concepts (e.g. 'harmony,' 'iron rice bowl'). The chapter places the language and culture synthesis advocated in the book, into an explanation of the development of Chinese employee relations in the larger socio-economic framework. What emerges is that Chinese language and culture hold unique characteristics, with underlying concepts, for example harmony, which is crucial for the understanding of Chinese employee relations.

Chapter 5, focusing on Italy, considers the notion of a 'gangmaster' to emphasize the role of translation in cross-national comparison and the intertwined relationship between language, culture, and law in the broad field of employee relations.

Chapter 6 considers the national system of plant-level employee representation in Germany, and the issues resulting from rendering specific terms in other languages, in this case focusing on the German works council, and thus acknowledging the cultural complexities that this exercise might generate. The German works council has been a particularly widespread model for employee representation, and therefore its language and cultural embedment in German employee relations is especially noteworthy.

The focus then, in Chapter 7, turns to the USA and the increasing ideologically driven divergence within the country between left-leaning 'equity and voice' states and right-leaning 'individual rights and efficiency' states. The chapter emphasizes the critical importance of terminology in employee relations and highlights the continued prominence of context and regional culture within the USA. Developing economies are increasingly influencing global economic developments and Chapter 8 centers in Nigeria. Nigeria's system of employee relations is discussed, as are the links between culture and labor relations, with a focus on the role of English and local languages in negotiations. A distinct focus of the chapter is how contextual factors, the broader socio-economic and political system, of the evolving economy, have an interdependent relationship with cultural prerogatives which are shaping the actors and institutions pertinent for employee relations.

The concluding Chapter 9 constitutes an attempt to summarize the findings gathered in this book and to point out that translation and language form part of interactions and relationships through which 'bundles of employment relational practices' are understood and performed. Such an approach will perhaps gain a better understanding of similarities and differences in employee relations, serving the purpose of comparative research.

BIBLIOGRAPHY

Blanpain, R., Bisom-Rapp, S., Corbett, W. R., Josephs, H. K. and Zimmer, M. J. 2007. *The Global Workplace: International and Comparative Employment Law*, Cambridge: Cambridge University Press.

Blanpain, R. and Blake, J. 2010. *Comparative Labour Law and Industrial Relations in Industrialized Market Economies*, the Netherlands: Kluwer International.

Bromwich, W. 2006. Lessico negoziale, contesto culturale e processi comunicativi nello sciopero nei servizi essenziali a New York. *Diritto Delle Relazioni Industriali, 2*(XVI), pp. 414–4.

Frege, C. and Kelly, J. 2013. *Comparative Employment Relations in the Global Economy*, London and New York: Routledge.

Green, G. D. 1994. *Industrial Relations Texts and Case Studies* (4th edn), London: Pitman Publishing.

Hotho, J. 2014. From typology to taxonomy: a configurational analysis of business systems and their explanatory power. *Organization Studies, 35*, pp. 671–702.

Hyman, R. 2005. Words and things: the problem of particularistic universalism. In Barbier, J. C. and Letablier, M. (eds), *Comparaisons internationales des politiques sociales, enjeux épistémologiques et méthodologiques/ Cross-national Comparison of Social Policies: Epistemological and Methodological Issues*, pp. 191–208, Brussels: Peter Lang.

Hyman, R. 2007. How can trade unions act strategically? *Transfer: European Review of Labour and Research, 13*(2), pp. 193–210.

Hyman, R. and Gumbrell-McCormick, R. 2013. *Trade Unions in Western Europe: Hard Times, Hard Choices*, Oxford: Oxford University Press.

Lu, Lung-Tan. 2012. 'Etic or emic'? Measuring culture in international business research. *International Business Research, 5*(5), pp. 109–15.

Manzella, P. 2015. Lost in translation: language and cross-national comparison in industrial relations. *The E-Journal of International and Comparative Labour Studies, 4*(1), pp. 1–21. Retrieved on 9 July 2019 from http://ejcls. adapt.it/index.php/ejcls_adapt/article/view/260/0.

Manzella, P. and Koch. K. 2017. Legal and cultural implications in managing multilingual and multicultural labor: selected translation issues from the US National Labor Relations Board. *Lebende Sprachen, 62*(1), pp. 59–78.

Meardi, G. 2011. Understanding trade union cultures. *Industrielle Beziehungen, 18*(4), pp. 336–45.

Pym, A. 2014. *Exploring Translation Theories*, Routledge: Abingdon.

Singam, P. and Koch, K. 1994. Industrial relations: problems of German concepts and terminology for the English translator. *Lebende Sprachen*, XXXIX(1), pp. 158–62.

Sorge, A., Noordherhaven, N. and Koen, C. 2015. *Comparative International Management*, London and New York: Routledge.

Tiraboschi, M. (ed.) 2003. *Marco Biagi: Selected Writings*, the Netherlands: Kluwer Law International.

World Economic Forum 2018. *The Global Competitive Report 2018*, Geneva: World Economic Forum.

PART I

Comparative employee relations in context

1. Employee Relations in Context: Globalization, Uncertainties, and Dynamics of Change

Aurora Trif and Valentina Paolucci

INTRODUCTION

Globalization, which refers to the process of increased integration between countries, has had significant effects on employee relations (Lansbury, 2018). Economic liberalism, a key feature of globalization, has fostered individualism and competition since the 1980s, hindering collective mechanisms aimed at limiting 'a race to the bottom' in labour standards in many countries (Doellgast et al., 2018). Despite being one of the causes of the 2008 financial crisis, the neo-liberal political discourse has become, over the past decade, a one-size-fits-all recipe for structural reforms with the blessing of international bodies, such as the International Monetary Fund (IMF), the World Bank and the European Union (EU). In the EU, most governments have sought to reduce unemployment and/or contain labour costs primarily by weakening the role of statutory and/or collective bargaining regulations in setting labour standards (Koukiadaki et al., 2016; Marginson, 2015). Thus, economic liberalism during the crisis has reduced the role of institutional mechanisms (e.g. collective bargaining and labour laws) and increased the role of market forces in the regulation of employee relations.

This chapter investigates the effects of recent global changes on employee relations. It examines the impact of major trends in the global environment on the two main mechanisms that regulate employee relations in capitalist societies, namely institutions and markets (Hall and Soskice, 2001). Considering the rise of individualism and unregulated labour markets across the world, it focuses on recent developments in employee relations in Eastern Europe, which can be considered an extreme case of radical change towards international liberalization since the 1990s, in a context of rather weak labour institutions (Bernaciak and Kahancova, 2017). It draws particularly on our qualitative empirical data gathered in 2015 for an EU project on the impact of the 2008 crisis on precarious work, focusing on nine Eastern European countries and Greece (Trif et al., 2016). The experiences of workers and employers in countries with limited workers' protection are becoming increasingly relevant for understanding the future of employee relations in developed countries, in a context where unregulated markets facilitate the transfer of labour practices from developing to developed countries (to reduce labour costs) rather than vice versa.

In addition, this chapter examines recent developments in two multinational corporations (MNCs) (based in developed countries) exemplifying the polar opposites of individualized approaches to managing people, namely 'hard' human resource management (HRM) in Ryanair and 'soft' HRM in Google. It is concluded that in this ever-changing global environment, work-related demands are not fundamentally different from those in the nineteenth century, when labour markets were unregulated. As such, they (only) have to be (re)framed by employee relations actors through the inclusive language of solidarity.

IMPACT OF RECENT GLOBAL CHANGES ON EMPLOYEE RELATIONS: A VICIOUS CYCLE?

Employee relations refers to managing interactions between workers and their representatives (e.g. trade unions, works' councils, workers' director etc.), on the one hand, and employers and their representatives (e.g. employers' associations or managers) on the other hand (Frege and Kelly, 2013). In contrast to a human resource management (HRM) perspective, which focuses on individual interactions between workers and their managers (and considers employee relations as an element of HRM), we use this term from an industrial relations perspective. Consequently, we focus on collective interactions between trade unions organized or unorganized employers which, in turn, frame the individual interactions between workers and managers. We consider that employee relations and HRM are interlinked as 'two sides of the same coin'.[1] The relationships between worker representatives and employers (i.e. social partners) are primarily contingent on the institutional and structural contexts in which they are embedded, as will be discussed next (Schmalz and Dörre, 2018).

Dynamics of Changes in Institutional Context: Is It All Worth It?

In capitalist countries, labour institutions consist of two inter-related elements, namely employment protection legislation and intermediary institutions that establish labour standards (Schmalz and Dörre, 2018). First, the legislation sets substantive outcomes for workers, such as minimum labour standards (e.g. minimum wage and maximum working time etc.) and procedural outcomes, such as job security (e.g. hiring and firing rules) and provisions concerning collective rights (e.g. freedom of association, collective bargaining and the right to strike). Second, intermediary institutions set the actual substantive (e.g. wages and working time) and procedural (e.g. how to deal with grievances) employment conditions contingent on the up-to-date context at a specific level (e.g. company, group of companies or sector and cross-sectoral). The two main parties that establish those regulations are trade unions or other worker representatives (e.g. works councils and workers' directors etc.) on the one side, and representatives of organized or unorganized employers, on the other. Collective bargaining is the main mechanism used by the social partners to reconcile their conflicting interests and set common rules on both substantive and procedural aspects of work at various levels. The outcome of this form of negotiation is a collective agreement that generally provides mutual benefits for both parties, including social peace and a degree of flexibility (Paolucci, 2017). In addition, trade unions, employers' associations and specialized government agencies can be involved in tri-partite cross-sectoral forums and consultations (e.g. regarding wages or a wider agenda resulting in social pacts) or provide input into social and economic policy at the national level.

Comparative employee relations literature indicates that recent changes in the global economy have primarily challenged the role of intermediary institutions in setting labour standards (Doellgast et al., 2018; Lansbury, 2018; Lévesque and Murray, 2002). The increased integration between countries achieved through the liberalization of international trades has presented governments with the challenge of adjusting their national institutions to improve economic performance. After 2008, in order to gain competitive advantage, most governments (with the notable exception of China) introduced policies seeking to reduce the influence of collective actors and institutions on the labour market, under the premise that solidaristic rules hinder economic growth (Koukiadaki et al., 2016).

Key Challenges for Workers

Policies aimed at deregulating the labour market have increased the scope for a 'race to the bottom' in labour standards (Marginson, 2015). First, it has become more difficult to reconcile the interests of workers and employers within bi-partite (e.g. collective bargaining) and/or tripartite forums; and, over time, the relationship between the social partners has deteriorated (Doellgast et al., 2018). Second, the decline of joint regulation has reduced the capacity of the social partners to maintain close bonds with their respective constituencies. As a result, fragmentation both within the labour movement and employers' associations has increased (Koukiadaki et al., 2016). Third, greater labour market flexibility has produced new forms of work that often escape national institutional arrangements (e.g. on shared platforms), leading to uncertainty for all stakeholders: workers, employers and society at large (Dundon, 2018). Although cross-country divergence still exists, contingent on the institutions which survived the 2008 crisis, the overall trend is towards weaker labour market regulation. Consequently, within countries variation in labour standards is increasing.

Apart from resulting in higher inequality in society (OECD, 2018), the declining role of collective bargaining as a joint mechanism to set working conditions has undermined unions' legitimacy (Trif and Stoiciu, 2017). Governments, often with the support of international financial institutions and/or the EU (e.g. via the European Semester), have undermined the mechanisms framing multi-employer bargaining fostering 'disorganized decentralization' (Marginson, 2015). This, in turn, has led to a reduction of collective bargaining coverage, particularly in countries where extension mechanisms were recognized by law (e.g. Greece and Romania) (Visser, 2016). Furthermore, bargaining decentralization has reduced the incentives for employers to enter into meaningful negotiations with trade unions at all levels, paving the way to concession bargaining whereby the employer sets the agenda and makes the most substantial gains. Moreover, the scope of collective bargaining has become narrower as individual employers have gained more leeway to unilaterally impose terms and conditions of employment, including pay, working time and workload (Müller et al., 2019). Finally, as a result of the reduction of institutional support, unions' actions have become more contingent on the values and principles of their leaders (Schurman et al., 2017).

Post-2008 legal changes have also undermined individual employment protection in many countries. First, the job security of employees on standard contracts was reduced by making it easier for employers to hire and fire employees (Rubery et al., 2016). Second, labour law changes have liberalized different forms of contracts for services, such as agency worker, self-employment (including workers on shared platforms) and outsourcing by using domestic or international suppliers (Lansbury, 2018). Third, new legal provisions have given employers more control over work schedules by removing existing restrictions on overtime and working hours both for standard and non-standard workers. For instance, recent legislation allows employers to increase or decrease the number of working hours per week of standard employees contingent on employers' needs, in countries such as Greece, Romania and Slovenia (Trif et al., 2016). As a result of both increased flexibility for employers to set working time and teleworking it has become more difficult for authorities (e.g. labour inspectors) to verify whether legal provisions concerning working time or minimum wage are applied.

Evidence in Eastern European countries reveals that these legal changes have led to a wide range of illegal or semi-legal practices, such as declaring shorter working hours, using part-time contracts for full-time workers and supplementing workers' income with untaxed cash-in-hand; this is done by employers primarily to reduce payroll taxes (Trif et al., 2016). Workers, on the other hand, tend to accept cash-in hand, enticed by short-term benefits and underestimating the negative impact that tax avoidance has on public service provisions: from pensions and social benefits to healthcare and education. In a context with limited institutional mechanisms to create incentives for employers (and workers) to observe labour standards, the enforcement of statutory and voluntary regulation has become increasingly contingent on the values of local managers.

The weakening of both individual and collective employment rights has eroded workers' solidarity (to various degrees across countries) (Doellgast et al., 2018). On the one hand, less individual protection, together with the emergence of new (flexible) forms of work, has fostered individualism and increased competition between workers, based on their personal characteristics (e.g. gender, age, ethnicity, skills, type of work contracts or union membership) (Schurman et al., 2017). On the other hand, the reduction of collective rights has diminished the legal protection offered to unions by the State thereby delegitimizing their role in society. The impact has been greater in Eastern Europe and in Anglo-Saxon countries where, prior to the 2008 crisis, labour institutions were already weak (Müller et al., 2019). Here, the lack of institutional support has forced unions to rely mainly on member action. As a result, it has become more difficult to defend the interests of the most vulnerable groups of workers who are generally not unionized. Also, protecting vulnerable workers, such as those on precarious contracts, can have indirect effects on the working conditions of union members who, over time, may become hostile. This growing division amongst workers has reduced the capacity of unions to build strength through solidarity and, as a result, also to improve labour standards.

In recent times, comparative studies have focused almost exclusively on the challenges faced by labour following the deterioration of institutional constraints (Schurman et al., 2017; Marginson, 2015). For instance, in their influential book on how to reduce precarious work in the current global environment, Doellgast et al. (2018) argue that employers profit from weak institutions and liberalized international markets because deregulation has a clear-cut, downward effect on labour costs in the short-term. Nonetheless, there is substantial evidence in the extant literature that labour market institutions, namely, collective bargaining, can have positive effects for companies in the long-term, by providing stability and facilitating mutually advantageous exchanges between employers and employees (e.g. Geary and Trif, 2011; Streeck, 1988). Hence, post-2008 labour market deregulation, particularly the decline of multi-employer bargaining arrangements, has reduced not only the capacity of unions to protect employees, but also the opportunity for employers to shape industrial policy.

Key Challenges for Employers

Although in recent years global changes have increased the leeway for employers to set unilaterally terms and conditions of employment, unregulated labour markets may also have been detrimental to employers (Streeck, 1988). The weakening of extension mechanisms for collective bargaining, together with the decline of collective bargaining coverage, makes it easier for unscrupulous employers to ignore labour laws (Koukiadaki et al., 2016). While large employers are in a stronger position to use legal loopholes to their advantage (e.g. outsourcing, agency work or relocation) (Doellgast et al., 2018), small and medium-sized enterprises (SMEs) are more likely to use illegal (e.g. no employment contracts) or semi-legal practices (e.g. cash-payments on top of minimum wage) to reduce labour costs (Schurman et al., 2017; Trif et al., 2016). In order to avoid unfair competition arising from the greater use of informal practices by SMEs, large temporary agencies (e.g. Addecco, Manpower etc.), which operate in one of the most deregulated and rapidly growing sectors post-2008, have recently set up their own employers' associations in Eastern Europe (Trif et al., 2016). These associations are trying to influence national policies by (re)shaping labour standards; the chairman of the Romanian association indicated that it was in favour of increased regulation, namely, obliging client companies (i.e. employers using agency workers) to provide the same (or better) working conditions for agency workers as for their direct employees (Trif et al., 2016).

Somewhat paradoxically, the international association of employers in the temporary agency work sector, the World Employment Confederation, is at the forefront of EU lobbying for more labour regulation to establish a level playing field for employers, albeit supporting an easy to hire-and-fire 'employment friendly' environment. Remarkably, this employers' organization argues that the strongest performing labour markets (e.g. those with the highest labour productivity) are in countries 'with a high level of social dialogue such as the Netherlands and Scandinavian countries where employers and trade unions typically work together to set specific market legislation that can then be adjusted in line with labour market changes' (World Employment Confederation, 2018: 35). In addition, it supports novel regulations to protect individuals rather than jobs, which could also suit the increasing number of (bogus) self-employed (World Employment Confederation, 2018). Thus, the challenges faced by employers in extremely deregulated labour markets has led to their (re)organizing as collective actors seeking to secure regulations that ensure mutually beneficial outcomes for workers and employers, as a means (as in the past) to reduce competition amongst employers.

Furthermore, the recognition by employers in the emerging unregulated labour markets of the mutual benefits of institutional constraints demonstrates that intermediary institutions can still generate benefits for capital. In countries with strong labour institutions, such as Denmark, the Netherlands and Finland, organized employers, together with trade unions, continue to maintain a strong incentive to protect their employment relations systems, due to the overall positive outcomes these secure for all parties involved (Müller et al., 2019). For instance, attempts by some employers to weaken collective bargaining in Denmark were unsuccessful (Doellgast et al., 2018) as it was impossible to uphold the neo-liberal discourse that this institution undermines competitiveness in a country with over 80 per cent collective bargaining coverage and one of the highest levels of labour productivity in the world (Visser, 2016).

In Denmark, the majority of employers consider that their organizations benefit from collective bargaining. Paolucci's study (2016) shows that both employers and HR managers value the opportunity to maintain an ongoing dialogue between social partners, seeking to develop joint actions to address the emerging economic and technological challenges posed by the crisis. In 2014, a senior official of one of the larger employers' associations in Denmark (Dansk Industry) reported:

> [M]any employers from other countries shake their heads when they hear how we deal with trade unions. We are not at war with trade unions; we negotiate with the best interest of Denmark in mind. For example, the energy sector is important and we are together with the unions on that. When we think that jobs may be moved from Denmark to foreign countries we join forces and we try to influence the government.

This respondent also indicated that:

> Training has become more and more important over the past ten years. I can't remember one sector level negotiation where training was not mentioned. Training helps employers to update the skills of unskilled employees and to train the skilled employees, making them better.[2]

The empirical evidence shows that it can be in the best interest of employers (and not just trade unions) to fight against the deterioration of labour institutions which guarantee stability and produce mutually beneficial outcomes for employers and their workers.

Despite an overall trend towards labour market deregulation, there is divergence in employers' preferences for labour institutions. On the one hand, collective bargaining continues to play an important role in countries with a strong (and stable) tradition of multi-employer arrangements, such as in Northern Europe (Müller et al., 2019). Collective bargaining is still supported by most Danish employers, because it enables them to gain competitiveness in the global market by relying on highly trained multi-functional employees (Paolucci, 2016). On the other hand, there have been timid attempts to restore the protection of the most vulnerable groups of workers in countries with very weak labour institutions, such as agency workers in Eastern Europe. Apart from organizing them, a significant recent development is the change in public discourse in relation to precarious work contracts. In Poland, for example, the perception of short-term civil contracts shifted from being seen as useful to boost employment, to being just 'junk contracts' (Mrozowicki et al., 2013). This diffident call to restore labour market institutions in extremely deregulated contexts supports Streeck's (1988: 421) prediction that 'capitalism may just be too important to be left to the capitalists – who arguably are the least capable of protecting it from its self-destructive tendency to pursue cheap and short-term advantages'. Although labour market deregulation increases the power imbalance in favour of capital, both parties in employee relations encounter challenges when the mutual long-term 'beneficial constraints' associated with collective regulation cease to exist.

Dynamics of Change in the Structural Context: Is the Market No One's Friend?

Recent changes in the global business context have made employee relations increasingly contingent on market forces (Myant and Drahokoupil, 2012). The liberalization of international trade, together with free flows of capital (and labour), has increased competition between firms pressurizing particularly domestic firms to reduce labour costs. These changes make it easier for capital to invest where labour standards are lower, while allowing foreign companies to compete with domestic ones (Batt, 2018). Nonetheless, very large MNCs are more likely than other firms to benefit from increased globalization. They have the financial resources to invest or relocate to countries with lower labour costs and/or low corporate tax; moreover, some of them have special tax arrangements with local governments and benefit from transfer pricing (able to declare their profits in countries with low corporation tax, such as Ireland) (Regan and Brazys, 2018). Furthermore, a significant share of their exports of goods and services is intra-firm and, therefore, determined by internal decisions, not external market prices (Lansbury, 2018). In addition, the emergence of shared platforms for different services (e.g. Uber, Airbnb etc.) have put pressure on traditional firms to reduce labour costs, as the workforce on shared platforms is not (yet) entitled to minimum statutory labour standards. These actions of a relatively small number of companies reduce the margin of profit for the other companies, which in turn, intensifies a quest for lower labour costs. Apart from fostering a hostile environment for labour, the increased market competition has also contributed to increased divisions amongst employers.

Besides, the growing interconnectivity of production/service networks across the world makes it difficult to determine where decisions concerning employee relations are made. First, shareholding (the dominant form of ownership) facilitates intricate equity ownership relations in funds and funds of funds, which makes it almost impossible to identify the owners (Lansbury, 2018). Second, the growing use of multiple tiers of suppliers by large companies makes it difficult to determine who sets the labour standards, particularly for the growing share of non-standard workers. The cost of labour for suppliers is often negotiated (or imposed) by the lead company in a supply chain, even for suppliers employing highly skilled workers with a greater capacity to disrupt services, such as pilots. For instance, the terms of the 2016 agreement in the US between Amazon and Atlas Air to transport their Prime products put pressure on the carrier to pay its pilots well below the prevailing market rate (Levy, 2017). Third, it is very difficult to find out which managers are responsible for labour standards in large MNCs with complex organizational structures; sometimes, local managers claim that decisions concerning labour are taken at higher levels, while regional (or headquarter) managers claim that decisions are taken by local managers (Trif and Stoiciu, 2017). Although increased interconnectivity and internationalization of production and services networks present a greater opportunity for workers to disrupt production (Silver, 2003), the ambiguity and fragmentation of employers and workers make it difficult (but not impossible) for workers to take collective action to disrupt production.

In addition, the intensification of labour emigration from countries with lower wages to those with higher wages enables employers to provide worse working conditions for migrants than non-migrant workers (Doellgast et al., 2018). For instance, in the EU, there has been an intensification of emigration from the east to the west after the EU accession of the post-communist countries in the 2000s (Eurostat, 2018). Although increased emigration led to a tighter labour market in Eastern Europe, it generally triggered wage increases only for managers and highly skilled professionals, as migrant workers from further east filled lower skilled jobs (e.g. Ukraine, Moldova, China and Vietnam) (Stan and Erne, 2015). Migrant workers are more likely to accept lower wages (and jobs below their qualifications) than non-migrant workers, as wages in their home country are often significantly lower than in the host countries (e.g. up to 10 times lower in Eastern Europe compared to Western Europe) (Eurostat, 2018).

Migrants, together with other vulnerable groups, particularly young workers, are more likely to accept different forms of insecure jobs which, in the long run, may undermine working conditions for the core labour force (Doellgast et al., 2018). In the past, it was primarily workers in low-skilled jobs who had precarious working conditions, while over the last decade it has become more common for highly skilled professionals, such as academics, engineers and researchers to experience insecurity during their careers (Harney et al., 2014). The increase in competition between individuals and/or various categories of workers to get (or retain) a stable job places pressure particularly on highly skilled workers and managers to work beyond the maximum legal working hours; this is not sustainable in the longer run, as either their health or the quality of their work (or both) is likely to deteriorate (Rubery et al., 2016). Thus, the current global business environment forces different categories of workers into a vicious cycle (Doellgast et al., 2018).

Moreover, technological changes introduced over the last 10 years allow employers to use individual workers as suppliers of services (Batt, 2018). Work contracts, ranging from (bogus) self-employed, to agency worker or outsourced/insourced worker, are used by companies to avoid paying payroll taxes and other benefits that employees with a contract of service are entitled to (Bernaciak and

Kahancova, 2017). Contingent on national culture and customs, other employers may argue that they have to use different forms of illegal or semi-legal contracts for their workers to avoid bankruptcy. Recent changes in technology have also led to the automation of many tasks and jobs, while somewhat paradoxically also supporting longer working hours, often above the legal limits. Not only does technology enable many workers to do their tasks remotely and outside office hours, it also makes it possible for consumers to use services 24/7 and for employers to control workers' activities (Lansbury, 2018). Thus, technological changes play a key role in blurring the boundaries between employers, workers and customers, trapping society in a culture of consumerism where each individual strives to maximize utility towards short-term benefits.

Overall, recent changes in the global environment have contributed to a shift in capitalism from a profit-seeking to a rent-seeking system, where shareholders accumulate significant amounts of profit without creating new wealth (Piketty, 2015). The 'rent' refers to Adam Smith's division of income into profit, wage, and *rent* (Stiglitz, 2012). In a traditional profit-seeking capitalist system value is created through work. The cost of labour is determined by the supply of and demand for labour (i.e. the market mechanism). The distribution of wealth is based on engaging in (so-called) mutually beneficial transactions between employers (buyers of labour) and workers (sellers of labour). Such 'mutually' beneficial transactions are a voluntary process of exchange based on rational choice, where both parties are better off. This does not necessarily mean that both parties benefit equally from such transactions (e.g. payday loans where a person takes a credit of 100 euro to make ends meet while s/he needs to pay back 200 euro is considered a mutually beneficial transaction). In a similar vein, in profit-seeking capitalism employee relations are based on a market mechanism that redistributes wealth in the form of profit for employers and wages for workers. However, in this process employers benefit far more than workers (Batt, 2018). Moreover, reliance on market mechanisms to set labour standards has contributed to a widening gap between high and low wage earners; in the US, the top 1 per cent of wages have increased by 150 per cent over the last three decades, while the bottom 90 per cent of wages have increased by only 15 per cent according to Stiglitz (2012).

In contrast to the traditional system, rent-seeking capitalism refers to shareholders accumulating income through legal or illegal methods that bypass market mechanisms, without creating new wealth (Piketty, 2015). Although rent-seeking, in the form of lobbying (or bribing) politicians for preferential economic regulations such as tariff protection, subsidies and corporate taxes, has been around for a very long time, the emergence of shared platforms that are 'rented' to sellers and buyers of services is a recent phenomenon (Dundon, 2018). These technological developments, together with the international liberalization of trades, have enabled platforms such as Uber, Airbnb and Deliveroo, to become dominant players in the global market, almost overnight, and to generate a significant income for shareholders without creating new wealth (Lansbury, 2018). There are limited market mechanisms to redistribute the income gained through the renting of such platforms, as they have limited (if any) competition for their services and do not act as employers (buyers of labour). Furthermore, many financial organizations also began to use principles of rent-seeking capitalism to increase the income of shareholders without producing wealth in different forms of services, such sub-prime mortgages (Piketty, 2015). Nevertheless, when these practices led to a financial crisis and bankruptcy, in most countries governments bailed banks out by externalizing the risks to society, by increasing taxes for workers and/ or by reducing services for the most vulnerable groups in society (e.g. children, people with disabilities etc.). Thus, technological progress and international liberalization continues to empower a minority of (wealthy) shareholders by shifting the burden of risk onto the majority of (far lower income) individuals.

The growth of rent-seeking capitalism has increased inequality by progressively reducing the capacity of the market to offer mechanisms of wealth redistribution towards mutually beneficial transactions between sellers and buyers of labour. In his seminal book entitled *The Price of Inequality*, Stiglitz (2012) indicates that the richest 1 per cent held 65 per cent of US national income gains in 2007, while their share increased to 93 per cent in 2010. He writes that: 'Paying attention to everyone else's self-interest – in other words to the common welfare – is in fact a precondition for one's own ultimate wellbeing . . . it isn't just good for the soul; it's good for business' (Stiglitz, 2012: 361). Like Streeck (1988), Stiglitz argues that mechanisms for cooperation should be restored to ensure benefits for all parties.

BEYOND INSTITUTIONS AND STRUCTURES: IS THE ALTERNATIVE INDIVIDUALIZATION OR COLLECTIVE ACTION?

Mechanisms aimed at fostering regulation have been dismantled to different degrees across countries in order to boost economic growth and enhance capital and labour mobility through competition (Baccaro and Howell, 2017). The picture we are left with after several decades of aggressive neo-liberal policies is polarized. The world is richer, but inequality is skyrocketing (Piketty, 2015; Stiglitz, 2012). Individuals' capacity to buy goods and services from virtually every corner of the planet has never been greater (Lansbury, 2018). Yet workers' purchasing power has declined due to reducing wages and deteriorating labour standards (Lévesque and Murray, 2002). Work is beyond flexible. Technologies, types of contracts and working hours have given employees the opportunity to redesign the boundaries of their jobs and work from everywhere. However, the perception of insecurity is pervasive and work-related anxiety is on the increase (Broughton, 2010). While the possibility for cross-border mobility expands, cultural cleavages are resurfacing along with requests for protection of national identities (Fukuyama, 2018).

In the ambivalence that permeates modern societies scholars have identified a common trend: *individualization* (Lansbury, 2018; Lévesque and Murray, 2002). This notion refers to the idea that each person can be responsible for her/his own present and future life. The logic of free-will and liberalization has reshaped society and fostered a 'me-first' attitude. Key features of the employee relationship too, such as autonomy and dependence, have been re-interpreted in terms of individual needs. Over the past thirty years, the field of HRM has played an important role in crystallizing this development. There is now agreement, especially amongst policy-makers, that work should be 'professionally managed' rather than 'socially negotiated' (Meardi, 2014: 595). HR managers can liberate individuals from organizational constraints, opening a path to personal growth and job satisfaction. In turn, employees will be productive and take ownership of their job security and employability (Boxall, 2014). As appealing as that sounds, this discourse has contributed to breaking the *link* between work and collective action which originated from *collectivism*; and, in a context where individual autonomy collides with solidarity, individuals have become more exposed to external risks and social exclusion (Crouch, 2015).

Scholars who questioned the sustainability of the current capitalist model have struggled to find a way out (Baccaro and Howell, 2017). Due to the significant deterioration in state-provided 'beneficial constraints' (Streeck, 1988) employers, employees and consumers all seem to be trapped in a vicious cycle of high dependence on the market, with reduced opportunities for cooperation (Doellgast et al., 2018). One of the casualties of this short-term, market driven, political agenda are workers and their labour organizations. It is undeniable that capitalism has never encountered less resistance from collective actors (Roche et al. 2014). However, capitalism has also posed challenges that employers can no longer escape. Meanwhile, new complex economic and societal demands are being formulated, especially with regard to equality (e.g. the *me too* movement) and sustainability. Thus, in this ever-changing scenario, one wonders: can workers' collective voice still be raised?

Ryanair's choice to recognize trade unions and Google protests have shaken the public debate by dispelling the myth that employee relations are irrelevant (Meardi, 2014). The surge of *collective* conflict in these two companies shows that even in large multinationals embedded in liberal market economies, employees can find opportunities for voicing their discontent and question employers' prerogatives. Despite the erosion of collective bargaining institutions, there are resources that employees can use to advance their demands. Solidarity, as well as conflict, might be silent at work but will never disappear. Old and new forms of labour organizations can revitalize collective action (Bernaciak and Kahancova, 2017).

From an employee relations perspective, Ryanair and Google share elements of similarity as well as difference. They are large internationalized organizations which are market leaders. They both employ highly skilled workers with sufficient structural resources to disrupt services in their respective industries, namely aviation and information technology (IT). Unitarism underpins management approaches in both Ryanair and Google and trade unions have never been recognized as legitimate representative of employees' interests. However, while Ryanair is one of the most notorious cases of hard HRM, Google is an exemplary case of soft HRM. Google has enhanced employees' participation through sophisticated high commitment practices, including individual (voice) channels that enable them to have an input into decision making. Whereas, Ryanair has openly repressed any form of internal disagreement (O'Sullivan and Gunnigle, 2009). Somewhat unexpectedly, neither hard nor soft HRM approaches prevented the emergence of workplace conflict and collective action of employees.

Michael O'Leary became the CEO of Ryanair in 1993. For over twenty years, his anti-union stance has led the company to engage in active resistance to independent forms of employee representation. Ryanair has invested in significant efforts to bend the law and reshape the institutional context both in Ireland and other host countries (O'Sullivan and Gunnigle, 2009). The company has relied on a mix of full-time employees and contractors in order to sidestep collective bargaining with pilots (Spero and Beesley, 2018). Moreover, there is a 'no-frills' policy in place for crew staff, who are paid below industry standards and often employed short-term. Over time, Ryanair has become a textbook case of poor personnel management. For many years employees have unsuccessfully demanded better pay and working conditions. Yet, they were unable to take advantage of favourable structural conditions, namely, the requirement for high skills (limited availability of qualified pilots, multiple languages and high mobility), a capital intensive sector (high cost of technology relative to labour) and a customer-driven business. While there were several strikes, until 2017 90 per cent of all flight schedules remained uninterrupted (Roberts and Griffith, 2018). The company maintained a highly competitive market position becoming the safest and most profitable low-carrier in Europe.

In September 2017, Ryanair employees took industrial action and, for the first time, the company was forced to cancel over 250 flights (BBC News, 18th September 2017). As Ryanair shares fell (down 13 per cent by October 2018), shareholders urged change. In a letter to the company, the Chairman of the Local Authority Pension Fund Forum stated: 'since the annual general meeting (AGM), it appears Ryanair faces a prolonged transition to a more stable employment model and improved IR. As long-term shareholders we believe that Ryanair can continue to grow and prosper, but also consider that this must involve change' (McLoughlin, 2018).

What was it that led to this unforeseen reverse in workers' power? Not only did Ireland provide Ryanair with a business-friendly institutional context, the company also has a history of deliberately circumventing local legislation when expanding into other European countries, by employing staff under Irish contracts (O'Sullivan and Gunnigle, 2009). Structural conditions too have remained relatively stable. Perhaps unsurprisingly, it was a grassroots initiative of self-organizing pilots which triggered this turnaround. They used several channels to strengthen their position vis-à-vis the company. First, after the Ryanair cancellation crisis in 2017 a large number of pilots joined trade unions. Second, they set up official company councils in order to 'facilitate and formalize negotiations in line with national and legal social requirements' (Air Traffic Management.net, 2018). Soon afterwards, the most infamous anti-union airline company was forced to capitulate: trade unions were publicly recognized. Third, the Ryanair Transnational Pilot Group was established in anonymity during the 2017 conference organized by the European Cockpit Association. Aided by social media, this international network has helped the Ryanair Employee Representative Councils to share resources (legal, political and technical know-how) as well as to develop negotiating skills. By acting transnationally and striking *en masse*, the group of workers with the strongest structural power – pilots – derailed Ryanair strategy to negotiate separate agreements with multiple Employee Representative Councils (Davies, 2018). While the battle in Ryanair is still ongoing, pilots initiated a pan European movement through which the lack of workers' institutional resources was, at least partly, overcome. This, in turn, has increased pilots' structural power and, with the support of trade unions, enabled other categories of employees (e.g. cabin crew) to put forward further demands.

The walk-out in Google is an equally fascinating development. The Google motto, 'Don't be evil', together with the autonomy given to employees to find solutions to current challenges contributed to the emergence of a new category of employee, namely 'Googlers'. Apart from having one of the highest wages in the US (Mautz, 2018), Googlers' reward packages include massages, catered meals, generous parental leaves, *in situ* pools, wellness programmes and other amazing benefits. Their generous reward package reflects the fact that they are considered vital for Google's success. The strategic focus that Google put on people management has heavily influenced the IT industry.

Moreover, Google's approach to employees is widely used for teaching purposes, as an exemplary case of soft HRM. It shows that companies which invest in employees can reap a return through productivity, quality and profitability while improving societal well-being (Boxall, 2014). In this unique work environment, dominated by the idea that each employee can make the world a better place to live – in a vaguely utopian form of individualism (Scheiber, 2018) – conflict does not exist. Googlers trust each other, management included, as they all equally strive to succeed. This is considered the living proof that a perfect alignment between a company's strategic objectives and its employees' needs is possible. The corporate culture offers everyone a purpose that is clear and direct: 'to organize the world's information and make it universally accessible and useful'. It is argued that managers are there to help, whereas trade unions hinder innovation. In this context, why should Googlers seek any form of collective representation?

However, about 20,000 Google employees all over the world staged a series of walk-outs in November 2018. This unprecedented form of collective action took place in Google after several allegations of sexual misconduct were made against senior executives, including one against Andy Rubin, the creator of Android mobile phone software. To secure his departure, the company paid a $90 million severance package. In response, employees opened a channel of international communication across all subsidiaries using social media (Walkout for Real Change, 2018) and other internal technologies. As in the Ryanair case, such technologies offered Googlers the opportunity to exploit their (hitherto unused) structural power and overcome the lack of institutional resources, such as their own independent forms of representation.

The demands of Googlers are at odds with that unitarist, individualistic culture celebrated by the company and seemingly shared by all its employees. Of the five specific requests that employees identified, three in particular clash with the claims of a soft HRM approach: (1) protesters asked for an end to forced arbitration in cases of harassment and discrimination, including the right of workers to bring a representative or other supporter when meeting HR; (2) protesters demanded to end pay and opportunity inequity, particularly concerning the gender, race and ethnicity compensation gap; and (3) in order to ensure that their demands are addressed by the management team, Googlers asked for an independent Employee Representative to join the Board of Directors and requested a higher status and additional resources for the existing Chief Diversity Officer (Walkout for Real Change, 2018). As highlighted by Scheiber

(2018), the most remarkable aspect of the walk out at Google is 'that organisers identified their action with a broader worker struggle, using language almost unheard-of among affluent tech employees' and arguably, many other industries (e.g. workers' solidarity). The Googlers' collective action can be seen as an example of economic liberalism leading to a reactionary countermovement whereby society seeks to re-entrench the economy and society by establishing social protection (Polanyi, 1944).

Interpreting recent developments in employee relations in the Ryanair and Google cases is not straightforward. The main lesson, however, is that collective action is still possible; both cases show that employee voice can become a powerful tool if individuals act together. These cases illustrate that workers' protests and solidarity are essential in reframing the mainstream discourse that highlights the benefits of economic liberalism and individualism to include consideration of its costs for workers and society. These companies used nineteenth-century practices, such as strikes and walk-outs, to advance social issues (equality, dignity and respect) that have yet to be solved. In Ryanair, the pilots' self-movement was a stepping-stone towards union recognition. It served as a way to mobilize an institutional resource, collective bargaining, which, albeit weakened, has existed since the twentieth century. In 2019, the Ryanair Chief People Officer, Eddie Wilson, was appointed as Chief Executive of the Ryanair airline, while Google has ended forced arbitration, following employee protests. Despite lacking institutions, Google workers were able to enact new structural resources, namely twenty-first century information technologies, reminding employers that they can (if they want to) exert power.

In other words, these two examples show that, when acting collectively, employees have the potential to turn any contingent resource (institutions and/or structures) into power, thereby advancing their demands. In both cases, technologies were essential for employees to establish international links, strengthen solidarity and gain publicity. This shows that technologies do not only make employees obsolete. On the contrary, they can empower them. As Kochan (2019) argues, technology is just a resource: it can be deployed to reshape the future of work in a productive and inclusive way. Perhaps what one should question is *agency*, namely the role and influence of existing channels for employee representation. Will unions be able to adapt to the current global environment? How will employers react if tensions intensify?

CONCLUSION

This chapter examined the impact of recent global changes on the two main mechanisms that regulate employee relations in capitalist societies, namely institutions and markets. First, it confirmed that prevailing policies of economic liberalization all around the world have weakened the role of labour institutions which set 'beneficial constraints' for labour and capital. While employers have benefited far more than workers from this development, their ability to seize the new opportunities offered by the global market varies greatly. Large multinational corporations have a greater capacity than small and medium size enterprises to take advantage of varying labour costs and tax regimes across countries.

Second, the growing share of direct links between sellers and individual buyers, facilitated by technology, has paradoxically undermined the role of the market mechanism in creating mutually beneficial transactions between buyers and sellers of labour. Fast-growing, online (.com) companies are escaping traditional rules governing the 'standard' employment relationship (minimum wage, working-time, health and safety and welfare entitlements) without considering the long-term effects not only on their profitability, but on society too, such as consumer backlash, conflict, and liability. Meanwhile, employers operating in many traditional industries such as manufacturing, retail, hospitality and other business services are been threatened by the growing role of rent-seeking capitalism (Lansbury, 2018). Both these developments are blurring the boundaries between the employer and the employee, while also increasing competition between employers.

Third, against a backdrop of loosening institutional constraints and uncertain market structures, this chapter highlighted the importance of collective action as an alternative to shake the status quo and create new incentives for cooperation between all societal actors. It is argued that employees with the strongest structural resources have the best opportunity to reinvent a more equal and sustainable workplace – they can take advantage of the visibility their companies have, and the technologies they helped develop, to lead a new (labour) movement. Young generations of highly demanding employees, who were hired to change the world (e.g. Googlers), can persuade their employers to abide by the ambitious ethical objectives they set for themselves. Social media offers a platform whereby disenfranchised workers can be heard.

Overall, the 'disruption' created by an increasingly *unregulated* global environment opens a 'Pandora's Box' of uncertainties: neither capital nor labour seems to know whether globalization helps or hinders their relative position in society. The issue is multifaceted and predictions are hard to make. However, this chapter shows that it is not impossible to exercise collective voice even in the highly individualized and competitive modern society. The cases of Ryanair and Google demonstrate that solidarity at work can certainly be rebuilt. It also highlights that workers' demands are the same as in the past and continue to remain unaddressed.

In the current context of weak institutions and volatile market structures, it is unclear whether the traditional employee relations actors – governments, employers and labour movements – will be able to address the challenges created by economic liberalism. Will these actors be willing and able to resort to each other's support to restate cooperation-enhancing institutions, such as collective bargaining or tripartite forums? Will Googlers play a leading role in shifting the dominant discourse from 'economic liberalism' to a global society that ensures 'dignity, equality and respect' for all, perhaps by using the new technology that they themselves create? Will policy-makers and employers consider the argument that it is not only human beings and natural resources that need protection, but that the capitalist system itself also needs to be sheltered from the potentially devastating effects of economic liberalism (Polanyi, 1944; Stiglitz, 2012; Streeck, 1988)? The answer lies with all of us, workers, employers and other groups in society. In particular, our social and political actions (or inaction) shape employee relations and the type of society that we work and live in.

NOTES

1. Professor Richard Hyman made this analogy during an informal discussion in the early 2000s.
2. Respondent interviewed by Valentina Paolucci for her 2016 study; these quotes were not used in her published work.

BIBLIOGRAPHY

Air Traffic Management.net 2018. Ryanair pilots signal birth of transnational group, 19 March, Key Publishing, accessed on 27 February 2019, https://

airtrafficmanagement.keypublishing.com/2018/03/19/ryanair-pilots-signal-birth-of-transnational-group/.

Baccaro, L. and Howell, C. 2017. *Trajectories of Neoliberal Transformation: European Industrial Relations Since the 1970s*, Cambridge: Cambridge University Press.

Batt, R. 2018. The financial model of the firm, the 'future of work', and employment relations, in A. Wilkinson, T. Dundon, J. Donaghey and A. Colvin (eds), *The Routledge Companion to Employment Relations* (pp. 465–79), London: Routledge.

BBC News 2017. Ryanair publishes full list of cancellations, 18 September, BBC, accessed on 8 March 2019, https://www.bbc.co.uk/news/business-41311603.

Beck, U. 2000. *Living Your Own Life in a Runaway World: Individualisation, Globalisation and Politics* (pp. 164–74), London: Jonathan Cape.

Bernaciak, M. and Kahancova, M. 2017. *Beyond the Crisis: Innovative Practices Within CEE Trade Union Movements*, Brussels: European Trade Union Institute.

Boxall, P. 2014. The future of employment relations from the perspective of human resource management. *Journal of Industrial Relations*, *56*(4), pp. 578–93.

Broughton, A. 2010. Work-related stress, Eurofound Dublin, accessed on 8 March 2019, https://www.eurofound.europa.eu/sites/default/files/ef_files/docs/ewco/tn1004059s/tn1004059s.pdf.

Crouch, C. 2015. *Governing Social Risks in Post-Crisis Europe*, Cheltenham, UK and Northampton, MA, USA: Edward Elgar Publishing.

Davies, R. 2018. Ryanair pilots form unofficial union in battle with Michael O'Leary. *The Guardian*, accessed on 8 March 2019, https://www.theguardian.com/business/2017/oct/02/ryanair-pilots-union-michael-o-leary.

Doellgast, V., Lillie, N. and Pulignano, V. (eds) 2018. *Reconstructing Solidarity: Labour Unions, Precarious Work, and the Politics of Institutional Change in Europe*, Oxford: Oxford University Press.

Dundon, T. 2018. The fracturing of work and employment relations. *Labour and Industry: A Journal of the Social and Economic Relations of Work*, *28*(1), pp. 1–13.

Eaton, A. E., Schurman, S. J. and Chen, M. A. (eds) 2017. *Informal Workers and Collective Action*, New York: Cornell University Press.

Eurostat 2018. Database, accessed on 8 November 2018, https://ec.europa.eu/eurostat/data/database.

Frege, C. and Kelly, J. 2013. *Comparative Employment Relations in the Global Economy*, London: Routledge.

Fukuyama, F. 2018. *Identity: Contemporary Identity Politics and the Struggle for Recognition*, London: Profile Books.

Geary, J. and Trif, A. 2011. Workplace partnership and the balance of advantage: a critical case analysis. *British Journal of Industrial Relations*, *49*(s1), pp. 44–69.

Hall, P. A. and Soskice, D. W. (eds) 2001. *Varieties of Capitalism: The Institutional Foundations of Comparative Advantage*, Oxford: Oxford University Press.

Harney, B., Monks, K., Alexopoulos, A., Buckley, F. and Hogan, T. 2014.

University research scientists as knowledge workers: contract status and employment opportunities. *The International Journal of Human Resource Management, 25*(16), pp. 2219–33.

Kochan, T. 2019. It is not technology that will steal your job, *Irish Times*, accessed on 13 January 2019 https://www.irishtimes.com/opinion/it-is-not-technology-that-will-steal-your-job-1.3753547.

Koukiadaki, A., Tavora, I. and Martínez-Lucio, M. 2016. *Joint Regulation and Labour Market Policy in Europe During the Crisis*, Brussels: European Trade Union Institute.

Lansbury, R. D. 2018. The changing world of work and employment relations: a multi-level institutional perspective of the future. *Labour and Industry: A Journal of the Social and Economic Relations of Work, 28*(1), pp. 5–20.

Lévesque, C. and Murray, G. 2002. Local versus global: activating local union power in the global economy. *Labor Studies Journal, 27*(3), pp. 39–65.

Levy, A. 2017. Amazon prime air pilots are heading to shareholders meeting to confront execs over low wages, CNBC 22 May 2017, accessed on 18 November 2018, https://www.cnbc.com/2017/05/22/amazon-shareholders-meeting-protest-prime-air-pilots.html.

Marginson, P. 2015. Coordinated bargaining in Europe: from incremental corrosion to frontal assault? *European Journal of Industrial Relations, 21*(2), pp. 97–114.

Mautz, S. 2018. Google, Facebook and Amazon just revealed their median pay and it's a major lesson in employee motivation, accessed on 21 December 2018, https://www.inc.com/scott-mautz/google-facebook-amazon-just-revealed-their-median-pay-its-a-major-lesson-in-employee-motivation.html.

McLoughlin, G. 2018. Ryanair investors want chairman replaced, *Irish Times* accessed on 15 December 2018 https://www.independent.ie/business/irish/ryanair-investor-wants-chairman-replaced-37467801.html.

Meardi, G. 2014. The (claimed) growing irrelevance of employment relations. *Journal of Industrial Relations, 56*(4), pp. 594–605.

Mrozowicki, A., Roosalu, T. and Senčar, T. B. 2013. Precarious work in the retail sector in Estonia, Poland and Slovenia: trade union responses in a time of economic crisis. *Transfer: European Review of Labour and Research, 19*(2), pp. 267–78.

Müller, T., Vandaele, K. and Waddington, J. (eds) 2019. *Collective Bargaining in Europe*, Brussels: European Trade Union Institute, forthcoming.

Myant, M. and Drahokoupil, J. 2012. International integration, varieties of capitalism and resilience to crisis in transition economies. *Europe-Asia Studies, 64*(1), pp. 1–33.

OECD 2018. Going for Growth 2018: An opportunity that governments should not miss, OECD, accessed on 8 March 2019, http://www.oecd.org/eco/going-for-growth.htm.

O'Sullivan, M. and Gunnigle, P. 2009. Bearing all the hallmarks of oppression. *Labor Studies Journal, 34*(2), pp. 252–70.

Paolucci, V. 2016. *The Role of Collective Bargaining in Addressing Flexibility and Security: A Multi-level Comparative Institutional Analysis of Three*

Countries and Four Companies within the Chemical and Pharmaceutical Sector, University of Warwick (IRRU) PhD.

Paolucci, V. 2017. The role of collective bargaining in addressing flexibility and security. *European Journal of Industrial Relations*, *23*(4), pp. 329–46.

Peters, J. 2008. Labour market deregulation and the decline of labour power in North America and Western Europe. *Policy and Society*, *27*(1), pp. 83–98.

Piketty, T. 2015. About capital in the twenty-first century. *American Economic Review*, *105*(5), pp. 48–53.

Polanyi, K. 1944. *The Great Transformation*, Boston: Beacon Press.

Regan, A. and Brazys, S. 2018. Celtic phoenix or leprechaun economics? The politics of an FDI-led growth model in Europe. *New Political Economy*, *23*(2), pp. 223–38.

Roberts, D. L., and Griffith, J. C. 2018. *A Tale of Two Airlines: A Comparative Case Study of High-Road Versus Low-Road Strategies in Customer Service and Reputation Management*, accessed on 8 March 2019, https://commons.erau.edu/publication/965.

Roche, W. K., Teague, P. and Colvin, A. J. 2014. Introduction: developments in conflict management, in W. K. Roche, P. Teague and A. J. Colvin (eds), *The Oxford Handbook of Conflict Management in Organizations* (pp. 1–29), Oxford: Oxford University Press.

Rubery, J., Keizer, A. and Grimshaw, D. 2016. Flexibility bites back: the multiple and hidden costs of flexible employment policies. *Human Resource Management Journal*, *26*(3), pp. 235–51.

Scheiber, N. 2018. Google workers reject Silicon Valley individualism in walkout, *The New York Times* online 6 November, accessed on 8 March 2019, https://www.nytimes.com/2018/11/06/business/google-employee-walkout-labor.html.

Schmalz, S. and Dörre, K. 2018. The power resources approach. Paper prepared for the project Trade Unions in Transformation, accessed on 8 March 2019, https://www.fes.de/index.php?eID=dumpFile&t=f&f=32816&token=e509820f9daab00a4fe1be4f4d052f9ef 7085fc9.

Schurman, S. J., Eaton, A. E. and Chen, M. A. 2017. Conclusion: expanding the boundaries of labour organising and collective bargaining, in A. E. Eaton, S. J. Schurman and M. A. Chen (eds), *Informal Workers and Collective Action* (pp. 217–37), Cornell: Cornell University Press.

Silver, B. J. 2003. *Forces of Labor: Workers' Movements and Globalization Since 1870*, Cambridge: Cambridge University Press.

Spero, J. and Beesley, A. 2018. Has Ryanair chief Michael O'Leary lost his cost-killing touch? *Financial Times* online, 4 October, accessed on 8 March 2019, https://www.ft.com/content/2d5671ec-c7d5-11e8-ba8f-ee390057b8c9.

Stan, S. and Erne, R. 2015. Is migration from Central and Eastern Europe an opportunity for trade unions to demand higher wages? Evidence from the Romanian health sector. *European Journal of Industrial Relations*, *22*(2), pp. 167–83.

Stiglitz, J. E. 2012. *The Price of Inequality: How Today's Divided Society Endangers Our Future*, New York: W. W. Norton & Company.

Streeck, W. 1988. Comment on Ronald Dore, rigidities in the labour market. *Government and Opposition*, *23*(4), pp. 413–23.

Taskin, L. and Devos, V. 2005. Paradoxes from the individualization of human resource management: the case of telework. *Journal of Business Ethics*, *62*(1), pp. 13–24.

Trif, A., Koukiadaki, A. and Kahancova, M. 2016. The rise of the dual labour market: fighting precarious employment in the new member states through industrial relations: comparative report (Croatia, Czechia, Greece, Hungary, Latvia, Lithuania, Poland, Romania, Slovakia and Slovenia). European Commission. Brussels, Belgium: European Commission.

Trif, A. and Stoiciu, V. 2017. Turning crisis into an opportunity: innovation within the Romanian trade union movement, in M. Bernaciak and M. Kahancova (eds), *Beyond the Crisis: Innovative Practices Within CEE Trade Union Movements* (pp. 161–77), Brussels: ETUI.

Visser, J. 2016. What happened to collective bargaining during the great recession? *IZA Journal of Labor Policy*, *5*(9), pp. 1–35.

Walkout for Real Change 2018. Google walkout for real change, Twitter Referencing Group, 1 November, accessed on 6 March 2019, https://www.nytimes.com/2018/11/06/business/google-employee-walkout-labor.html.

World Employment Confederation 2018. Economic report 2017, WEC, accessed on 15 December 2018, https://www.wecglobal.org/fileadmin/media/pdf/WEC_Economic_Report_2018_Edition.pdf.

2. Comparative Employee Relations: An Overview of Contemporary Developments and Scholarship

Chris Brewster

INTRODUCTION

This chapter builds from the first one, examining not so much what is happening in employment relations, as focusing on contextual differences between employee relations in different countries, and the way work is changing and how work is and will get done. The chapter also picks up the 'language' theme of the book and notes the symbiotic relationship between words such as 'work' and 'employment', and 'employment relations', and the way scholars are addressing these issues.

The book as a whole examines the way that notions of employment and employment relations vary around the world and how different uses of language, and the different languages used in different countries, both inform and reflect that. It is worth reiterating here that language is fundamental to the way we discuss concepts. How we discuss any issue is rooted in the words and the language we use and the definitions we attribute to our terms. This chapter therefore examines these issues, considers the world of work and the way we discuss it, its relationship to the kinds of developments around the world flagged in Chapter 1 and, in particular, the effects of developments in technology that are impacting the world of work, of employment and of employment relations and the different scenarios that are found in different countries.

Background

When the International Labour Organization (ILO) was founded at the end of the First World War, the focus was on the imperial powers and the way work was being conducted there. Under pressure from the Bolshevik revolution in Russia, it was felt important to ameliorate the worst features of capitalism for workers. The ILO was comprised of representatives of three partners – governments, employers and trade unions – and dealt with the relationships between these parties within specific national contexts and the outcomes of these relationships in terms of the employment contracts of workers (Davies and Woodward, 2014). It was obvious to the Organization that it was these relationships that determined 'industrial relations', the way people were employed in the manufacturing sector (and, as an afterthought, other sectors).

There was initially little attention paid to the unorganised sectors of the economy – it was assumed that these would decrease as organisation spread – and little attention paid to the way people worked, often outside 'employment', in the less developed countries of the world. In the colonial territories, the powers tended to feel either that, since these were not manufacturing centres, trade unions were irrelevant or, in some cases, they simply tried to replicate their own industrial relations in the colonial territories. The ILO operated through 'conventions' (159 of them) creating labour rights in all the countries that signed up to them.

A century later we can look back on developments since then and see that, whilst initially manufacturing and 'Taylorist' management spread rapidly, it never conquered the world and for much of the second half of the period it has been in decline. New kinds and forms of working patterns, not all by any means requiring either traditional or indeed any employment, have developed. Different societies rose and fell in the international firmament (and different countries were absorbed into or separated from others), but most countries remained poor and never developed the tradition of regular employment or the strength of trade unionism found in some of the developed countries. We can also see that trade unionism itself has been declining even in those countries it which it was once strong (Kelly, 2015). In response the ILO was reduced in size, but its mandate was expanded to 'decent work', a much less precise terminology that allowed it to continue in business, often advising on the same 'organisational' models of employment relations, even as the proportion of the world covered by trade unions reduced dramatically (Standing, 2008).

Employers and, to a large extent, governments responded to the changes not just by pressuring the ILO but more seriously by changing their approach to the role of trade unionism, and then to the ILO itself, by taking a less co-operative stance. Governments refused to support trade unions in the ways they had in the past and introduced 'cost-effective' rather than exemplary approaches into their own relationships with the people they employed in the public sector. Employers refused to be bound by ILO Directives, refused to pass further Directives, and lobbied governments to allow them more scope in the way people were employed. They rebranded their 'personnel administration' or 'industrial relations' departments as 'human resource management' departments and then, latterly, restricted them to their elites by rebranding them again, this time as 'talent management' departments. The ILO responded by, effectively, giving up on the idea of persuading governments to accept ILO Directives into enforceable legislation and decide to operate through 'soft law' principles (Hassel, 2008), preferring that governments should be constrained by self-regulation, shifting the emphasis from labour rights to principles – which are much more difficult to define and to enforce (Alston, 2004).

We academics responded, in part, by changing our focus and language: our terminology. Thus 'industrial relations' gave way to 'employment relations' or 'employee relations'. Like industrial relations, employee relations was assumed to, and generally did, though there were interesting exceptions, apply to relationships within the nation state. Cross-border trade unions or trade unions operating beyond national boundaries were rare, although international trade union federations existed even before the time of the founding of the ILO. In general, however, industrial relations, and employee relations, was and is nationally bound.

The Language of Employee Relations

As Chapter 1 notes, employee relations refers to managing interactions between workers and their representatives (e.g. trade unions, works' councils, workers' director etc.), on the one side, and employers and their representatives (e.g. employers' associations or managers) on the other side (Frege and Kelly, 2013). It was argued that what was important was not so much the relationship between the two (employer and union) parties involved, as the way that such relationships were managed. In many cases the subject was restricted to the relationship between the two main parties in each separate workplace: trade unions, representing the employees, and management, as employees representing the employer. Note that the definition and the language here discusses 'workers' but that the overall terminology and the general practice assumes that workers are 'employees' only. However, not all workers are employees (a point we return to below), and peripheral employees such as temporary staff, part-time staff, and so on are often not included. There is also here an explicit assumption (shared in most countries other than the Nordic ones, where most employees, including managers, tended to be trade union members) that employees are on one side of the table and managers, although themselves employees, are on the other. Note, too, that one further difference between 'employee relations' and 'industrial relations' is that the latter normally includes some reference to the system and the other parties that define the ground on which the relationship will be based. The definition of employee relations narrows the field to the relationship between trade unions, or other representative groups, and employers: the state no longer has a key role to play.

The terminology does mention 'employees' as well as 'their representatives', recognising that in many cases these are not two parties as such: there is only management on one side and highly differentiated groups of, or even single, individual, employees on the other. As it began to be understood that between the parties it was generally management that had the greatest power, with the other parties tending to be responsive to them, and as management's power became increasingly obvious, academics started to study 'human resource management'. However, 'whilst terminology and (some) practices change, the concerns [the employment relationship, power and employee performance and productivity] remain the same' (Nienhüser and Warhurst, 2018: 214). Language is important, but not all important.

It should be emphasised that none of the changes noted above was clean or complete. In the way that work was organised and conducted, in the way that governments, employers and management responded and in the reactions of scholars, the changes were messy, incoherent and swept back and forth around the globe, gaining adherents at different times in different places and occasionally experiencing push-back and reversals. There are elements of all stages still existing somewhere today.

Driving all these changes are underlying, and continuing, changes to the context in which work is conducted, changes to the nature of work and changes to the nature of work in relationship to employment. Such changes inevitably impact experience of and, perhaps belatedly, our understanding of employment relations. It is worth setting this in context. For the majority of people around the world, work has never been connected to employment. Even for that minority that had employment, they only had 'employment relations' in the very general sense that there were interactions between employees and management: in most cases those interactions involved deployment and control rather than consultation or negotiation.

Employment was in a sense one of the key inventions that made the Industrial Revolution possible. Before the Industrial Revolution most people had been in some sort of servitude to their masters (or few mistresses), or had worked as independent farmers, bakers or manufacturers, or had simply grown and operated their homes from their own family resources (subsistence farming). The first Industrial Revolution developed concomitantly with employment, where people sold their time to other people in exchange for doing the work they were deployed and ordered to do. Although much of this work was still done outside (manu)factories, in what was at the time the most technologically advanced country, the United Kingdom, the effect of bringing such workers together as employees sowed the seeds of collective action and trade unionism. The Industrial Revolution created not just employment but also industrial relations.

Subsequent revolutions made huge changes to the way work is conceived and carried out. In hindsight, people identified a 'second Industrial Revolution' (Schwarb, 2016), mass assembly and production. This increased employment massively: having a ready supply of labour was crucial, and the massing of labour together created the possibility of workers operating in concert, developing and strengthening trade unions and giving rise to the notion of industrial relations. Technology moves inexorably on and the third (automation and computerisation) and the fourth (robotisation and artificial intelligence) revolutions are leading us (back to) an increasing separation of work and employment (Schwarb, 2016).

It is against this background that this chapter explores employment relations around the world.

COMPARATIVE EMPLOYMENT RELATIONS

There is little debate about the fact that employee relations (the catch-all term adopted by this book and used here) is a national phenomenon. There is plenty of evidence (Bamber et al., 2016; Brewster et al., 2007; Nienhüser and Warhurst, 2018; Wood and Brewster, 2007) that employment relations varies markedly from country to country. Indeed, although there have been attempts at direct comparisons (Barry and Wilkinson, 2011; Frege and Kelly, 2013; van Ruysseveldt et al., 1995; Wilkinson et al., 2014), many books on 'comparative employment relations' (Bamber et al., 2016; Wood and Brewster, 2007) are fundamentally compilations of chapters on different countries. Of course, and as evidenced elsewhere in this book, employment relations has some common themes across all countries: it generally relies on notions of paid employment, it is concerned with employment contracts and how they are determined (Kaufman, 2004), pay and conditions are at its heart, communications between representatives of employers and employees or representatives of employees are crucial, and for all the parties involved (including here governments, employers, employees and those who depend on them) the critical outcome is employee output and productivity. This is a critical outcome because governments rely on the success of businesses to enable them to levy taxes and to provide services for the citizens; employers rely to some extent or other on successful organisations for their competitiveness, their income and their growth; and it is crucial to employees and the families and communities who depend on them, because without competitive levels of productivity such employment will be at risk.

Employee relations varies, of course, and, as evidenced elsewhere in this book, not just between countries but also within nation states, most markedly between larger and smaller employers, but also between sectors of the economy, and sometimes regionally. Adopting an international comparative lens means focusing on the differences between employment relations at the country level; it is like focusing a telescope (Brewster, 1995), examining employee relations at different levels means some things come more clearly into focus and others blur – what is being observed does not change, but the comparisons you use and the conclusions you can draw do change.

What scholars find when they compare employee relations internationally depends to some extent on what they are looking for

(Nienhüser and Warhurst, 2018): employee relations can be, and has been, examined through different disciplinary lenses – economics, sociology (including labour process), social psychology and the psychological contract, political economy and the 'new institutionalism' (Frege and Kelly, 2013). Each discipline has ways of thinking and language they use that restricts its accessibility to other ways of thinking. At the internationally comparative level, the main explanations advanced so far for comparative differences are institutionally based and culturally based (Brewster et al., 2018). Both explanations are widely conceived but have leading authorities that have dominated the debate in both cases, tending to narrow understanding. Thus, a wide view of institutionalism would discuss the impact on employee relations of factors such as the size, topography and wealth of a country as well as the industrial structures, and political, legislative, educational, welfare and labour market systems typically discussed by scholars using the analyses of Hall and Soskice (2001), Amable (2003) and Whitley (1999). A wide view of culture would discuss historical trajectories, ethnic groupings, masculine domination and the effects of colonialism as well as the national values analyses typically based on the work of Hofstede (1980) or the GLOBE studies (House et al., 2004).

We can see some simple differences between countries, at least in stereotypical form, if we, briefly, compare employment relations in the UK, Japan and Argentina (for details on China, Nigeria, USA, Germany and Italy, see the relevant chapters in this book). We outline these below and then address the questions of the reality of these stereotypes and of change.

The UK was where the original Industrial Revolution began, and it was a precursor of industrial relations (or employee relations). Many other countries set up their industrial relations systems as copies of, or in reaction to, the British model. Industrial relations in the UK developed in a typically pragmatic and haphazard manner – reflecting a culture of 'trying stuff out and keeping what worked'. Thus, each workplace developed its own system of trade unions and it was only later that they combined, usually for reasons of effectiveness (they were facing the same employer) or for reasons of efficiency (it was more cost-effective to combine). The result was unionism that had strong roots at the workplace level combined into a patchwork of industrial, occupational and often competing unions at national level. The central national trade union body, the Trades Union Congress (TUC), was dominant (although there were smaller, weaker competitors) but had little other than symbolic power. Over time, as union membership increased the unions became richer and more powerful. Then, as membership decreased, the bureaucracies that had been created found it difficult to adjust and the efficiency rationale came to the fore with more and more unions combining into cheaper-to-run general unions, while some powerful occupational unions maintained their independence. With union membership in the country now covering perhaps less than a fifth of all workers, the influence of the unions and the TUC has declined to the point where, except for one or two occupations, they are almost more lobby groups than negotiators of contracts.

Trade unionism in Japan is more recent. Japan has more than twice the population of the UK and is significantly richer. At one time, in the 1960s and 1970s, Japan was held up as a model economy (Aoki and Dore, 1994), but economic problems put an end to that and allowed the re-establishment of the 'dominant' US-based model (Smith and Meiksins, 1995). Trade unionism in Japan had early shoots but was developed effectively after the First World War. The unions generally cover only the largest firms and the public sector and, as elsewhere, are in decline. For these larger firms, and in the public sector (though never in the majority of workplaces), employment was traditionally built on the three pillars of long-term employment, seniority-based pay enterprise unions. Although these are all in decline, pushed particularly by high use of technology and big increases in atypical work, employee relations in Japan is still idiosyncratic. What strikes an outsider looking at the country is the co-operative nature of employee relations. It may be, as Kaufman et al. (2018) show, that even in the antagonistic USA employee relations in most cases is generally felt to be 'OK', but Japan rarely experiences overt conflict.

On yet another continent, South America, Argentina is a large country but with a population two-thirds the size of the UK. It was one of the earliest countries to develop economically, indeed before the First World War it was the tenth richest country in the world (Eiras and Schaefer, 2001). However, a series of economic and political crises have meant that the country is now much less successful. In employee relations terms the country has had a relatively stable system for decades as a result of the Peronist inclusion of labour and trade union rights in the national constitution. The trade union movement was controlled by the populist President Peron and on the demise of Peronism split between those who wanted to maintain the fight to legitimise the labour law and those who wanted to fight increasingly right-wing or military governments (James, 1988). From the 1990s onward privatisations and massive deregulation of the labour market led to a significant increase in atypical employment and reductions of labour rights (ILO, 2009). Currently the situation is contested. The Argentine workers movements is, for South America, unusually centralised in the CGT and membership remains high, although precise figures are hard to establish. Collective agreements, led by the CGT's member unions and federations, were usually industry based and set minimum wages levels with company-level bargaining above that, but that has changed, and most agreements are now at firm-level. The union movement continues to rely on a close relationship with supportive politicians. Still, however, most workers are not trade union members.

CONVERGENCE AND DIVERGENCE

These differences, combined with some similar trends, force us to revisit the debates about convergence and divergence. So far, much of this debate has been cast in terms of globalisation versus national specificities. The question that has been raised is whether globalisation is forcing increasing standardisation around the world: in other words, with the increasing globalisation of the world economy are these differences in employment relations around the world decreasing? Does the increasing influence of multinational enterprises, spreading their human resource management practices around the world, mean that employment relations are being globalised too? We have increasing evidence about this, for the developed countries at least. We know that although trade union membership has been falling in nearly all countries the countries tend to stay in the same relationship with each other: the ones that have higher membership figures tend to remain the ones with the higher membership figures, even at lower overall levels of membership.

More importantly, however, the approach to employment relations tends to stay the same. Thus, Japan and the Nordic countries are categorised as co-ordinated market economies, where taxes are high, social services are excellent and, importantly for us here, trade union membership figures are higher. In the Nordic countries, for example, most workers are trade union members and managers still tend automatically to discuss crucial work-related issues with employees and representatives of employees. The common view is that such processes may take longer but generally lead to better and more acceptable decisions. In turn, the trade unions continue to see their role as challenging management with the aim of ensuring the success of their enterprise. Their argument is that only if their organisation is successful will their members be secure in their jobs and the employer be able to continue paying decent wages. For most businesses, competition is based on quality. The Nordic countries are amongst the richest in the world, with very low levels of poverty, so it is widely believed, on all sides, that the system works. Nevertheless, there are pressures in these countries to move towards a 'more competitive' (lower cost) neo-liberal market.

The Anglo-Saxon liberal markets, including the UK's ex-colonial countries, have inherited a liberal market tradition and management and unions continue to see their role as antagonistic. This is based on a zero-sum game analysis: whatever one side gets (as either dividends or salaries), is then not available to the other side. Hence employers try to give employees as little information as they can get away with, and to keep the wage bill as tightly controlled as possible; and employees distrust even the information they are given and wherever they can push for wage increases. Much competition is on the basis of low-cost production. As will be evident elsewhere in this book, the liberal market democracies are not a homogenous whole: each country has a different cultural and institutional make-up and, consequently, different employee relations.

The market position of the South American countries is less clear: they are not included in the typical analyses by Hall and Soskice (2001), Amable (2003) or Whitley (1999). Those authors were concerned to identify why the co-ordinated market policies of Germany and the Rhineland countries, the Nordic countries and Japan did things completely differently from the 'one size fits all' economic policies pushed by the international organisations (as noted in Chapter 1) and yet were equally successful. So South America was not within their scope. Other authors have argued that South American countries are part of a hierarchical market economy (Schneider, 2009).

These distinctions are based in long-standing institutional and cultural differences that are slow to change. It is unlikely that all the elements would combine to change together towards one of the other forms of capitalisms and so countries, and market economies, tend to maintain their distinctiveness. In other words, convergence is unlikely. It remains important to understand the comparative perspective on employee relations.

In short, national differences continue to matter.

BEHIND THE CHANGES IN EMPLOYMENT RELATIONS: CHANGES IN WORK

Obviously, history, and economics are behind these differences and the changes that have occurred in every country. But we might argue, like Karl Marx, that underlying all these developments is technology. And that is what is going to drive employment relations in the future. It was the technology, the accompanying economic structures, and the political and social structures that they spawned that created employment and the differing and changing employment relations in the UK, Japan, Argentina; in the other countries covered in this book; and in all other countries. Initially the technology created 'employment' in workplaces where trade unionism could flourish and provide political and social opportunities to those trade union movements. And it is the new technologies that are causing the worldwide (if nationally distinct) declines in trade union memberships.

The changes are created by new technologies: by robotisation, and particularly by the development of information and communication technology and, more recently, artificial intelligence. Work is changing – and becoming increasingly divorced from employment (Brewster and Holland, 2019).

Much of this work takes place in what is known, apparently without irony, as the 'sharing' economy, or the 'gig' economy or, less argumentatively, as the platform economy. There are now numerous texts, and journal special issues, trying to capture the business and management implications of these ways of working (De Stefano, 2016; Forde et al, 2017; Frenken and Schor, 2017; Howcroft and Bergvall-Kåreborn, 2018; Kirchner and Schüßler, 2019). They are only rarely addressed in the employee relations literature, presumably because the language of 'employee relations' is predicated on 'employment' – and these workers are not employees. Various types of platform work have been identified. These cover three main categories: (1) platform-based on-demand work (e.g. Uber); (2) virtual or be-clouded work (e.g. Amazon's Mechanical Turk); and (3) work via online marketplaces (e.g. Taskrabbit) (Srnicek, 2017; Veen et al., 2019). What is significant about these platforms is that they are rentiers, taking value out of the work chain but investing very little. Workers take their tasks from the platform and are paid by the end-user or customer. No 'employer' is involved. Proponents of the platform economy, and there are many, argue that, like previous industrial revolutions, it will create new economic opportunities for workers, more transparent and efficient markets, and enable more, and more self-controlled, flexible work arrangement (Goods et al., 2019; Mulcahy, 2017; Peticca-Harris et al., 2018; Srnicek, 2017). What it is definitely doing is causing an increasing dislocation of work and a separation between work and employment (Brewster and Holland, 2019; De Stefano, 2016). There are choices in how this is viewed: does it herald a new dawn with workers able to control their own work and no longer dependent on employers? Or does it take us back to the days before the invention of employment (and, of course, employee relations) and closer to the way that most people throughout the world have worked throughout history – including perhaps sharing their minimal standards of living and security?

Because this expanding proportion of the workforce (Huws et al., 2018) is not 'employed', platform work tests the boundaries of employee relations regulatory regimes. There has been a series of attempts in North America, Europe and Australasia to bring at least members of the 'platform work on-demand' category of workers under employment legislation (Rubery et al., 2018), but it remains to be seen whether the regulations can cope with these new ways of working.

The platform economy exists alongside a raft of 'self-employment', where employers ask their workers to continue to do the same work but to go 'self-employed', which frees the ex-employer from many routine administrative tasks, to accept short-term contracts, or to take unpaid or lowly paid internships (Batt, 2018; Bernaciak and Kahancova, 2017; Lansbury, 2018). Such arrangements help businesses to get work done without having to accept the employment responsibilities that have traditionally gone with such work. In the UK there are estimates of up to 5.5 million people out of a workforce of 32.5 million who are 'working' but are not 'employed'. Some of them are entrepreneurs, running their own businesses; some are doing tasks that look suspiciously like the employment they used to have; many work in the platform economy, 'managed' by programmes and algorithms. They log in and find the next fare, or delivery, or piece of computer work; they do it and the customer pays them (the system takes a proportion), and they are responsible for arranging their own tax and insurance affairs, their own equipment, and their own holidays (they only get paid when they work). They are 'independent'. Although there have been one or two high profile exceptions, in most cases these workers are isolated and not represented by a trade union or by anyone. They work for themselves. Some people like this, others hate it – most accept it.

The effect of this huge section of the workforce working this way is to increase yet further the pressure on people working as employees. This is very visible in retail establishments where increasingly customers are expected to 'cash-out' themselves: as the number of automatic cash-out machines increases, the number of employees falls. The same pattern is repeated in warehousing, in insurance offices and in distribution.

At the time of writing the result is, as noted by Fleming (2018), not unemployment but an expanding proportion of poor work. Again, a comparative perspective expands the picture. A key drive for employers is to keep costs to a minimum consistent with being able to offer the goods or services that customers want. For most organisations, labour costs are the largest single component of their variable costs. There are ways to reduce labour costs: in some cases they can be outsourced to poorer countries.

Where work cannot be taken to other countries (care homes, agriculture, etc.) then labour costs can be reduced by bringing cheaper labour from poorer countries into the location where the work must be performed. We should not let our focus on comparative employee relations between nations blind us to the increasing interconnections between work and workers across national boundaries. Not only has there been, as noted, substantial moves to place work where the workers are cheaper, but workers are now increasingly moving to other countries to find work. The figures are estimates and are probably rather dubious but the United Nations, for example, suggests that by 2017 there were more than 250 million people living outside their home country, with around half of them working. The figures have grown significantly in recent years and are projected to grow further. A small percentage of these people are the elite, and much studied, expatriates; many more of them are economic migrants, moving to better themselves and their families (remittances from such people back to their usually poor home countries amounted to over $600 billion in 2015, according to World Bank estimates (World Bank Group, 2016: xii)). Around $450 billion of that went to developing countries, nearly three times the amount of official development assistance. The actual amount of remittances, including unrecorded flows through formal and informal channels, is believed to be significantly larger. Many are people who have been forced out of their own countries by natural disaster, climate change, political oppression or war: or sometimes a combination of several of those factors. Such people need work. Governments often make legal work difficult for them. And getting a job is often hard for such disadvantaged workers, even if they speak the local language well. As a consequence, they are often provided with very poor salaries and working conditions. Not only does this mean the employer has an immediate decrease in labour costs, but it may serve to depress labour costs generally in the area or the industry (Doellgast et al., 2018). Migrants do this because they may be desperate to get and hold jobs, or because the terms and conditions offered are significantly better than those they face at home. Whether their employment conditions are seen as an example of migrants reducing working conditions for locals or as an example of exploitation by employers is a political question.

Or, the employer can use robotisation, but only where the managers are comfortable with it (managers are often more resistant to the introduction of robotisation and computerisation than their workers) and there are clear cost savings. Alternatively, the employer can use the technology – or use the threat of technology – to drive down costs by reducing the terms and conditions of workers. Thus, the outcome of computerisation and robotisation may be not unemployment but poorer working conditions and salaries (Fleming, 2018).

And where robotisation, computerisation and the platform economy have taken workers out of employment they simply drop from the visibility of governments, policy makers, trade unions and employee relations scholars focused, as so many of us are, on 'employment'.

CONCLUSIONS

Our language and the baggage that it brings with it are important. It is important to explore this at a national level. Words cannot always be translated directly or exactly into other languages' and words always come with 'background' and 'meaning' and have implications. The way each country talks about employee relations has a symbiotic relationship with practice. But words have a meaning more generally. A focus on 'employee relations' moves us beyond industrial relations and employment relations, allowing us to consider employment relationships that may not be covered by or dependent on trade unions or collective bargaining. It adds the whole field of non-unionism into our discourse and indeed allows or even privileges the whole field of individual employer (or manager) to individual employee relationships. By standing apart from human resource management, it allows us to explore issues beyond the needs or wishes of employers and enables us to examine issues of labour markets, employment and resistance from a more neutral point of view.

However, the language of employee relations as a terminology restricts our analysis to employment issues. By definition, it excludes relationships that do not involve employment. Crucial issues of work in the global value chain are placed outside our scope. In the Rana Plaza tragedy, well over 1,000 people were crushed and killed when five factories collapsed (Chowdhury, 2017). These low-paid workers were making goods for world-famous brands from 31 different companies in buildings that some said were locked so that the people inside could not leave before the end of their shift. The workers were making goods for world-famous brands; but were not employed by those brands, but by outsourced suppliers. The brands disclaimed any responsibility. The continuing, sometimes brutal or even murderous, exploitation of workers in countries with weak institutions, lacking similar notions of employment rights to those found in the more advanced economies, are excluded from the purview of employee relations. Similarly, the developments in technology that are leading to work being undertaken by robots or through artificial intelligence are excluded. It will be many years before these changes become so widespread as to threaten our scholarly endeavours in the subject of 'employee relations'. In the meantime, a focus on international comparisons helps us to set employee relations in context and to appreciate that the language we use to describe it impacts on how we understand the ways (and the range of ways) that employee relations are organised in each country.

Eventually, inevitably, as work gets increasingly divorced from employment, as work gets moved around the world, and as it gets done by 'the machines', employee relations will become a restrictive terminology. And we will have to turn to different terminology, different language, to understand the way the world works.

REFERENCES

Alston, P. (2004). Core labour standards and the transformation of the international labour rights regime. *European Journal of International Law*, 15(3): 457–521.

Amable, B. (2003). *The Diversity of Modern Capitalism*. Oxford: Oxford University Press.

Aoki, M. and Dore, R. P. (1994). *The Japanese Firm: The Sources of Competitive Strength*. New York: Oxford University Press.

Bamber, G., Lansbury, R. D., Wailes, N. and Wright, C. F. (2016). *International and Comparative Employment Relations* (6th edn). Sydney: Allen & Unwin.

Barry, M. and Wilkinson, A. (eds) (2011). *Research Handbook of Comparative Employment Relations*. Cheltenham, UK and Northampton, MA, USA: Edward Elgar Publishing.

Batt, R. (2018). The financial model of the firm, the 'future of work', and employment relations. In A. Wilkinson, T. Dundon, J. Donaghey and A. Colvin (eds), *The Routledge Companion to Employment Relations*. London: Routledge, pp. 465–79.

Bernaciak, M. and Kahancova, M. (2017). *Innovative Union Practices in Central-Eastern Europe*. Brussels: European Trade Union Institute (ETUI).

Brewster, C. (1995). Towards a 'European' model of human resource management. *Journal of International Business Studies*, 26(1): 1–21.

Brewster, C. and Holland, P. (2019). Work 'or' employment in the 21st century? In A. Wilkinson and M. Barry (eds), *The Research Agenda for the Future of Work*. Cheltenham, UK and Northampton, MA, USA: Edward Elgar Publishing.

Brewster, C., Mayrhofer, W. and Farndale, E. (eds) (2018). *Handbook of Research on Comparative Human Resource Management* (2nd edn). Cheltenham, UK and Northampton, MA, USA: Edward Elgar Publishing.

Brewster, C., Wood, G., Croucher, C. and Brookes, M. (2007). Are works councils and joint consultative committees a threat to trade unions? A comparative analysis. *Economic and Industrial Democracy*, 28(1): 53–81.

Chowdhury, R. (2017). The Rana Plaza disaster and the complicit behavior of elite NGOs. *Organization*, 24(6): 938–49.

Davies, M. D. V. and Woodward, R. (2014). *International Organizations*. Cheltenham, UK and Northampton, MA, USA: Edward Elgar Publishing.

De Stefano, V. (2016). The rise of the 'just-in-time workforce': on-demand work, crowdwork, and labor protection in the 'gig-economy'. *Comparative Labor Law and Policy Journal*, 37(2): 471–504.

Doellgast, V., Lillie, N. and Pulignano, V. (eds) (2018). *Reconstructing Solidarity: Labour Unions, Precarious Work, and the Politics of Institutional Change in Europe*. Oxford: Oxford University Press.

Eiras, A. and Schaefer, B. (2001). Argentina's economic crisis: an 'absence of capitalism'. Executive Summary. Washington, DC. Heritage Foundation.

Fleming, P. (2018). Robots and organization studies: why robots might not want to steal your job. *Organization Studies*, 40(1): 23–38.

Forde, C., Stuart, M., Joyce, S., Oliver, L., Valizade, D., Alberti, G., Hardy, K., Trappmann, V., Umney, C. and Carson, C. (2017). The social protection of workers in the collaborative economy, *Report for European Parliament Employment and Social Affairs Committee*.

Frege, C. and Kelly, J. (2013). *Comparative Employment Relations in the Global Economy*. London: Routledge.

Frenken, K. and Schor, J. (2017). Putting the sharing economy into perspective. *Environmental Innovation and Societal Transitions*, 23: 3–10.

Goods, C., Veen, A. and Barratt, T. (2019). 'Is your gig any good?' Analysing job quality in the Australian platform-based food-delivery sector. *Journal of Industrial Relations*, DOI:0022185618817069.

Hall, P. and Soskice, D. (2001). *Varieties of Capitalism: The Institutional Foundations of Comparative Advantage*. New York: Oxford University Press.

Hassel, A. 2008. The evolution of a global governance regime. *Governance*, 21(2): 231–51.

Hofstede, G. (1980). *Culture's Consequences: International Differences in Work-Related Values*. Beverly Hills: Sage Publications.

House, R. J., Hanges, P. J., Javidan, M., Dorfman, P. W. and Gupta, V. (eds) (2004). *Culture, Leadership, and Organizations: The GLOBE Study of 62 Societies*. Thousand Oaks, CA: Sage Publications.

Howcroft, D. and Bergvall-Kåreborn, B. (2018). A typology of crowdwork platforms. *Work, Employment and Society*, 33(1): 21–38.

Huws, U., Spencer, N. H. and Syrdal, D. S. (2018). Online, on call: the spread of digitally organised just-in-time working and its implications for standard employment models. *New Technology, Work and Employment*, 33(2): 113–29.

ILO (2009). *Industrial Relations and Collective Bargaining: Argentina, Brazil and Mexico Compared*. ILO Working Paper No 5, by A. Cardoso and J. Gindin. Geneva: International Labour Office.

James, D. (1988). *Resistance and Integration: Peronism and the Argentine Working Class 1946–1976*. Cambridge, Cambridge University Press.

Kaufman, B. E. (2004). Employment relations and the employment relations system: a guide to theorizing. In B. E. Kaufman (ed.), *Theoretical Perspectives on Work and the Employment Relationship*. Champaign, IL: Industrial Relations Research Association, pp. 41–75.

Kaufman, B. E., Barry, M., Gomez, R. and Wilkinson, A. (2018). Evaluating the state of the employment relationship: A balanced scorecard approach built on Mackenzie King's model of an industrial relations system. *Relations industrielles/Industrial Relations*, 73(4): 664–701.

Kelly, J. (2015). Trade union membership and power in comparative perspective. *Economic and Labour Relations Review*, 26(4): 526–44.

Kirchner, S. and Schüßler, E. (2019). The organization of digital marketplaces: unmasking the role of Internet platforms in the sharing economy. In G. Ahrne and N. Brunsson (eds), *Organization Outside Organizations. The Abundance of Partial Organization in Social Life*. Cambridge Cambridge University Press, pp. 131–54.

Lansbury, R. D. (2018). The changing world of work and employment relations: a multi-level institutional perspective of the future. *Labour & Industry: A Journal of the Social and Economic Relations of Work*, 28(1): 5–20.

Mulcahy, D. (2017). *The Gig Economy: The Complete Guide to Getting Better Work, Taking More Time Off, and Financing the Life You Want*. New York: American Mangement Association.

Nienhüser, W. and Warhurst, C. (2018). Comparative employment relations: definitional, disciplinary and development issues. In C. Brewster, W. Mayrhofer and E. Farndale (eds), *Handbook of Research on Comparative Human Resource Management*. Cheltenham, UK and Northampton, MA, USA: Edward Elgar Publishing, pp. 200–22.

Peticca-Harris, A., de Gama, N. and Ravishankar, M. N. (2018). Postcapitalist precarious work and those in the 'drivers' seat: exploring the motivations and lived experiences of Uber drivers in Canada. *Organization*, DOI:1350508418757332.

Rubery, J., Grimshaw, D. and Keizer, A. (2018). Challenges and contradictions in the 'normalising' of precarious work. *Work, Employment and Society*, 32: 509–27.

Schneider, B. (2009). Hierarchical market economies and varieties of capitalism in Latin America. *Journal of Latin American Studies*, 41(3): 553–75.

Schwarb, K. (2016). *The Fourth Industrial Revolution*. Switzerland: World Economic Forum.

Smith, C. and Meiksins, P. (1995). System, society and dominance effects in cross-national organisational analysis. *Work, Employment and Society*, 9(2): 241–67.

Srnicek, N. (2017). *Platform Capitalism*. Cambridge: Polity Press.

Standing, G. (2008). The ILO: an agency for globalization? *Development and Change*, 39(3): 355–84.

van Ruysseveldt, J., Huiskamp, R. and van Hoof, J. (1995). *Comparative Industrial and Employment Relations*. London: Sage Publications.

Veen, A., Oliver, D., Goods, C. and Barratt, T. (2019). The 'gigification' of work: consideration of the challenges and opportunities. In R. D. Lansbury, D. van den Broek and A. Johnson (eds), *Contemporary Issues in Work and Organisations, Actors and Institutions*. London, Routledge.

Whitley, R. (1999). *Divergent Capitalisms: The Social Structuring and Change of Business Systems*. Oxford: Oxford University Press.

Wilkinson, A., Wood, G. T. and Deeg, R. (2014). *The Oxford Handbook of Employment Relations*. Oxford: Oxford University Press.

Wood, G. T. and Brewster, C. (eds) (2007). *Industrial Relations in Africa.* London, Palgrave.

World Bank Group (2016). *Migration and Remittances Factbook* (3rd edn). New York: International Bank for Reconstruction and Development, The World Bank, http://www.worldbank.org/en/research/brief/migration-and-re mittances (accessed 18 July 2019).

3.   A New Approach: The Incorporation of Culture, Language and Translation Elements in Comparative Employee Relations

Pietro Manzella and Karl and Koch

INTRODUCTION

The primary aim of this chapter is to provide a new conceptual framework for evaluating the linked areas of culture, language and the translation process when analysing employee relations in international comparative perspective. It therefore expands and deepens the existing scholarship in the international comparative field which has added much to our understanding of, for example, state institutions, trade unions, employers' associations and the practices of negotiations and collective bargaining.

However, the interconnectivity of world society, through globalisation and the rapid evolution of international communication, requires both attention and understanding of cultural differences when employee relations are internationally compared and contrasted. This necessitates creating new conceptual research perspectives that specifically are transdisciplinary and have a focus on culture. An important principal theoretical approach in this respect has been the recent refinement of the concept 'cultural turn' by Bachmann-Medick (2016); turn meaning that culture focuses on new areas and generates new analytical categories. International comparative employee relations, with its transdisciplinary methodology, certainly belongs to this category and allows a specific focus on culture and language.

A useful starting point is the perceptive analysis of the significance of translation in the area of business research that concluded 'by advocating that the translation process be reformed as a process of intercultural interaction, rather than a lexical transfer of meaning' (Chidlow et al., 2014: 562). What is striking is the recognition of not only the centrality of cultural factors but the dynamic nature required to create a deeper conceptual approach to the translation process. This approach can be considered as complementing some of the major contemporary translation theories, such as, for example, the sociolinguistic approach, the semiotic approach, the communicative approach, the literary approach, and the hermeneutic approach.

In practical terms, such an approach allows the contours underlying the concepts used in languages to describe business, management and employee relations to emerge as well as revealing differences when contrasting and comparing them in the international context. However, there is a further critical issue, namely the transfer of correct interpretations of cultural elements from one national employee relations system to another.

Employee participation – a central feature of employee relations systems – effectively illustrates how the inclusion of cultural factors allows the deeper contours of different national practices to surface. For instance, focusing on three designations, the German concept of Mitbestimmung, co-determination, the notion of 'voice' in the USA, and the fundamental underlying issue of collective bargaining in the UK, demonstrates the significance of an inclusive comparative approach.

Co-determination has linkages to both the establishment of democracy and the social partnership concept, underlying the social market economy in its original conception. The societal paradigm in the Federal Republic of Germany, therefore, not only supports the acceptance of co-determination but has an embedment in historical roots. Importantly, German co-determination is also linked to German labour law, that is, the provision of representation of employees at enterprise board level. The principle enshrined, accepted by employers, is that there is a fundamental right for employees to have a collective mechanism in decision-making affecting employment relations. This perspective leads to the conclusion that comparison with the USA and UK, and their respective related designation of 'voice' and 'collective bargaining', are problematic if a holistic approach is not employed.

Employee voice is regarded as providing a mechanism in organisations that enables employees to be involved, to contribute their views and ideas, and to raise concerns. In practical terms, this aspect leads to many consequences, but there is a fundamental principle of individual rights, as is the case in the USA, underpinning this form of employee participation. Thus in the USA employers do not regard collective employee representation as a fundamental right, instead encouraging and fostering a variety of communication structures, as, for example, quality circles. The recourse to employee participation in decision-making processes is not generally acceptable. In contrast to Germany and the UK labour law, the USA preserves the traditional prerogatives of management from legitimate trade union interests.

The UK stands out in two respects. First, employee participation has no universal framework, despite the fact that it is regarded as an essential requirement of the working environment. Second, where employee participation exists – more commonly designated as worker participation – trade unions are by far the most frequent representation of employees in organisations. The dominance of trade unions as employee participation bodies can be explained in part by the persistent cultural characteristic of the idea of collective bargaining being intimately linked to the original historic concept of industrial democracy, which facilitates collective workers' participation.

The succinct and abbreviated three employee participation models described reveal complex historical genesis, reflections of socio-political differences, and an underlying deeper significance for each of the three countries. Excluding these characteristics leads one to overlook the crucial linkage between language and culture and, consequently, the efficacy of overtly including the cultural dimension in translation.

The interlinkage between translation and culture in comparative research can be summarised by what Sztompka defines as the incommensurability of concepts (Sztompka, 1990). This aspect is fundamental to fully appreciate the notions scrutinised when engaging in comparative analysis. In other words, notions originate from a given cultural framework: coming to terms with the cultural dimension of the concepts at issue is therefore pivotal when attempting to find the closest equivalent in other languages. We have just seen how social and cultural differences might hamper understanding of employee relations institutions cross-nationally. Employee relations literature brims with examples of practices that are not fully comprehended or face translation problems in the target language, which in the context of this chapter denotes the language which is being translated into (Shuttleworth, 2014). This is due to major cultural differences between the source and the target employee relations system. This is a point made by Hofstede, who argues that language is the most apparent component of culture (1995), therefore the cultural component plays a key role in comparative employee relations. 'Contextualisation is therefore important in comparative analysis' (Nienhüser and Warhurst, 2018: 210) and all the more so in comparative employee relations. Unfortunately, 'too often, that contextualisation is ignored' (Nienhüser and Warhurst, 2018: 210), frustrating our appreciation of the practices being compared. One aspect that is frequently disregarded when engaging in comparative analysis in employee relations is that culture is dynamic and undergoes constant change. Language mirrors culture, because words refer to the beliefs and practices of a given society (Nida, 2001). For this reason, language needs to adapt to such changes – in order to grasp the proper meaning of evolving practices – and so does translation. The shifting nature of culture and the need of translation to adapt to such changes at the time of rendering notions in other languages is evident if one looks at the English notion of 'gangmaster' and its Italian translation, which will be dealt with at length later on in this book. Until recently, a gangmaster could have been defined as someone who illegally hired casual labourers to employ them in agriculture or in the building sector. However, following the 2004 Gangmasters (Licensing) Act, efforts were made to legalise the activity of gangmasters. So they can now legally perform their work, as long as they obtain a licence. As a result, this term no longer conveys the idea of malpractice, as it is now possible to be a gangmaster and operate in full compliance with the law. The notion of a gangmaster in the English language has undergone a somewhat cultural shift from being illegal to being legal. Consequently, consideration should be given to the more neutral cultural nuance this term has been given when translating this notion into other languages. In Italy's employee relations, the word usually employed to render this concept is *caporale*, while the activity is called *caporalato*. As discussed further on, the problem with this translation is that major differences exist between the two concepts. While in the UK gangmasters are now regarded as those who obtain a licence and perform their duties in compliance with the law, *caporali* in Italy still operate outside the law, as organising the work of casual labourers is not allowed. Consequently, new terminology is needed to provide a proper rendering of 'gangmaster' in Italian that takes account of the new cultural connotations in the target language. As the example above illustrates, words can be assigned new meanings as a result of social and cultural changes that need to be understood and transposed in the target language. This is particularly true in the case of employee relations, where terminology frequently arises from bargaining and negotiations and faces constant adaptation. Translation can, therefore, only provide a narrow lens revealing the most appropriate contextual equivalent of a given text; the inclusion of the cultural perspective becomes clearly evident. However, culture as a topic and concept has long been subject to scholarship and debate in numerous subjects and disciplines, anthropology, literature, art and society are some examples. The approach in this book proposes a synthesis of selected cultural characteristics which impact and apply to employee relations within the international framework.

CULTURAL FRAMEWORK

The term culture has been subject to numerous analyses and interpretations across disciplines and subject areas. Consequently, the application of the concept is dependent on the precise area of its intended usage. The complexity of conceptual frameworks for specific areas of research has been emphasised by the multi-disciplinary approach that has become increasingly required. A similar approach is fundamental, given the objective to construct an appropriate conceptual framework to link culture and language for an insight into the deeper underlying structures of the semantics and concepts in employee relation systems.

It is, therefore, appropriate to perceive culture in the specific paradigm of comparative employee relations and construct a focused definition accordingly. Intimately connected to this is that the definition is embedded in the construct of the systems approach, which has proved such a rich source for comparative research. The original institutional-based studies of comparative industrial relations were firmly based on social systems theories. Mention should be made of the specific approach of Dunlop (1958) who identified industrial relations as a system. The incorporation of culture into these models is supported by the expansion of Luhmann's (1984) theory of society to include the notion of communication. The central point of this theoretical proposition of communication is understanding that social systems or, more generally – the terms of the social world – are composed entirely, and only, through communication. The essence of this is the centrality of communication. Society manifests innumerable interaction systems and a valid interpretation is that components will vary according to specific social systems that are characterised.

A cultural system is consequently a useful starting point, drawing on its historical connections and evolution, the information it deals with and the inferences which can be drawn from this. Each cultural system thus reflects specific meanings and brings together a unique group of variables. These might, for example, include behavioural patterns, customs, and clearly the all-encompassing language element. The notion of system in this paradigm includes the continuous modification of both output and input, thus Luhmann's argument of autopoiesis, that is the independent function of systems, as a contributor to these dynamic changes.

Recent research has demonstrated a deeper underlying structure pertinent to cultural systems, the role and impact of cultural memory. Cultural memory has increasingly been recognised as a vital factor in determining defined cultural systems and has been underpinned by its linkage, from neuroscience research, to a biological base. Assmann's (2000) seminal study has come to the conclusion that all human groups share a continuous common past and concluded that this is a defining characteristic of societies. However, he refined this by distinguishing between communicative memory, derived from communication, and tradition as a central factor for cultural memory. Tradition in this context 'is a special case of communication in which cultural memory is stored and handed down over long periods of time' (Velicu, 2011: 2) This is a succinct formulation of the dynamic nature required for an understanding of cultural memory in a wider context.

Culture is intimately linked to language and this relates to the understanding and knowledge derived from the enormous corpus of linguistics research and scholarship. In addition, this too has a parallel field of language analysis from neuroscience, having its genesis in the early work of Chomsky (1968), and the recognition that linguistic rules are generated from brain functions. But contemporary research has moved far beyond this, and evidence is accumulating that what might be termed deep cultural ancestry, that is the deeper evolutionary descent, has a significant impact on human development, even if the extent of impact remains controversial (Sookias et al., 2018).

Taking all these characteristics into consideration reveals that the contextual methodology of interpreting meaning in the classic mode of Firth (1968) that 'context of situation' is a crucial element to language study in general and meaning in particular, clearly is too superficial. What is required is a holistic approach incorporating the critical selected variables as related to the subject of this book – that is, employee relations – and the cultural context in the field of international comparative scholarship.

This posits two operational factors in constructing a conceptual model incorporating cultural systems. First, the intimate nature of language as a component and, second, the recognition that cultural characteristics lead not only to deeper analysis but expand the semantic field more comprehensively, for example, in fully understanding employee relations in different national contexts. A starting point is the selection of factors specifically pertinent to the focus of cultural characteristics linked to the linguistic output in the context of comparative employee relations.

Figure 3.1 summarises the selected characteristic for a definition of culture that supports a holistic approach to the analysis of employee

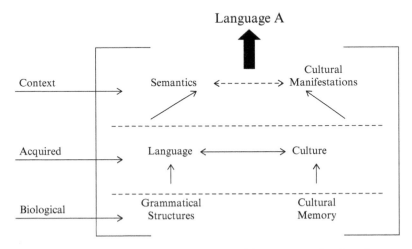

Figure 3.1   Conceptual model of selected language and cultural characteristics

relations in the international comparative framework explored in this volume. Significantly 'culture is intimately linked to language, is deeply embedded in societal behavioural patterns, is a determining factor in defining perceptions, attitudes and actions on specific foci in social systems, and is underpinned by a biological base' (Manzella and Koch, 2017: 63).

It is, of course, a matter of debate which selected variables are the most applicable, but from a pragmatic perspective, for comprehending comparative aspects focusing on employee relations, those listed in Figure 3.1 provide a useful basis. The model clearly differentiates between the inherent internal variables, acquisition through biological processes and the external societal contextual factor. Finally, the model distinctly posits that the outcome, in terms of a specific language and its communication function, is a fusion of the constituent characteristics of the model.

Culture becomes an indispensable part of descriptions, explanations, and analysis when employee relations systems are subject to international comparisons. In addition the model allows an insight into the dynamics of shifting cultural and language factors, inclusive of translation, the first adapting and the latter expanding concepts and terminologies. This is of particular significance as a major component of the dynamic nature of employee relations has been the impact of the globalisation process in transfer of ideas and structures in the international environment.

But globalisation also means that increasingly new geographical areas of the globe are acquiring economic significance and therefore new languages and culture in these areas need understanding. The historical domination by a few continents, and a small group of countries, is being supplemented by new areas, such as, for example, Southeast Asia and Latin America. The proposed conceptual cultural model can be applied for deeper analysis and understanding for these international developments, which also incorporate comparative employee relations.

LANGUAGE AND TRANSLATION

Scholars in the domain of translation studies and legal translation have closely examined the struggle resulting from transposing concepts and institutions in different languages. Yet, and barring a few exceptions (e.g. Bromwich, 2006; Manzella, 2015), academics in these fields have given scant consideration to language-related issues in employee relations and, specifically, to translation issues arising at the time of comparing and contrasting different employee relations practices. This might be due, at least in part, to the fact that employee relation terminology is often regarded as being part of legal discourse. While this might be true, the terminology that is peculiar to this domain is frequently the result of interactions in collective bargaining and talks between actors involved in negotiations, to the extent that 'the subject has developed its own language' (Green, 1994: 2), leading one to speak of a discursive genre per se, which deserves further analysis. This is also because the focus of discourse in employee relations 'has been for the most part . . . labour market structure and changes, employment trends, trade union growth and decline, labour law reforms, aggregate dispute data, macro-economic wage analyses, and political interlinkage' (Joseph, 2004: 2). Dealing with interactions between employers and employees, Kelly (1998) reinforced this point, taking the view that:

> [T]he arguments and discussions that take place among activists, fellow workers, and employers in what McAdam calls the 'micromobilisation context' involves debates about the most appropriate ways of 'framing' issues and problems. In other words, they are debates about the most appropriate linguistic categories to use in describing and accounting for employers' actions and inactions, and study of the day-to-day language, or discourse of industrial relations is therefore of major significance. (Kelly, 1998: 127)

Significantly, it has primarily been scholars in the discipline of employee relations that have pointed out terminological and translation challenges when engaging in comparative analysis (Hyman, 2005; Manzella and Koch, 2017; Schregle, 1981; Whiteside, 2005). Some of them have stressed the ambiguities resulting from transposing national practices and institutions in other languages (Hyman, 2007a; Singam and Koch, 1994) when 'attempting equivalent translations of national systems' (Singam and Koch, 1994: 158). Others (Blanpain and Baker, 2010) have emphasised the lack of equivalent practices – and therefore of adequate translation – in the employee relations systems being compared, calling for the need 'to recognise the problems which language poses for comparative research' (Blanpain and Baker, 2010: 6) because 'institutional realities differ cross-nationally and cross-linguistically' (Hyman, 2009: 18). More recently, and with special reference to the translation of employee relations concepts in EU documentation, attempts have been made to point out cases of ambiguous renderings by examining different language versions of the same documents (Manzella, 2015).

The pragmatic application of cultural perceptions is particularly significant and intimately linked to the process of translation. In the case of employee relations this is implicitly understood but not always subject to analysis. Blanpain correctly identified that this is linked to the specific understanding of realities: 'one of the main difficulties, which presents a real pitfall for the comparative scholar, is the fact that identical words in different languages might have different meanings, while the corresponding terms may embrace wholly different realities' (Blanpain and Baker, 2010: 16). Comparative research in employee relations is thus confronted with translation challenges. Expressing concepts which pertain to another legal system in a different language is a problematic task, for they are context-bound and only rarely value-neutral. The relevant literature is replete with instances of ambiguous translations in these fields. To give a few examples, Singam and Koch (1994) take the views that the German *Gewerkschaft* is not the same as the British 'union'. However, while the former is usually (and functionally) translated as 'trade union', this rendering fails to convey the particular organisation of the German bodies representing workers. The same can be said of the German *Arbeitgeberverband*, which is translated as 'employers' association' into English, though some major differences can be detected as regards their organisation. As the authors postulate, the examples below point out 'the inherent difficulties of translating culture-specific terms and the limits placed on translation' in the domains examined (Singam and Koch, 1994: 158). Still on the same issue, it would be highly misleading, though it is often done, to translate the Italian notion of *ricollocazione* as outplacement. Outplacement refers to measures put in place to head off workers' dismissal and exit from the labour market while still at work. Conversely, relevant legislation refers to *ricollocazione* as a set of targeted initiatives implemented to help workers who have been out of work for at least four months to re-enter the market, also by means of intensive job-search support.

Therefore, language does have much bearing on comparative research, for contrasting highly differentiated notions entails knowledge of both the systems under scrutiny and the language of the countries covered. This holds even truer in employee relations, where most terminology identifying practices and institutions is frequently crafted out of negotiation processes. After all, the battle of ideas is often carried out through a battle of words (Hyman, 2007b) instantiated in collective bargaining, social dialogue and concertation. Yet it would be erroneous to assume that linguistic problems in comparative analysis bear relevance only at the highest levels of abstraction. This is far from the case, especially in today's labour market, where massive changes in global migration patterns have generated a growing multilingual and multicultural workforce. Furthermore, Frege posits that: 'Despite the increasing convergence of employment institutions and practices throughout the advanced industrialized world and despite the increasing international com-munication and interaction among the research communities' (Frege, 2007: 18) distinctive national research patterns remain in employee relations, which seem astonishingly resistant to the processes of universalisation or modernisation. Therefore, misinterpretations of rules and practices cross-linguistically might give rise to ambiguities and confusion as regards workers' union rights, health and safety, and working conditions. One might argue that the use of English as a lingua franca might facilitate understanding when comparing and contrasting national institutions cross-linguistically. Yet this is far from the case, even when comparative analysis of industrial rela-tions practices involves countries making use of the same language (Hyman, 2005: 204). This is due to two reasons. First, the use of dif-ferent 'Englishes' – among which is that used as Eurospeak – might affect our appreciation of non-national institutions in comparative employee relations. For instance, what is known as direct discrimina-tion in the UK – that is, when someone is treated less favourably because the person belongs to one of the protected groups – is fre-quently referred to as disparate treatment in the US (Blanpain et al., 2007). Conversely, positive discrimination – that is, giving an advan-tage to those groups in society that are often treated unfairly because of their race, sex – is known as reverse discrimination or affirmative action across the pond (Blanpain et al., 2007). Still, compassionate leave, that in the UK is time off from work to deal with the death of a close relative, can be termed bereavement leave in the US. Second, 'linguistic standardisation due to the universal use of English is not always matched by a similarity of structures and functions' (Tiraboschi, 2003: 192).

The challenges posed by language at the time of contrasting employee relations practices have led Hyman and Gumbrell-McCormick to argue that 'serious comparative research requires the capacity at least to read the languages of the countries covered' (Hyman and Gumbrell-McCormick, 2013: vii). While this is certainly true, it is likewise important to understand how and what to compare. Blanpain stated clearly that 'in order to compare what is in fact comparable, one needs to compare the functions institutions perform rather than institutions themselves' (Blanpain and Baker, 2010: 13).

Of course, relevance should be given to the cultural dimension at the time of comparing employee relations practices cross-linguistically. Meardi speaks of 'the neglect of culture by comparative industrial relations . . . Culture is left aside, as a convenient "emergency" variable, to account for the unexplained residua' (Meardi, 2011: 336). Recently, Manzella and Koch (2017) have made an attempt in stressing the significance of culture, and its close relationship with language, in understanding context-bound meanings and national employee relations practices, coming to the conclusion that 'it is imperative that the cultural factors become an intrinsic element of translations on which crucial interpretations, are dependent' (Manzella and Koch, 2017: 68).

Failing to consider the cultural dimension in translating employee relations practices might result in misleading interpretations of industrial relations concepts when transposing institutions from one language, and one system, into the other.

Consequently, an attempt is made here to integrate the cultural and translation factors to enable those involved in the international dimensions of employee relations to be aware of system differentials at a deeper level of understanding. Specifically, this book will focus on 'interlingual translation', which according to Pym (2014) is concerned with the 'rewording between languages' (Pym, 2014: 146) and with how culture affects comprehension of industrial relations concepts and institutions in this transposition process.

RECIPROCAL AUGMENTATION: CULTURE AND LANGUAGE

The construction of a conceptual model for both comprehension and pragmatic application, based on an explicit link between the cultural definition and translation perspective adopted above, has to meet two clear objectives. First, the cultural characteristics are distinctly interconnected to the comparative and international framework of employee relations. In a broader sense, this encompasses the enormous scholarship spanning Human Resource Management and Industrial Relations, among others. Second, translation is required to incorporate the cultural dimension in the specific context of comparative employee relations to provide a holistic spectrum of meaning for specific terminological descriptions.

The conceptual approach developed in this chapter differs from the assumption, frequently made, that translation can be defined as an intercultural practice, where culture and translation converge at a given point (Martinez-Sierra, 2010). Instead the schism between the two fields of study are recognised and bridged by what might be described as a reciprocal augmentation, thus understanding the link, as well as the specific and distinctive nature of each of them. Translation and culture are embedded in language, which facilitates and transmits the shifting nuances of meaning according to numerous variables, for example context, historical prerogatives and the explicit subject area, in this case employee relations.

Reciprocal augmentation indicates an intimate link between two variables but with distinctive differences in their origin. Culture with its profounder fundament of cultural memory, on the one hand, and language, the vehicle of communication, on the other, can be perceived in such a manner. A critical distinction between culture and language is that the former has a plurality of unique cultural constructs, whereas the latter has an underpinning of universal characteristics. The consequence of such perceptions points to a holistic conceptual understanding underlying a meaningful translation process.

This supplements the interest expressed by studies in the field of cultural translation, which has been a peripheral field of scholarship for some time, in social sciences and anthropology, by specifically focusing on employee relations. Although a recent and informative publication (Maitland, 2017) presents a strong case for expanding translation to cover contemporary cultural phenomena in the globalised and multicultural world, which is still based on the great tradition of the humanities. An applicable and vital point Maitland makes is that meaning is always produced by communication, it is determined in relation to context, and that the process is continuous and dynamic, as we have seen in the example above about the rendering of 'gangmaster' in Italian. For now, what matters is that this approach certainly applies to any translation concerned with different employee relations systems and reinforces the proposal for an encompassing culture and language conceptual model. It is interesting to note that Martin Ruano (2018) points out that 'in our ever more polylingual, heterogeneous, and increasingly hybrid cultures, different (post)identities and sensibilities are continuously being confronted in acts of translation, which thus calls for an enhanced awareness of the limits and possibilities of recontextualising and renegotiating differences' (Martin Ruano, 2018: 260). In a similar vein, House (2016) posits that one should look at culture as a diversified entity that is dynamic, fluid and hybrid with cultural borders being increasingly difficult to be determined in a globalised world. This is a recurrent practice when contrasting employee relations practices, because of the increasingly diverse workforce resulting from globalisation and because of the assumption that 'Institutions differ cross-nationally; so do modes of thought' (Hyman, 2005: 205). Consequently, with culture that is embedded in language, the meaning of any linguistic item can only be properly understood with reference to the context enveloping it (House, 2016). Among other things, the model put forward aims to guide employee relations practitioners to recontextualise national practices, taking into account the nuanced and ever-changing meanings which might be lost in translation when engaging in cross-national comparison.

The above considerations suggest that a functional approach to explain the interconnectivity between the identified interrelated factors, relevant for international comparisons of employee relations systems, provide both awareness and deeper understanding. Figure 3.2 puts forward a systematic conceptual methodology when translating from language A into language B with the selected variables from the domain of language and culture, as described for Figure 3.1. The designation domain indicates a complex area which has its identifiable internal structures and relationships, cultural memory being an excellent example where the interaction of numerous elements result in a specific cultural indicator.

The progression outlined in Figure 3.2 recognises the bond between the designated domains in terms of reciprocal augmentation, particularly the synergy between the domains in broad terms, of language and culture. The model further suggests that the translation

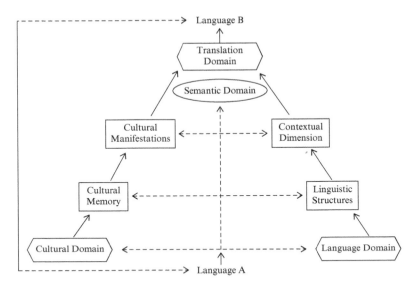

Figure 3.2   Dynamics of language and culture in translation process

process, with this method, is dynamic and system based, continuously enriching and expanding its effectiveness.

The practical application of the conceptual model in Figure 3.2 can be illustrated through following the pathway of translating the German concept of *Friedenspflicht*, as applied in the employee relations context, into English. In the broad sense the German word defines the relationship between the representatives of capital, employers' associations, and labour, trade unions, when agreements have been reached through negotiations. The obvious literal rendering into English results in 'peace obligation'; a phrase which has a very wide semantic field and is not applied, for example, in the English language context of employee relations. But the German word *Friedenspflicht*, as applied in the employee relations case, distinctly reveals that the word is a composites of such characteristics as ideas, values, and historical experiences. In effect the relationship between the domains, explained above, for example, culture and language, embedded cultural memory and language context, reveals precisely the underlying cooperative relationship of employee relations in Germany and the mechanisms for the avoidance of industrial conflict. It is these cumulative aspects, the progressive path illustrated in Figure 3.2, which ultimately allows the semantic and translation domain, to achieve an appropriate translation. English has no all-embracing equivalent to *Friedenspflicht*; in the UK the deep cultural premise of legitimate conflict as a consequence of historical class divisions necessitates a context-specific word.

CONCLUSION

Employee relations have been, and continue to be, subject to enormous changes leading to continuous adaptations, transformations and understanding and flexibility from the stakeholders. The globalised environment presents a strong case for translations to embrace contemporary cultural practices and become accustomed to rapid changes in the interconnected world of work. This implies that international comparative employee relations research and scholarship require a high awareness of both the socio-economic shifts and the dramatic transformation of the concept of 'work' caused by fundamental changes in work organisation from skills demand focused on automation and digitalisation.

The approach suggested rests on a selected group of variables, as set out in the conceptual model above, to establish a link between culture, language, translation practice, and with a specific focus on international comparative employee relations analysis. Clearly, there exist a number of limitations, given the diversity of these major areas and the vast scholarship. First, definitions of culture are highly exclusive to individual disciplines, for example anthropology, humanities, management, and defined aspects of sociology. Therefore, the interdisciplinary approach, as proposed by the conceptual model in this chapter, is not intended to provide a general model. Second, and related to this, is the fact that it does not provide a predictive model for the future of work. This is an important aspect as a recent study estimates that from 75 to 375 million people – that is, from 3 per cent to 14 per cent of the global workforce – will need to embrace new occupational categories (Bughin et al., 2018). Third, the model provides parameters to facilitate deeper understanding and awareness, when contrasting and comparing international differences and similarities in the field of employee relations. Yet further development is needed for providing a practical tool, for example, for translators.

Reciprocal augmentation provides a method for a holistic approach, the essence being that it provides a mutual enhancement of the selected variables, thereby giving a clearer perception of underlying structures which shape individual employee relations systems.

Significantly, the model put forward elaborates on a number of Translation Theories arguing that – in order to be effective – translation should be carried out not as a stand-alone activity, but considering context, which includes situational, sociological, and political factors; 'psychological (cognitive) aspects; social and cultural effects of translation; culture-bound concepts' (Tyulenev, 2012: 46). In relation to the discipline under scrutiny here, it is also important to remember that translating and adapting employee relations concepts require an awareness that this domain has elaborated its own terminology. Consequently, one should also be aware that employee relations terminology differs in important respects from the legal one strictly speaking, though they frequently overlap. The reason for this can be found in the definition of industrial relations provided by Hyman, namely 'the study of the processes of control over work relations, and among these processes, those involving collective worker organisation and action are of particular concern' (Hyman, 1975: 12). If the focus is on the employment relation and not only on the institutions of labour, management, and government, then examining industrial relations terminology only through the lens of legal translation can provide too narrow a tool. This is particularly the case if one considers that employee relations terminology frequently, though not always, arises out of 'the result of interactions in collective bargaining and talks between actors involved in negotiations' (Manzella, 2017: 346). As a result, the model suggested is justified by the need to consider translation of employee relations concepts in context, on the one hand, and on the specificity of employee relations terminology, on the other hand, with the latter that frequently originates from societal and political practices in use at the national level.

The reciprocal augmentation concept allows a reconfiguration of the methods in which studies in international comparisons of employee relations can be understood at a deeper level in the continuing globalised environments by the inclusion of customs and traditions, underlying beliefs, and networks and flows within the systems.

REFERENCES

Assmann, J 2000, *Religion und kulturelles Gedächtnis*, Beck: Munich.

Bachmann-Medick, D 2016, *Cultural Turns: New Orientations in the Study of Culture*, De Gruyeter: Berlin/Boston (German version, 5th edn. Reinbeck: Rowohlt, 2014).

Blanpain, R and Baker, J (eds) 2010, *Comparative Labour Law and Industrial Relations in Industrialized Market Economies*, Kluwer International: The Hague.

Blanpain, R, Bisom-Rapp, S, Corbett, W R, Josephs, H K and Zimmer, M J 2007, *The Global Workplace – International and Comparative Employment Law*, Cambridge University Press: Cambridge.

Bromwich, W 2006, 'Lessico negoziale, contesto culturale e processi comunicativi nello sciopero nei servizi essenziali a New York', *Diritto Delle Relazioni Industriali*, vol. 2, no. XVI, pp. 414–26.

Bughin, J, Hazan, E, Lund, S, Dahlström, P, Subramaniam, A and Wiesinger, A 2018, *Skill Shift: Automation and the Future of the Work Force*, Discussion Paper, McKinsey Global Institute, pp 1–84, viewed 30 July 2018, https://www.mckinsey.com/featured-insights/future-of-organizations-and-work/skill-shift-automation-and-the-future-of-the-workforce?smid=nytcore-ios-share.

Chidlow, A, Plakoyiannaki, E and Welch, C 2014, 'Translation in Cross-language International Business Research: Beyond Equivalence', *Journal of International Business Studies*, vol. 45, no. 5, pp. 562–82.

Chomsky, N 1968, *Language and Mind*, Harcourt Brace and World: San Diego, CA.

Dunlop, J T 1958, *Industrial Relations Systems*, Holt: New York.

Firth, J R 1968, 'Linguistic Analysis as a Study of Meaning' in F R Palmer (ed.), *Selected Papers of J R Firth*, Longmans Linguistic Library: London, pp. 12–26.

Frege, C M 2007, *Employment Research and State Traditions. A Comparative History of Britain, Germany and the United States*, Oxford University Press: New York.

Green, G D 1994, *Industrial Relations Texts and Case Studies* (4th edn), Pitman Publishing: London.

Hofstede, G 1995, 'The Cultural Relativity of Organisational Practices and Theories' in J Drew (ed.), *Readings in International Enterprise*, Routledge: London, pp. 141–58.

House, J 2016, *Translation as Communication across Languages and Cultures*, Routledge: Abingdon.

Hyman, R 1975, *Industrial Relations Theory: A Marxist Introduction*, Macmillan: Basingstoke.

Hyman, R 2005, 'Words and Things: The Problem of Particularistic Universalism' in J C Barbier and M T Letablier (eds), *Comparaisons internationales des politiques sociales, enjeux épistémologiques et méthodologiques/Cross-national Comparison of Social Policies: Epistemological and Methodological Issues*, PIE-Peter Lang: Brussels, pp. 191–208.

Hyman, R 2007a, 'An Anglo-European Perspective on Industrial Relations Research', *Arbetsmarknad & Arbetsliv*, vol. 13, no. 3–4, pp. 29–41.

Hyman, R 2007b, 'How Can Trade Unions Act Strategically?', *Transfer: European Review of Labour and Research*, vol. 13, no. 2, pp. 193–210.

Hyman, R 2009, 'How Can We Study Industrial Relations Comparatively' in R Blanpain (ed.), *The Modernization of Labour Law and Industrial Relations in a Comparative Perspective – The Bulletin of Comparative Labour Relations*, Kluwer Law International: Amsterdam, pp. 3–23.

Hyman, R and Gumbrell-McCormick, R 2013, *Trade Unions in Western Europe – Hard Times, Hard Choices*, Oxford University Press: Oxford.

Joseph, J 2004, *Industrial Relations: Towards a Theory of Negotiated Connectedness*, Response Books: New Delhi.

Kelly, J 1998, *Rethinking Industrial Relations: Mobilisation, Collectivism, and Long Waves*, Routledge: London/New York.

Luhmann, N 1984, *Soziale Systeme, Grundriß einer allgemeinen Theorie*, Suhrkamp: Frankfurt.

Maitland, S 2017, *What is Cultural Translation?*, Bloomsbury Academic: London and New York.

Manzella, P 2015, 'Lost in Translation: Language and Cross-national Comparison in Industrial Relations', *The E-Journal of International and Comparative Labour Studies*, vol. 4, no. 1, pp. 1–21.

Manzella, P 2017, 'Multilingual Translation of Industrial Relations Practices in Official EU Documents: The Case of Italy's Cassa Integrazione Guadagni', *Perspectives: Studies in Translation Theory and Practice*, vol. 26, no. 3, pp. 344–56.

Manzella, P and Koch, K 2017, 'Legal and Cultural Implications Inherent in Managing Multilingual and Multicultural Labor: Selected Translation Issues from the US National Labor Relations Board', *Lebende Sprachen*, vol. 62, no. 1. pp. 59–78.

Martin Ruano, M 2018, 'Issues in Cultural Translation: Sensitivity, Politeness, Taboo, Censorship', in S A Harding and O C Cortes (eds), *The Routledge Handbook of Translation and Culture*, Routledge: Abingdon, pp. 258–79.

Martinez-Sierra, J 2010, 'Building Bridges Between Cultural Studies and Translation Studies: With Reference to the Audiovisual Field', *Journal of Language & Translation*, vol. 11, no. 1, pp. 115–36.

Meardi, G 2011, 'Understanding Trade Union Culture', *Industrielle Beziehungen*, vol. 18, no. 4, pp. 336–45.

Nida, E 2001, *Contexts in Translating*, Benjamins: Amsterdam.

Nienhüser, W and Warhurst, C 2018, 'Comparative Employment Relations: Definitional, Disciplinary and Development Issues' in C Brewster, W Mayrhofer and E Farndale (eds), *Handbook of Research on Comparative Human Resource Management: Second Edition*, Edward Elgar Publishing: Cheltenham, UK and Northampton, MA, pp. 200–22.

Pym, A 2014, *Exploring Translation Theories*, Routledge: London.

Schregle, J 1981, 'Comparative Industrial Relations: Pitfalls and Potential', *The International Labour Review*, vol. 120, no. 1, pp. 15–30.

Shuttleworth, M 2014, *Dictionary of Translation Studies*, Routledge: Abingdon.

Singam, P and Koch, K 1994, 'Industrial Relations – Problems of German Concepts and Terminology for the English Translator', *Lebende Sprachen*, vol. 39, no. 1, pp. 158–62.

Sookias, R B, Passmore, S and Atkinson, Q D 2018, 'Deep Cultural Ancestry and Human Development Indicators Across Nation States', *Royal Society Open Science*, vol. 5, no. 171411, pp. 2–14, viewed 10 September 2018, http://rsos.royalsocietypublishing.org/content/royopensci/5/4/171411.full.pdf.

Sztompka, P 1990, 'Cultural Frameworks in Comparative Enquiry: Convergent or Divergent?' in M Albrow and E Kings (eds), *Globalisation, Knowledge and Society*, Sage Publications: London, pp. 47–61.

Tiraboschi, M 2003, *Marco Biagi's Selected Writings*, Kluwer Law International: The Hague.

Tyulenev, S 2012, *Applying Luhmann to Translation Studies: Translation in Society*, Routledge: London and New York.,

Velicu, A 2011, 'Cultural Memory between the National and the Transnational', *Journal of Aesthetics and Culture*, vol. 3, no. 1. pp. 1–4.

Whiteside, N 2005, 'Comparing Welfare States. Conventions, Institutions and Political Frameworks of Pension Reform in France and Britain after the Second World War', in J C Barbier and M T Letablier (eds), *Comparaisons internationales des politiques sociales, enjeux épistémologiques et méthodologiques/Cross-national Comparison of Social Policies: Epistemological and Methodological Issues*, PIE-Peter Lang: Brussels, pp. 211–28.

PART II
Employee relations in the national context

4. Employee Relations and Harmony in China

Jing Xi

This chapter presents a profile of Chinese employee relations (ERs) from the beginning of China's industrialization early in the 1910s to the giant changes today. The Chinese economic reform, starting in 1978, was a key turning point that involved changing from a planned economic system to a socialist market-oriented economy. One consequence of this economic reform was that it created the diverse and complex employee relations that can be seen in China today, which originated from three branches: the traditional cultural heritage, the communist ideology and the impacts of the marketing economy.

EMPLOYEE RELATIONS: LOST IN TRANSLATION

When talking about the translations of employee relations, researchers found that it is a quite complicated thing. Early reports from the literature review proved that the correspondent term with employee relations was translated as 产业关系 (chan ye guan xi), but Chinese word chan ye traditionally refers to the manufacturing industries. Later when Marxism-perspective industrial relations theories were introduced in China, people used to analyze the industrial relations from a social conflict point of view. Actually, for quite a long time, scholars in China used the term 'labour relations' instead of industrial relations to generalize the relations between employers and employees (Cheng, 2002: 3). In China, someone who gets paid to work for an organization or for another person can be called an employee. But the term 'employee' is always confused or misused with other terms such as labourers, workers, staff members and so on.

When using the term labour relations, it refers mainly to the relations between capital and labourers, emphasizing the contradictory features from two sides. The term industrial relations 劳工关系 (lao gong guan xi) in Chinese is an employee-centred concept, and includes concerns about employees' organization, the trade union, and the process for collective bargaining with employers (Cheng, 2002).

Another Chinese term in employee relations is 劳雇关系 (lao gu guan xi) which referred to the legitimate relations between employees and employers in their responsibilities and accountabilities. Later on, Chinese scholars adopted a new term of employer relations 劳使关系 (lao shi guan xi) from Japanese empirical studies (Cheng, 2002) which had more emphasis on the technical issues of management, but less care about value judgement, took more measures on creating mild and intimate relationships, but with less confrontational structures.

More or less, the study of relations between trade unions, management and government in China has included every layer under the principles of a socialist system with Chinese characteristics. The connotation of employee relations or employment relations in China is not the same as that of a Western cultural context, and mistakes always occur because of wrong interpretation.

In this chapter, the term of employee relations is translated as 劳动关系 (lao dong guan xi), which used to be translated as labour relations (LRs) 产业关系 (chan ye guan xi) by some Chinese scholars (Cheng, 2002; Chang, 2005) because LRs have featured too many ideological characteristics. It is necessary, with China being the world's second largest economic entity, to focus on mass labour-intensive industry in China, which is one of the typical features in China's employment system, thus, study of the tripartite relationship between trade unions, management and government takes on more significance than human resources management.

ERs RESEARCH THEORIES FROM CHINA

In mainland China, there have been various expressions used to deliver the meaning of employee relations, such as industrial relations, employee relations, labour–capital relations, as well as employment relations.

Qin (1995) noted that employee relations referred to the relations generated in the labouring process between the labour and the employees, like enterprises and other units. It is an important content in productive relations, which has a direct impact on productivity. Judging from the main body of text, this is a narrow conception of employee relations, however, the contents of which belong to a relatively broad concept.

Hei (2004) saw employee relations as a combined relation derived from the group of social work, including labourers like the trade unions, as well as users of the labour force, like the Enterprise Manager Association and the Employer Association. These two parts form the main body of social employee relations. Obviously, this is a broad definition of employee relations.

Cheng (2002) believes that employee relations come from employment organizations studying the relevant issues about the employment management, showing the total sum of the cooperation, conflicts, strength and power. This defines the labour relation from the aspect of the management of employee relations in companies.

Chang (2005) argues that labour relations refers to the actual labour within the productive relationship. Specifically speaking, it is a social economic relation combined by the labourer in terms of working, and the user of that labour force, which is a relatively comprehensive concept, as well as the concrete manifestation of the combination between the production materials and the labourers in the process of social production.

The study of ERs in China shall look at three actors and their performances in the respective periods of Chinese history. China's industrialization started in the 1910s, soon after the collapse of China's Qing Empire, which is why Dunlop's actors' framework is used to illustrate that the roles of actors may be played differently due to the changes in China's social and cultural environments (Dunlop, 1958).

China has a tradition of authoritarian regimes since long before the Zhou Dynasty, a feudal political structure that was established 2,700 years ago. This political cultural heritage has had a deep impact, even from the beginning of China's capitalist revival in the late nineteenth century. China's industrialization, driven by both government intention and capital from overseas Chinese, started at the beginning of the twentieth century because of the then-government's defeat by the British Empire. A famous statement from Mr Wei Yuan, a well-known translator and senior official in the Qing dynasty, said that China must take the national strategy of 'learning merits from the foreign to conquer the foreign'. Industrialization was undoubtedly one solution for 'learning merits' at the time. Early factors of employee relations in China actually had two components: the management itself was the representative of government or state agencies, while for the private industry, China has strong family business characteristics.

In the 1920s, in light of the success of China's Revolution of 1911, the foundation of a new government and the Republic of China, China's industrialization developed into a new epoch, a more thriving stage, with private capital involved in large proportions in some special industrial areas, such as agriculture, textiles and so on. The tripartite conflicts between government, management and employees were the driving forces leading to industrial actions and some social revolutions.

In the 1950s, after the liberation of new China, the communist party dominated government, private capitals were demolished almost totally in the process of socialization and corporate employees became 'the masters of the country'. The trade union organization changed its character, functioning as a government body. The tripartite relationship between government, management and employees became merged as one body.

After 1978, the Open Door Policy in economics swept across China. Private economy was encouraged and special economic zones where entrepreneurs could enjoy special tax-free privileges were set up in the Pearl River Delta in South China. The tripartite relationship returned to three independent factors in the private economy. According to China's Xinhua news agency, the private economy accounted for more than 60 per cent of national GDP, and more than 90 per cent of new employment positions were offered by the private economy until 2012 (Xinhua News, 2012), while in state-owned corporations, factors of employee relations still retained the characteristics of the socialist structure. The metaphor of the 'iron rice bowl' and the 'golden rice bowl', was used to describe work opportunities in the state-owned enterprises and the public sector respectively, the latter still being the dream job for the young generation.

CHINESE EMPLOYEE RELATIONS: A HISTORICAL REVIEW

From a Marxist point of view, China was a country of feudalism for more than 2,000 years, where peasantry was the dominant relationship between landlords and peasants. This legacy is deeply embedded in Chinese society. In 1840, the Opium War between China's Qing Dynasty and the British Empire broke out. China lost this war and signed the Nanjing Contract with the British government, under which British businessmen were allowed to set up factories in five chartered trade cities, namely Canton, Fu Zhou, Xia Men, Ning Bo and Shanghai. By 1894, there were 34,000 labourers working in 191 foreign-owned enterprises, and 40,000 in 48 state-owned enterprises, with another 27,000 to 30,000 workers in 135 private enterprises (Liu, 1985).

Formation of Chinese ERs from its Early Industrialization

In 1911, the Xinhai Revolution broke out, and China's Qing Emperor was replaced by the Republic of China. With regard to the organization of labour, from 1840, the Opium War, to the collapse of the Qing Dynasty in 1911, there was no formal trade union organization, but labourers were organized into so-called 'Townsmen's Associations', referring to people from the same regions. The Qing Emperor strictly prohibited any type of industrial action. During the Xinhai Revolution, with the appealing slogan of 'Three Principles for the People: the people's democracy, the people's rights, and the people's wellbeing', the new government advocated the establishment of labour organizations. In addition, a series of labour laws and regulations were released (Wagner, 1938), covering labour organizations, labour disputes, security, and the working environment.

However, this situation changed quickly with the influence of the Russian revolution in 1917, as the expansion of Marxism drew the attention of the Chinese intelligence. Marxist learning teams were founded in the big cities of Beijing, Shanghai and Canton. On 4 May 1919, the news that China had lost its own land in Shan Dong Province, which used to be a German concession, came to Beijing.[1] Students from Peking Universities rushed into the streets and demonstrated for the refusal to sign the Treaty of Versailles. This May Fourth demonstration developed as an unprecedented movement in support of Chinese democracy, freedom, and science. Historians, since then, have talked about the 'May Fourth Spirits'. College students, along with labour workers, played an important role in this movement. Two years later, in July 1921, Marxism learning teams, scattered throughout the main cities of China, organized their first representative session in Shanghai, in which the

Communist Party of China (CPC) was officially founded. In its first session, the CPC clearly stated that the Party's essential mission was to conduct research, to lead labour movements with different forms and to strengthen its control of the trade unions. Both the CPC and Kuomintang, then the ruling government party, realized the importance of the thriving labour power in China. Since then, the control of China's ERs has been a powder keg between the two parties and the trade unions.

Trade unions were split into two groups: one group was led by the CPC, the other by the Kuomintang Party. Early in December 1920, the first 'modernized trade union', compared with the old labours' Townsmen's Associations, which was named the Shanghai Trade Union of Machinery, was founded under the guidance of Chinese communist activists. After the foundation of the CPC in 1921, a new branch, the General Secretary Department of All China Trade Union (GSDACTU), was formed, directed by Zhang Guotao. Later in May 1925, GSDACTU was replaced by a new All China Federation of Trade Unions (ACFTU), which continues today (Gao, 2008: 85).

As for the Kuomintang Party, after holding power, notably after the impact of the May Fourth Movement, the Kuomintang-controlled government issued a series of regulations to earn support from the working class. In February 1922, the first Chinese Law of Trade Union Regulations was released, and soon after that, in 1938, the Sino–Japan War broke out. The Kuomintang government had ameliorated a series of laws relating to employee relations. They are: the Trade Union Law, amended in 1929, 1931, 1932 and 1934; the Enterprises Regulations, released in 1929 and amended in 1932; the Regulations of Labour Dispute Process, released in 1930, amended in 1932 and 1933; the Law of Collective Contract, released in 1930; the Labour Contract Law, released in 1936; the Minimum Wage Law, released in 1936; and the Law of Mineral Enterprises, released in 1936 (Gao, 2008: 58). But there were critics, for example:

> The accomplishment of labours' law is a great leap forward for our government and our country. It is unprecedented progress in the Far East countries, but it is almost hopeless in practice. So far, our government has not been ready to make it happen: those regulations are just waste papers. (Translated by the author) (Gao, 2008: 58)

Nevertheless, the legitimated labour construction had a positive influence on social stability and created a government-for-the-people reputation in international society. China was one of the founding members of the International Labour Organization (ILO) (Gao, 2008: 59). From 1919 to 1928, China appointed overseas diplomatic staff as representatives to attend the ILO conference. Starting in 1929, the Kuomintang government sent a delegation, including members standing for government, employers and labourers, to attend the ILO conference. In 1944, China became a permanent member of the ILO.

Born from the 'half feudalism and half colonialism environment', China's trade unions were growing, with a strong influence on ideology. They had close relations with local customs, political regimes and investment orientation.

Employee Relations During the Planned Economy (from 1949 to 1978)

The period between 1949 and 1978 was a time when the CPC adopted a pattern, partly learnt from the Soviet Union, and partly from localized Marxist interpretations, to guide its employee relations under the planned economic environment. An analysis of the employee relations came from its economic-rational roots, with macro and micro aspects (Taylor et al., 2003):

> Micro-analysis examines work-based employment relations, examining a range of workplace-based employment issues, and the operation of the labour process ... while, the macro-analysis focuses on social-level institutions, such as the state, trade union organs and employers' organizations, and maps the overall employee relations framework within society. (Taylor et al., 2003: 3)

After the liberation in 1949, the CPC-controlled government paid much attention to dealing with employee relations. A cradle-to-grave welfare system was set up and private enterprises almost disappeared from the country. The working class was the leading class and the masters of the country. The wages, employment, and welfare provisions were all taken by the government, which was called the 'iron rice bowl' (tie fan wan). An employment unit, namely Danwei, functioned as a small country, offering not just working facilities, but also the necessary services, such as hospitals, schools, grocery shops, cinemas, and even clubs.

From a macro perspective, the workers' employer was the Party (government), which had a special name, Zhi Gong (worker and staff). The term 'Zhi Gong' includes workers in workshops, administrators in the office, engineers, technicians, and all the people working inside the Danwei (working unit). During the period of the planned economy, all the enterprises were just workshops of the state-factory. Following this socialist ideology, the interests of labour (workers), enterprises, and country (government) became the same, while trade unions lost their function from the previous period of civil and anti-colonial wars, but became an assistant and subsidiary department of government organs. Wang (1992: 143) concluded that the objective of trade unions in the planned economy was to 'organize labour contests, technical innovations, and increased production drives and propagandizing worker's management of such activities as organizing sports and entertainment events for workers, supervising the implementation of occupational health and safety and providing sanatoriums, rest homes and public welfare services for workers'. In other words, the trade union, ACFTU, was acting as a 'transmission belt' between the Party (government) and workers and staff in the planned economy, with a strong unitarist ideology.

A Dynamic Change of Current Employee Relations: The Role of the Party (Government) and Legalization

The unitarist ideology faced challenges beginning in 1978. On 18 December 1978, the CPC held its third Plenary Session of the 11th Party Central Committee in Beijing. This historical plenary session had two themes: one was to criticize the 'Two Whatevers' guidance (whatever Chairman Mao says is right; whatever Chairman Mao demands, we shall follow), saying 'practice is the only way to evaluate the truth'; the second was to stop the wrongdoing in the Cultural Revolution, change the Party's job from 'taking the fight between classes' to 'taking economic construction as the key job of the people and the country'. The Party was trying to adopt a market economy as an effective way to reimburse its losses during the Cultural Revolution period.

The Party subsequently promoted a series of economic reforms, and released new policies encouraging private business and township collective business. With the development of China's economic reform, foreign capital as well as investments from Hong Kong and Taiwan rushed into mainland China because of its cheap labour and its convenient and well-constructed infrastructure. Within 30 years, China's GDP was growing by two digits per year, which is quite rare in the history of the world economy. In 2001, China entered the WTO and enhanced its cooperation with world developed economies. China became the wonderland for global enterprises. The workers were no more than masters of the enterprises, and there were divergent employee relations. Statistics showed that the number of employees working in the State Owned Enterprises (SOEs) industries shrank from 112.61 million in 1995 to 76.40 million in 2001: a loss of almost one-third (NBSC, 2003).

It was a hard time for those people who were laid off (xia gang): statistics showed (Luo, 2011) that each year between 1988 and 2011, seven to nine million people were laid off, until there were about 40 million laid-off workers in China. Most of those laid-off workers, of whom females tended to be aged 40 and over and males tended to be aged 50 and over, came from China's old industrial bases and undeveloped economic territories: for example, 25 per cent of them were from the North-East part of China, an old industrial belt in the 1950s.

The increasing complexity of employee relations forced the Party to bring its policy up to date. In terms of social public management, the aims of the Party (government) were as follows:

(1) Maintaining a planned economic system

The actions and policies for the market economy were very cautious, because traditionally the Party believed that the free market economy violated the spirit of socialism and was typical of capitalism. From 1978 to 1992, the economic policy was 'giving first place to the planned economy and second place to market regulation' (jihuajingjiweizhu, shichangtiaojieweifu) (Fan, 1994: 130). Unemployment was another challenge for the government. During the Cultural Revolution, nearly 17 million urban youth were assigned to the countryside to accept 're-education' according to Chairman Mao's allegation. To ease the crises, the State Bureau of Labour (1981) instituted a policy to perfect the employment situation in urban areas: in contrast to the previous system of job allocations by the government, people were allowed to find employment through recommendations from any of the state-run labour service departments, the provision of jobs by voluntary organizations, or by finding jobs for themselves.

To attempt a new style of employment relations, the government introduced the 'economic zone' policy. In 1980, four coastal cities were defined as special economic zones. They are Shen Zhen near Hong Kong, Zhu Hai near Macao, Shan Tou and Xia Men near Taiwan. A principle of 'special treatment inside the special economic zone, and a new policy for new things' (teshiteban, xinshixinban) was applied in the economic zones (Ke, 1988). Generally speaking, there was co-existence of different wage systems, overall application of labour contracts in all enterprises, wage levels were generally higher than in inland cities, and the labour social security system was widely applied. Government in economic zones set up special departments for labour service and labour insurance (Ke, 1988). The experience in economic zones later expanded and is being applied widely in China.

(2) Filling in the 'gap' between the two systems

For quite a long time, two systems of employment existed: the state-controlled enterprises and those workers working for Township and Village Owned Enterprises (TOEs, VOEs), or Joint-venture Enterprises (JVEs). Social provisions varied and a gap emerged. Plus, large surplus labour resources from the countryside were rushing into cities. Those peasant workers (migrant workers) offered cheap labour for the enterprises, but competition with the urban workers caused social conflicts in some areas. Migrant workers were required to apply for work permits from local governments before they could legally move into cities. Dealing with the conflicts because of the gap at the micro level was a key job for the government, as the former minister of labour once said:

> Labour administrative departments . . . must make efforts to establish and perfect a macro-control mechanism over labour and wages which can be compatible with the operation of the market. On one hand, resorting to the market as a means to allocate the labour force; on the other hand, employing the plan, by taking its advantages of overall balance and emphasis on the long-term, to compensate for the absence in the former. (Ruan, 1996: 77–9)

(3) Function of establishing a market mechanism

The initiative and driving forces for economic reform were to 'bring order out of chaos' (bo luan fan zhen). China's new leaders realized that the old extreme 'left' way was pushing China into chaos. Deng Xiaoping once said, 'It is a death road if we do not follow the socialism principle, do not take the opening policy, do not develop economics, and do not change people's life for the better' (Li, 2012:

23). The government realized that low economic efficiency was the key problem of China's State Owned Enterprises. The 'iron rice bowl' must be broken. In 1993, the Third Plenum of the 14th CC-CPC released a decision on 'Some Issues of Establishing a Socialist Market Economy'. Following this principle, the Chinese labour market is a 'labour force employment market' (lao dong li jiu ye shi chang), as explained by the Ministry of Labour and Social Security (MoLSS), in which all parties can come to buy or sell labour with no need for a trade union, collective bargaining, and so on (Taylor et al., 2003).

At the beginning of the economic reform, the government believed that the old employment system was a barrier hindering enterprises' rights to employability. After 1993, the government announced that it would give enterprises entitled autonomies in a variety of aspects of personnel management. A new system of social security was built to meet the demands of SOEs changes: for example, the housing welfare system (Tang and Xi, 1994). Early in 1987, the government called for an individual contract between workers and enterprises, and proclaimed it as a means to establish new employment relations. Since then, the government has gradually withdrawn its management at the micro level of internal employee relations, instead taking care of employee relations at the macro level. In 2007, the new Labour Contract Law enforced the necessity for collective contracts, and has attempted to establish a harmonious and self-adjusting mechanism for employee relations.

Apart from the above functions, the government has been attempting other roles. The government is a regulator, inspector and arbitrator. As a regulator, the government issued a number of regulations and laws, such as the new Labour Law (2007), the Regulation for Collective Bargaining (2004), the Law of Trade Union (Reversion) (2001), the Labour Tribunal (2007), the Employment Promotion Law (2007) and so on. Obviously, the government is trying to put China's labour regulation into a legislative trajectory. As an arbitrator, the government has given more autonomy to the enterprises and focused on social stability, social status and collective bargaining with workers, and on maintaining a harmonious tripartite relationship among trade unions, enterprises and management. As an inspector, the government holds the power to stop any acts against the labour laws, and to order rectification where appropriate. But the government's intention to act as a third party has failed due to Chinese tradition and cultural heritage, as workers are ultimately much more reliant on direct appeals to the government when there are unresolved labour disputes.

As a country with thousands of years of authoritarian tradition, China's government officials take unlimited responsibility towards the people. For example, if one official is nominated as a prefect, people may call him/her a Parent-like Official (fu mu guan), and people living in the prefecture area are just like his/her children. From the other side, the prefect will take endless responsibility to take good care of his citizens. This family concept of administrative patterns has created a stable and long-lasting social structure in China: even today, the CPC warns its officials to be a good fu mu guan for the people. In cases relating to IR actions, however, the parent-like management can be troublesome for the government, because people will not choose a legitimate way to solve labour disputes when they arise, but rather will appeal directly to the higher government authority (shang fang) by demonstration, threatening suicide or any other action which may draw the attention of the media or society.

By and large, any successful reform taken in China should involve combined power from top-to-bottom, from the government, and bottom-to-top, from the ordinary citizens. An influential siege that occurred in the south of China, the Wukan Protests (Wikipedia, 2011)[2] proved that, in China, effective solutions for social disputes can be achieved only if both government and villages approach consensus: otherwise, setbacks can easily destroy people's efforts.

TRADE UNIONS

The general principle to the CPC Constitution (2018 version) states that the CPC leadership is 'the essential part of constructing socialism with Chinese characteristics'. Thus, it is clear that Marxist ideology has been the dominant theory since its foundation in the 1920s. Earlier in the nineteenth century, trade union organizations in China originated, in most periods, from 'townsmen's associations', which are still active today in some underground trade unions in South China, with some trade unions being manipulated by the capitalists. Since its foundation, the ACFTU has been assigned the function of 'transmission belt' and the responsibly to transmit the government's policies (Taylor et al., 2003). For example, in the latter half of the

1980s, the ACFTU tried to free itself from the control of the CPC and to be independent, but failed (Jiang, 1996). The new Trade Union Law (2001) stated that the trade union shall abide by the leadership of the CPC. The highest body of the ACFTU is the National Congress of Trade Union and the Executive Committee elected by the national congress, while the chairperson of the ACFTU is usually among the most powerful political leaders: that is, a member of the China politburo.

In the time of the planned economy, the trade union was acting as an assistant or subsidiary department of government organs. Its main function was to assist government or enterprises' management in order to urge workers or staff to accomplish the production targets set by the central government. In the time of absolute planned economy, combining the experience of the Soviet Union and practices in China, there was a 'three-in-one' guideline for trade unions, which meant 'taking production as the central task, and paying attention to workers' living and education' (Taylor et al., 2003: 106). Thus, it is no surprise that trade unions at the enterprise level were busy organizing labour contests,[3] technical innovations and increased production drives and propagandizing workers' political and ideological thinking.

Since the market economy, the ACFTU has faced a contradictory situation. On the one hand, it is the representative of the workers, but since 1978, with the expansion of the private economy and the loosening policy for citizen mobility, the situation has become more complex. Statistics showed that in 2009 there were 200 million migrant workers who were the core parts of China's manufacturing industry. It is becoming a challenge for the ACFTU to attract more workers and stabilize the workforce in the process of reform. On the other hand, ordinary workers and staff require the ACFTU to represent their interests and protect their rights. Recent cases of industrial actions such as strikes and demonstrations, and even rival/illegal unions, have stimulated changes in the official trade unions. The ACFTU is attempting democracy-oriented reform in some cities. A pattern of direct election of trade union leadership has been applied in some FDI enterprises and SOEs, such as the Japanese direct invested 'Ricoh Shenzhen Subsidiary',[4] 'Panasonic Shenzhen Subsidiary',[5] and the state-owned 'Yantian International Container Terminals' (YICT) (China Newsweek, 2012). It could be predicted that such reform might lead to uncertainty for official trade union career paths and disrupt bureaucratic stability, but the ACFTU is making the experiment work with democracy-oriented working arrangements.

WORKERS AND STAFF

Definition

There have been debates over the definition of the term 'workers', because it carries both a descriptive and an ideological significance. Following the traditional Marxist definition, the working class is a definite social group, whose common identity is their lack of means of production and thus independent survival, selling their labour power for wages and holding the status of employees (Braverman, 1974). However, at the time of China's revolutionary history, there was a successful revolt against feudalism, and many more jobs relied on peasant mobilization. Thus, in the first official version of the Chinese Constitution, both the working class and the peasant class were defined as the key parts of the state socialist system (Chapter 1, Article 1). Thus, some scholars argued that the main body of the working class was industrial workers, but it also included commercial and agricultural workers who were registered as permanent residents in urban localities (chengshihukou). More than that, some researchers insisted that the working class may also have included other staff and intellectuals engaged in educational, scientific and health work units (Chang, 1988; Kuang, 1984). Therefore, the new concept of 'working class' was composed of four social strata: 'blue-collar' workers who provide their physical labour (tililaodong), 'white-collar' workers who provide their mental labour (naolilaodong), intellectuals engaging in educational or scientific work, and civil servants/managerial cadres working in the public sector (Liu, 2002). Given that the CPC has been a political party of the Chinese working class since its foundation, the challenge that it faces in the new era is to maintain a social ideology in the context of a market economy (see Figure 4.1).

On 9 November 2014, the Third Plenum of the 18th CPC Central Committee was successfully held in the building of the People's Congress in Beijing. It was a conference of power-switching in which was founded a new poli-bureau leadership directed by Mr Xi Jinping. Moreover, the Communiqué released in the plenum

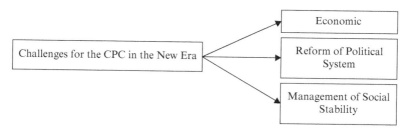

Figure 4.1   Challenges for the government in the new era

answered questions on how the CPC would implement a series of policies ensuring social development; further, the new government published a set of Explanatory Notes for the 'Decision of the Central CPC of China on Some Major Issues Concerning Comprehensively Deepening the Reform', from which more specific measures and policies being taken by the government were explained.

To understand the policies that central government is taking, three aspects should be take into consideration. The first is the function of free marketing principles: for a long time, the CPC did not admit the function of market-oriented economy – instead, a socialist planned market system dominated China's economy for more than thirty years until Mr Deng Xiaoping undertook economic reform from 1978. The direct consequence of the planned market system led to extremely low efficiency of output, to more than 40 million laid-off workers, and to severe damage to the Chinese nation's competitiveness in the world. Economic construction is still the essential strategy for the CPC government, which was clearly expressed in the Communiqué of the 3rd Plenum of the 18th CPC, which stated that, 'in the coming 10 years, we should respect the function of the market-oriented economy, let the market play a decisive role in allocating resources', and that the government should leave the free market alone, with less interference.

Second, in the coming ten years, the CPC should take great care with political system reforms: its targets are to achieve a less authoritarian but more democratic government, and one that is more effective and less corrupt. According to China's Xinhua news agency in 2014, the Xi government cracked down on a group of corrupt senior officials: nearly 50 government senior officials above the provincial governor level have been arrested and given jail sentences since Xi's new government was founded in 2013 (Xinhua News, 2013). This anti-corruption storm has set up a much more positive image of the CPC to Chinese people and the international community, and also strengthened the power and administrative capability of the new government.

Third, maintenance of social stability is another challenge for Xi's government: that is, in the coming ten years, the government should 'explore social equality and justice, further promote social harmony and stability, and further improve the Party's leadership and governance' (adopted from the Decision, translated by author). Given the constant social riots, demonstrations and industrial strikes taking place in recent years, people appeal for their benefits by any possible channel, legal or illegal ways. The question for the new government is how to create a more 'just, transparent, harmonious, and ecological society' in the course of China's industrialization and urbanization. Today, if one walks into a village in the countryside, no matter which province it is in, one remarkable thing is that there are only old people and teenagers living in it: most of the young people have left their home towns and gone to the cities as migrant workers (nong min gong).[6] New types of employee relations, different from that of the traditional state-owned enterprises, are formed and challenge the tripartite relations.

WORKERS AND STAFF IN THE PLANNED ECONOMY PERIOD

During the planned economy period, the premises where workers and staff worked, known as Danwei,[7] were strengthened with the birth of SOEs in 1950s. There are different opinions on the origins of Danwei (Lu, 1997; Sil, 1997; Yeh, 1997), but they supplied almost all the social needs of their workers and staff, such as housing, schools, medical care and recreation. They thus became the basic administrative unit of urban society during the planned economy. Workers and staff earned their privileges through different types of Danwei, and stood as an elite group in the working class of China.

However, this 'cradle-to-grave' welfare system has encountered unprecedented challenges since China's second generation of leadership held power in 1978. Extremely low efficiency of productivity, nepotism, and political favouritism forced the government to undertake a 'socialist style economic reform'. All the SOEs were required to follow the principle of economic reform: that is, 'increasing efficiency by downsizing staff'. The government subsequently released a series of policies encouraging workers and staff who had earned a certain skill or competence to develop private businesses, termed Xiahai (go swimming in the sea), while those who lacked skills or were disadvantaged by their age or financial supports were required to Xiagang (be laid off), and step down from their working position.

CHANGING PATTERNS IN THE TRANSITIONAL ECONOMIC PERIOD

In the four decades since 1978, the government has undertaken new economic reforms, aiming to increase efficiency. One remarkable change is the decreasing number of SOEs, with an increasing number of private enterprises and a new legal structure for firms. These changed employment patterns have caused considerable variation in labour standards and employment conditions. For example, in terms of standard wages, who will make the decision on the price of labour? It is not simply determined by the state as usual, but by the employer and employees. An open labour market may let the employees leave their Danwei to find new jobs. Statistics show that in private and FDI enterprises, labour disputes, collective bargaining, and industrial action are increasing due to the improvement of workers' awareness of their social identities and their right to a better life, and more importantly to the formation of grass-root trade unions. For most people, being a skilled or white-collar worker in a foreign invested enterprise, or securing any job in an SOE, is still the ultimate pursuit.

CULTURAL CHARACTERISTICS OF MAINLAND CHINESE EMPLOYEES IN FOREIGN ENTERPRISES

Schneider (1988) once noted that human resources policies are related not only to organizational culture but also to the national culture of where the subsidiary company is located. Therefore, practices of human resources management (HRM) such as planning and employment, performance evaluation and rewards, selection, and socialization should not only match with the enterprise strategy but also adapt to the culture of subsidiary company.

Holton (1990), by conducting multiple in-depth interviews with employees from Sino–foreign joint ventures, found that there are several cultural characteristics of Mainland Chinese employees:

- Employees attach importance to interpersonal harmony and fear losing face. Therefore, managers who are accustomed to Western enterprises should make alterations to their management pattern. In terms of staff training and performance evaluation, they are suggested to keep a reserved and low-key profile.
- Long surrounded by Chinese state-run enterprises, employees expect job security and crave the 'iron rice bowl'.
- Employees tend to be obedient and unwilling to shoulder responsibility; in the meantime, they are averse to 'initiative' or 'innovative' ways of doing things for fear that the internal harmony of the organization could be broken. Mainland Chinese managers are less courageous to shoulder responsibility but more willing to obey orders.
- Mainland Chinese managers are reluctant to conduct horizontal communication inside the organization and they perform poorly in cross-functional coordination.
- They tend towards economic egalitarianism and believe that there should not be a large gap between the salary of a high-level employee and that of a low-level one.
- In Chinese social culture, seniors are widely venerated for their rich experience and wisdom and are often regarded as 'sages'.
- A lack of technical employees, engineers and managers, with skills that are not easily transferred.
- Abundant grass-roots employees who are willing to be trained, but supervision is needed to sustain their performance.

SOME OBSERVATIONS ON THE DEVELOPMENT OF CHINA ERs

In a time of industrial upgrading initiated from 2010, employee relations in China are facing a new round of challenges in many aspects. As for the structure of labour law, it is not much different from that in other countries, but is has been substantially influenced by international labour standards.

The legacy of China's traditional hierarchical culture has had an impact on work law legislation, and it can be predicted that this hierarchy may reflect the economic and ideological assumption for a long time. In China, different categories of workers enjoy different payment and welfare. For example, Cooney et al. (2013) sorted out six entitlement of workers in China, sequencing from higher to lower degrees of protection. The six positions of workers are: (1) permanent workers; (2) workers engaged directly by employers under fixed contracts; (3) workers engaged in fixed contracts on labour hire arrangements; (4) casual workers; (5) so-called employees who are not engaged in labour; and (6) independent contractors. In shop-floor operations inside the enterprises, the Labour Contract Law does much to protect the conditions of the first three sets of workers, and largely neglects the other three (Cooney et al., 2013: 146).

Any changes, following the authoritarian tradition in China, in law and regulations of work situations, must be stat-centric. The involvement of civil society participation will be marginalized due to the need of social stability. Unlike the social structure in Western countries, non-governmental organizations are vulnerable and conflicted in Chinese employee relations. But the government may take extra-legal methods of implementation to promote innovative legal norms and processes.

LEGITIMACY AWARENESS

Traditionally, China has been thought of as an authoritarian country for many years, but the situation is changing thanks to 35 years of Open Reform policies taken since Deng's government. This reform movement was taken from the top to the bottom social classes by advocating the belief of 'ruling the country by law'. On one hand, China has the world's most complete legitimated rules regulating employee relations, such as the Trade Union Law, which requires a trade union organization in every company when the number of employees reaches a certain point, and the Regulations of Collective Bargaining, which call for legal procedures in trade unions' negotiations with employers, but on the other hand, trouble might arise if one company does everything following the laws and regulations without taking cultural factors into consideration. Thus, it is suggested that ERs in China need complete consideration of cultural factors as well as references to laws and regulations.

INTERFERENCE OF TRADITIONAL VALUE SYSTEMS

The value of culture in guiding us as to what is good and what is not worthy of doing plays an important role in reconciling the conflicts of ERs. The collectivism featured in Chinese culture plays a special role in ERs. Theories that are well-developed and verified in the West may not work in the East: for instance, Fan and Bjorkman (2003) investigated 62 MNCs in China to examine the relationship between HRM and firm performance, and found that the cultural environment can function as leverage to amend the connections of HRM and firm performance. Expatriates in MNCs may find that the work is easy to accomplish if a previous understanding is established or a short training programme relating to Chinese traditional value systems is taken before coming to China.

It is noted that value systems may advance with the times in contemporary Chinese society. The big changes to the economic and political structure have overturned a number of China's traditional values. For example, old Chinese philosophies taught that a man developing his career in society should follow the principles of 'cultivating one's moral character and governing one's family, and, last, managing the state', which was the creed for life. Today, the concepts of family and state may not be prioritized by young men looking for a job and a decent and comfortable life with better treatment at work is the new Chinese dream for ordinary people.

Nevertheless, traditional values control people invisibly, so insight into local culture and customs is important for expatriate managers when dealing with employees.

ROLE OF THE TRADE UNION: A DOUBLE-EDGED SWORD

Unlike the situation in the West, the trade union is taken as a serious organization in company administration, for example, there are no trade unions or similar organizations in the American MNCs such as Wal-Mart, KFC, McDonalds or some hi-tech companies, nor in the IT giants such as Microsoft and Apple Inc. But when the above companies set up subsidiaries in China, trade unions became a reliable partner in many cases.

There are always two edges to a sword: if trade unions, as research has found in the south of China, work together with the managers, this may greatly improve the output of products (see Figure 4.2). Misunderstandings about the role of trade unions might arise for the MNCs' managers because of the cultural and ideological differences and interference from their home country. The following reasons might be relevant:

- Taking a trade union organization as a political construction, which will have a negative impact and hinder the company's business;

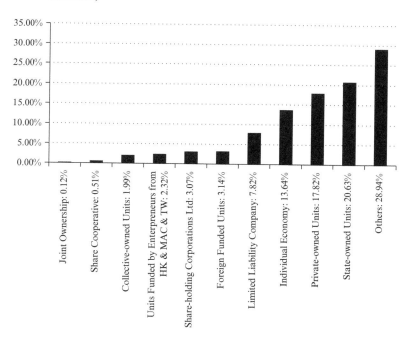

Source: State Council Information Center (2009).

Figure 4.2 Urban employment distribution in different ownership structures

● Concern that the trade union and management will have two opposite parts, which will threaten the company's development.

Another situation deterring the development of trade unions could be concluded as follows:

● Employees tend to be poorly motivated with regard to joining a trade union because most companies are labour-intensive and young women with comparatively lower education make up the majority of workers. There might also be negative attitudes and lack of support from the companies' management towards the trade union organization;
● Even if the trade union is set up by the requirements of law, it might not work effectively because of employees' strong mobility, rapid turnover, and internal management system;
● The confusing attitude from the grass-roots trade union organization, which takes MNCs as a special zone, is hard to communicate, and helping MNCs to set up a trade union is often a thankless job.

CONCLUSION

The same actors and institutions can be identified in Chinese employee relations, but there are marked differences. Their interests and nature of function are similar to their counterparts in the western world. But, due to the historical, economic and cultural reasons, the actors in China's employee relations hold unique characteristics in this system. To give a complete image of Chinese cultural characteristics, it is necessary to analyze it from four angles: first, to think of the influence of Chinese tradition; second, to look at the connection of religious impact; third, to take the impact of communist ideology into account, and fourth, to observe the value changes since the implementation of Open Door policies since the 1980s. Today, the Chinese government proclaims the way of socialism is to approach its modernization (Xi, 2014), which requires the construction of both material and spiritual progress. In the course of socialist modernization, one vital issue is that the construction of spiritual progress lags behind material progress, which leads to various noxious phenomena, such as corruption, money-centricity and malfeasance. Therefore, considering the essence of Confucianism has had a significant impact on China's spiritual progress in the present day. Since 1949, communist doctrines have prevailed in Chinese social life. Ideas from Karl Marx's socialist theories and Leninism from the Soviet Union, as well as Maoist concepts, have become dominant philosophies. Traditional Confucianism was criticized and rejected at the time, but some of its tenets were combined with Marxism and evolved as new patterns of Chinese political ideology: for example, egalitarianism meets traditional collectivism, Confucius's assertions about harmony assertion were accepted by proletarian unions, and the superiority of moral over legalistic obligations was welcomed by socialists' moral expectations. Egalitarianism, harmony, moral paradigm and paternalism came to be typical characteristics of the nation's state-owned company management.

A typical example is that the ACFTU is not just a union, but a quasi-government organ in which there are different opinions in its internal system on how to achieve the aim of maintaining social peace, a harmonious relationship for social stability. More than that, 'differences between public and private, between orientations to managerial authority and the application of government legislation are all different from liberal capitalist institutional arrangements' (Taylor et al., 2003: 207). Across the market economy period, the government tried to change its emphasis from the traditional control of everything to a focus on more general macro-level management: for example, to regulate the private sector and its employee relations via the adaptation of union organization, collective bargaining and labour provisions. The government is still playing an important role in employee relations and the positions of workers are steadily declining, while overt conflicts of interest are becoming more pronounced.

After four decades of economic development, there has been a two-digit increase in annual GDP. China's economy is still performing strongly, and has been called the locomotive of the world's economy. The various forms of employment relations, along with the complex international economic situation, mean that China's employee relations represent a more provocative issue, not just relating to China's political and economic life, but also to that of the world.

NOTES

1. When the First World War came to an end, the Chinese people, having long suffered from imperialist aggression and full of hopes for national independence, had hailed 'the victory of truth over might' and the '14 Articles of Peace' put forward by US President Wilson. But the method of dealing with the Shandong issue at the Paris Peace Conference rid the Chinese people of their illusion and made them realize that they themselves needed to 'take direct action'. The May Fourth Movement thus broke out. Source: https://www.britannica.com/event/May-Fourth-Movement (accessed 29 July 2019).

2. The Wukan protest, also known as the Siege of Wukan, was an anti-corruption protest that began in September 2011, and escalated in December 2011 with the expulsion of officials by villagers, the siege of the town by police, and subsequent hostilities in the southern Chinese village of Wukan (pop. 12,000).

3. From 1975 to 1978, trade unions in *Danwei*, state owned industries and the public sector organized some sporting events and competitive performances as a means of stimulating labour motivation and maintaining political control.

4. In October 2010, workers in the Japanese Ricoh Shenzhen Subsidiary went on strike. Workers asked for re-election of their own trade union representative, and furthermore, considering the background of the two Ricoh subsidiaries undergoing amalgamation, workers demanded compensation for those who lost their jobs and higher salaries for those who remained working in the new amalgamated enterprise.

5. On 24 May 2012, in Oumu Electronics Ltd., the Japanese Panasonic subsidiary in China, a new trade union chairman was elected by the workers, not appointed by the enterprise, which was the model being used by most Chinese enterprises. The newly elected chairman of the trade union was one of the achievements of three months' demonstration and strike by workers. After this action, the Oumu Electronics executive expressed to the media that the enterprise would emphasize four issues in the future: first, to provide a budget of 100,000 Yuan each year to support the trade union management; second, to set up a system for collective negotiation between the enterprise management and trade union, including acceptance of employees' complaints, and to release the enterprise's annual report twice a year; third, to address the employees' salary standard though a collective bargaining system directed by the trade union; and fourth, to pay attention to the training of trade union leaders from the ordinary workers. Source: http://www.gdftu.org.cn/zghd/xxlgjy/mtgz/201209/t20120912_317791.htm (accessed 29 July 2019).

6. The term 'migrant worker' has different official meanings and connotations in different parts of the world. The United Nations' definition is broad, including any people working outside of their home country. Some of these are called expatriates. Several countries have millions of foreign workers. Some have millions of illegal immigrants, most of them being workers also. The term can also be used to describe someone who migrates within a country, possibly their own, in order to pursue work such as seasonal work. Overall, the Chinese government has tacitly supported migration as a means of providing labour for factories and construction sites and for the long-term goals of transforming China from a rural-based economy to an urban-based one. Some inland cities have started providing migrants with social security, including pensions and other insurance. In 2012, there were a reported 167 million migrant workers, but with trends of working closer to home (within their own or a neighbouring province, a wage drop of 21 per cent). Migrant workers in China are notoriously marginalized, especially by the hukou system of residency permits, which tie one stated residence to all social

welfare benefits (source: http://www.doc88.com/p-4833124170574.html, accessed 29 July 2019).

7. *Danwei* in China has been described as a 'small city' which was able to meet all the basic social and welfare requirements of urban living and in which 'individuals are born, live, work, and die' (Naughton, 1997: 170).

BIBLIOGRAPHY

Braverman, Harry. 1974. *Labour and Monopoly Capital: The Degradation of Work in the Twentieth Century*. New York: Monthly Review Press.

Chang, Kai. 1988. *Compendium of Trade Union Science* (*Lilun Gonghuixue Gailun*). Beijing: Economic Management Press.

Chang, Kai. 2005. *Labour Relations Science* (*Laodong Guanxi Xue*). Press of China Labour Social Securities. Zhongguo laodong guanxi baozhang chubanshe.

Cheng, Yanyuan. 2002. *Industrial Relations* (*Laodong Guanxi*). Press of China People's University, Zhongguo renmin daxue chubanshe, Beijing.

China Newsweek. 2012. https://www.clssn.com/html/Home/report/59500-1. htm (accessed 29 July 2019).

Cooney, S. Biddulph, S. and Zhu, Y. 2013. *Law and Fair Work in China*. Abingdon: Routledge.

Dunlop, John. 1958. *Industrial Relations Systems*. New York: Entry Holt.

Fan, Gang (ed.). 1994. *Toward Market (1978–1993: An Analysis of the Economy of China* (*Zhouxiangshichang (1978–1993): Zhongguojingjifenxi*). Shanghai: Shanghai People's Press.

Fan, X. Che and Bjorkman, Ingmar. 2003. Human recourse management and the performance of foreign invested enterprises in China. *Journal of Management Sciences in China*, 6(2): 54–9.

Fang, T. 2003. A critique of Hofstede's fifth national culture dimension. *International Journal of Cross Cultural Management*, 3(3): 347–68.

Gao, Ai-di. 2008. *A History of China Labour Movement* (*Zhongguo Gong Renyun Dong Shi*). Beijing: Press of China Labour and Social Security.

Hei, Qiming. 2004. Scientific definition of ten essential categories in the research of industrial relations (Laodong guanxi yanjiu shida jiben fanchou de kexue jieding). *Theory and Modernization* (*Lilun yu Xiandaihua*), 6: 73–5.

Holton, R. H. 1990. Human resource management in the People's Republic of China. *Management International Review*, 30: 121–36.

Jiang, Kaiven. 1996. The conflicts between trade union and the party-state: the reform of Chinese trade unions in the 1980s (Gonghuiyu dang-guojia de chongtu: bashiniandaiyilai de zhongguogonghuigaige). *Hong Kong Journal of Social Sciences*, 8: 121–58.

Ke, Huangrui. 1988. Labour law and regulations in the economic zone (jingjitequlaodongfaluzhidu). *Journal of Ganshu Institute of Political Science and Law*, 2: 67–70.

Kuang, Kuang. 1984. *Working Class in China* (*ZhongguoGongrenJieji*). Changchun: Jinlin People's Press.

Li, Zongfu. 2012. Review Deng's conversation in South of China, firmly develop the opening reform policies (ChongwenDengxiaopingNanfang Tanhua, JiandingBuyiTuijin Gaige Kaifang). *Journal of Qunyan*, 4: 23–5.

Liu, Mingkui. 1985. *Historical Situation of China Working Class (ZhongGuo Gong Ren JieJi Li SHi Zhuang Kuang)*. Beijing: China Communist History Press, 2–56.

Liu, Yufang. 2002. On the changes occurred within the structure of working class (Qiantangongrenjiejiduiwuneibujiegoubianhua). *Journal of Shijiazhuang CPC Party College*, 1: 21.

Lu, Xiaobo. 1997. Minor public economy: the revolutionary origins of the Danwei. In Xiaobo Lu and Elizabeth J. Perry (eds), *Danwei: The Changing Chinese Workplace in Historical and Comparative Perspective*. Armonk: M. E. Sharpe, 12–13.

Luo, Xiuyun. 2011. *Second Largest Poor Group in China: The Lay-off Workers*. http://www.360doc.com/content/11/0306/11/5177773_98574464. shtml (accessed 29 July 2019).

Naughton, B. 1997. *Danwei: The Changing Chinese Workplace in Historical and Comparative Perspective*. London: M. E. Sharpe.

NBSC. 2003. National Bureau of Statistic of China, http://www.stats.gov.cn/ (accessed June 2009).

Qin, Liuqing. 1995. Improving the strengthens of state-owned enterprises by properly managing the in-depth conflicts (Chuli hao guoyouqiye shengcengci de maodun, zengqiang guoyouqiye huoli). *Lingnan Journal*, 2: 26–8.

Ruan, Chongwu. 1996. Speech at the national conference of directors of labour bureaus (Zaiquanguolaodongtijuzhanghuiyi de jianghua), 15 December 1992, in Jianxin Wan (ed.), *China Labour Yearbook: 1992–1994*. Beijing: China Labour Press, 77–9.

Schneider, S. C. 1988. National vs. corporate culture: implications for HRM. *Human Resource Management*, 27(2): 231–46.

Sil, Rudra. 1997. The Russian 'village in the city' and the Stalinist system of enterprise management: the origins of worker alienation in the Soviet state system. In Xiaobo Lu and Elizabeth J. Perry (eds), *Danwei: the Changing Chinese Workplace in Historical and Comparative Perspective*. Armonk: M. E. Sharpe, Chapter 5.

State Bureau of Labour. 1981. http://www.stats.gov.cn/english (accessed 15 October 2019).

State Council Information Center. 2009. http://english.gov.cn/ (accessed 29 July 2019).

Tang, Shurong and Xi, Ongsheng (eds). 1994. *A Complete Works of Application of Labour Law, Laodongfashiwuquanshu*. Beijing: China Workers Press.

Taylor, Bill, Kai, Chang and Qi, Li. 2003. *Industrial Relations in China*. Cheltenham, UK and Northampton, MA, USA: Edward Elgar Publishing.

Wagner, Augusta. 1938. *Labour Legislation in China, Peking*. Cited in Chen Guo-jun, 1960, *Labour Legislation (Lao Gong Li Faxinlun)*. Taipei: Zhengzhong Publishing House.

Wang, Yongxi. 1992. *History of Chinese Trade Union (Zhongguogongyunshi)*. Beijing: Dangshi Publishing House.

Wikipedia. 2011. https://en.m.wikipedia.org/wiki/Wukan_protests (accessed 29 July 2019).

Xi, Jinping. 2014. *The Governance of China*. Beijing: Foreign Language Press.

Xinhua News. 2012. http://news.xinhuanet.com/2012-05/25/c_112036687.htm (accessed 29 July 2019).

Xinhua News. 2013. http://finance.sina.com.cn/china/20130411/153215117440. shtml (accessed 29 July 2019).

Yeh, Wenshin. 1997. Republican origins of the Danwei: the case of Shanghai's Bank of China. In Xiaobo Lu and Elizabeth J. Perry (eds), *Danwei: The Changing Chinese Workplace in Historical and Comparative Perspective*. Armonk: M. E. Sharpe, 43–5.

5. Culture, Language and Translation in Comparative Employee Relations: The Case of the Italian *Caporalato*

Pietro Manzella

INTRODUCTORY REMARKS

This chapter aims to illustrate the way culture affects translation in the broad field of comparative employee relations (ER). Specifically, the chapter will look at how cultural shifts taking place in ER cause practices to take on new shades of meanings. Arguments will be made in support of the view that these cultural changes need to be taken into account when engaging in comparative analysis. Translation plays a key role when attempting to convey the meaning of the practices under examination – along with their cultural connotations – and transposing them into the language of the ER system being compared. We will also see how ER is continuously evolving, along with the terminology employed to define institutions thereof, which thus needs continuous adaptation. As Hyman would put it 'tradition is potent, words themselves change their meaning with time' (Hyman, 1995: 20). Consequently, a term that was appropriate to translate a given ER institution into the language of the employee relations under comparison might need reviewing, as the cultural changes referred to above might load it with different nuances of meanings.

In order to stress the linkage between culture, language, and translation in comparative ER and to substantiate the previous arguments, the Italian and the UK ER systems will be considered. Specifically, the Italian concept of *caporalato*, and also *caporale*, will be looked at, along with the terminology used to translate them into English – for example, 'gangmaster system' and 'gangmaster' – to see if these terms can be seen as proper equivalents in UK employee relations. As will be seen, these terms have undergone a shift of meaning, following legislation that was passed in the UK that legalized gangmasters' activity. This legal change – which is also a cultural one, as it affects people's perception of the ER practice under scrutiny – has not taken place in Italy, so differences emerge between the two countries concerning the collective sentiment towards gangmasters and their work. Before engaging in the examination of the concepts and their transposition into the target ER systems, the theoretical background will be provided, which will be followed by some definitional aspects. Some concluding remarks will summarize the findings.

THEORETICAL BACKGROUND

It must be said at the outset that the discussion concerning the significance of culture in comparative ER is not new. ER scholars have acknowledged the relevance of culture to inform employment relations (Gennard et al., 2016; Hofstede, 1980; Price, 2010; Verma et al., 1999; Wilkinson et al., 2014). While it has been posited that 'comparative employment relations that focus too exclusively on cultural dimensions alone are likely to miss important geopolitical influences' (Dundon and Collings, 2011: 214 quoting Jackson), the form which industrial relations takes in any one nation does markedly reflect the culture concerned (Blum, 1981). Accordingly, culture constitutes a major aspect of ER, even more so when two ER systems are compared. One point that should be stressed is that when conducting comparative research in ER, culture, and institutions should not be seen as conflicting elements. In this sense, Meardi (2011) insists that 'Sometimes, the theoretical opposition between institutional and cultural explanations is just a matter of wording and (undefined) definitions' (Meardi, 2011: 337). This is even more so if one considers that ER practices might be peculiar to a particular cultural context, that is, they are culture-specific. The appreciation of culture-bound work and employment features is essential and greatly benefits from an understanding of national institutions. Therefore, the cultural and institutional components of an ER system should be jointly examined in order to provide a comprehensive picture of the system under scrutiny.

When there are different ER practices cross-nationally, the relevance of translation is evident. Like culture – and its weight in the domain considered – the challenges posed by language and translation do not represent a novelty, at least among ER comparative scholars. Hyman has examined many translation issues at the time of comparing ER institutions, going as far as to argue that 'words, especially when they undergo translation, are not always what they seem' (Hyman, 2001: 38). Blanpain and Baker have also stressed the difficulties resulting from translating concepts pertaining to specific national ER contexts, reasserting the need to move beyond 'labels' and to compare functions, rather than institutions (Blanpain and Baker, 2010). In a similar vein, Meardi (2011) reminds us of 'the naïve assumptions that words mean the same in all national contexts' (Meardi, 2011: 336), while Bean (1999) postulates that attempts to contrast institutions on an international basis are confronted with immediate difficulties of terminology, in that bodies with the same name might perform different functions.

If in ER, words are particularly important in order to understand 'the reciprocal interdependence of language and concepts, concepts and theories, theories and realities' (Hyman, 1995: 19), and if translation is germane to fully appreciating the functioning of practices cross-nationally, the fact that this discipline has attracted little consideration on behalf of Translation Studies (TS) scholars is somewhat surprising. This is especially the case in consideration of the fact that ER terminology is laden with nuanced meanings conveying national and cultural values which are difficult to render in other languages. If we limit our discussion to the Italian–English pair, among ER-related TS research, mention should be made of the work of Bromwich (2006) who considered the difficulties stemming from translating terms in union discourse from Italian into English. Reference should also be made to Manzella (2017), who has recently stressed the hurdles of translating Italian ER concepts into English, providing examples of ambiguous translations in EU documentation. In this respect, he has posited that ER jargon 'while sharing common aspects legal discourse, can be regarded as making up a distinct genre, since words employed in this domain are often the result of negotiations, and informal interactions and practices, which therefore deserve special attention when engaging in comparative research' (Manzella, 2017: 345).

As for the notions under discussion here – for example, *caporale* and *caporalato* – and their English translation, no research has been conducted so far, based on the author's knowledge. Accordingly, this chapter aims to fulfill a two-fold purpose. First, it intends to fill this research gap, looking at the difficulties resulting from translating ER notions. Examining the issue from a TS perspective will provide a fresh approach. This might hold, especially considering the vast amount of ER literature discussing translation issues in this discipline, as compared to little TS research available in this field. Second, and more generally, this work wants to serve as a call to TS to take up ER as a field of research. The distinctive features of comparative ER make it a fascinating and inspiring field of investigation from a TS standpoint. For this reason, TS research would significantly contribute to the understanding of ER practices and institutions when engaging in comparative research.

DEFINITIONS

This section will attempt to provide definitions for gangmaster and *caporale*, respectively in the UK and Italian ER systems, and will help to appreciate the notions at hand better, as well as to identify possible commonalities and differences. In addition, the analysis of these definitions will present us with the opportunity to comprehend the relationship between culture, language, and translation and to what extent the cultural changes taking place in the source language and ER system affect the terminology employed in the target language and ER system to render the preliminary concepts. Starting with 'gangmaster,' a suitable definition is afforded by Strauss (2014), who argues that: 'In the UK, labor contractors, intermediaries, and agencies that provide workers mostly for the agricultural, horticultural and shellfish sectors are known as gangmaster. Those who employ workers in 'gangs' and are hired on a short-term seasonal basis to meet the demand for cheap labor in these sectors' (Strauss, 2014: 165). This terminology resonated with undeclared work in the UK and was given significant media coverage in 2004, following an incident which took place on a beach in the northwest of England and was ever since known as the Morecambe Bay tragedy. A gang of illegal Chinese migrants thought to be brought into the UK by a criminal association (i.e. the Chinese Triads) was put to work collecting cockles. They attempted to leave the beach, but they were overwhelmed by the sea. Reportedly, 23 'cocklers' passed away because of drowning or hypothermia. The episode was such resounding news that, as pointed out by Byrne and Smith (2016), it introduced the British public to a new word, namely, the gangmaster. The following investigations led to the conclusion that the liberalization of labour was detrimental, as it favoured migrants' exploitation.

Consequently, the Morecambe Bay tragedy was seen as the last straw and prompted legislation regulating the intermediation activity of gangmasters. Specifically, the UK government adopted the Gangmasters (Licensing) Act 2004, making provisions for the licensing of activities concerning the supply of workers in a number of sectors (agricultural work, gathering shellfish; processing or packaging agricultural produce or shellfish or fish products). According to this legislation, an appointed body (e.g. the Gangmasters Licensing Authority) issues licenses to gangmasters, closely monitoring their activities (Sargeant and Lewis, 2008). Consequently, while in the past these illegal gangmasters provided labour to individuals and companies with no questions asked (Byrne and Smith, 2016), now those who serve as gangmasters without being awarded a license or with forged documents are guilty of an offence. In this sense, unlicensed gangmasters might face imprisonment.

Concerning Italy's *caporali*, these are individuals who organize casual labour, especially in agricultural work. The term *caporale* refers to a historical personage from feudal southern Italy. He was pivotal to the organization of agricultural labour, and the term is loaded with connotations of bullying, brutality, and exploitation. Nowadays, *caporale* is employed to denote the archetypal labour trafficker (Howard, 2016). The activity of *caporali* is, of course, illegal, yet they play a significant role, in that they are in charge of liaising with farmers, sourcing workers, transporting them to and from the fields and ensure that work is fulfilled and workers are paid. *Caporalato*, that is the illegal form of intermediation provided by *caporali*, has been a long-standing issue in Italy. As it was with the UK, a number of incidents taking place in Italy of gang labourers suffering from extremely hard working conditions have attracted public attention over time, making the prevention of this form of employment a matter of urgency. The problem of gangmasters is such an important one that the news frequently reports incidents concerning their activity. In this sense, the death of 12 gang labourers who died in August 2018 in Foggia while going to work was given much coverage. They were packed into the back of a van which hit an articulated lorry. It is also because of the many deadly accidents suffered by workers led by *caporali* that a new piece of legislation was passed in Italy in 2016.

Specifically, this law provides that those engaged in illicit interme- diation and labour exploitation can now face up to six years in prison and a fine for each labourer hired. Eventually, making legislation stricter would help to tackle this issue. One might note that legisla- tion in the UK and Italy concerning gangmasters have attempted to pursue the same objective through a different strategy. In the UK, lawmakers have tried to legalize this form of employment, by issuing licenses regulating activity.

Conversely, in Italy efforts have been made to repress gangmasters' work, by strengthening penalties. The approaches adopted to deal with the same issue are also the result of cultural differences between the two countries which had a play in the legislative measures enforced. As we shall see in the next sections, these cultural and legal divergences need to be taken into account because they also affect the terminology used to refer to the notion of *caporalato*, and its translation in the language examined. Bound to a particular legal system, each language of the law is the product of a specific history and culture (Sarcevic, 1998). The same of course applies to employee relations discourse, the terminology of which is influenced by national–specific aspects and factors (Manzella, 2017). So, once again, the relationship between law, culture, and translation comes to the fore.

EMPLOYEE RELATIONS AND TRANSLATION ISSUES

With a view to substantiate the arguments put forward above con- cerning the way cultural change affects language, and thus transla- tion, in comparative ER, some examples will be provided about how the notion of *caporalato* (or that of *caporale*) has been translated into English in official documents. Rather than a systematic terminologi- cal analysis, the examples supplied are intended to be illustrative, as they serve to highlight the challenges emanating from rendering over- seas concepts following cultural and legal changes taking place in the ER source system. To this end, a number of documents containing the word *caporalato* or *caporale*, produced by the European Union in

Italian and then translated into English, have been examined to discover how translators at the EU have attempted to navigate the issue of rendering this concept in English. Significantly, all the documents from which the examples are taken were produced after 2004 – that is, the year the Gangmasters (Licensing) Act came into force – that is to say after the notion of a gangmaster in English acquired a more neutral tone.

For example, looking at Table 5.1, one can see that the concept at hand has been translated into English as 'gangmaster system'.

Similarly, Table 5.2 describes how *caporali*, namely those engaged in illicit activity, has been rendered in English as 'gangmasters'.

Table 5.1   English translation of caporalato *in EU documents (emphasis added)*

Italian version	English version
Oggetto: *Caporalato* e diritti dei migranti	Subject: The *gangmaster system* and the rights of migrant workers
Recenti notizie pubblicate su giornali locali italiani portano alla luce nuove vicende legate alla triste piaga del *caporalato*	Recent reports published in several local Italian newspapers have brought to light yet more incidents linked with the terrible scourge of the *gangmaster system*

Source: Written questions by Members of the European Parliament and their answers given by a European Union institution (2014/C 357/01), 2014.

Table 5.2   English translation of caporali *in EU documents (emphasis added)*

Italian version	English version
Rapporti di lavoro di questo tipo non sono dissimili da quelli che intercorrono tradizionalmente tra i lavoratori occasionali o a giornata e gli intermediari di manodopera (i cosiddetti '*caporali*')	There are similarities between such relationships and the position of the traditional casual or day labourer, a type of work with the use of *gangmasters* that everyone thought had been consigned to the past

Source: Opinion of the European Economic and Social Committee on 'Abuse of the status of self-employed' (own-initiative opinion) (2013/C 161/03), 2013.

Looking at the foregoing examples, one might argue that translating *caporalato* or *caporali* respectively with 'gangmaster system' or 'gangmasters' might perplex the English language reader. 'Gangmaster' somewhat moves away from the source-text meaning. Following the Gangmasters (Licensing) Act, gangmasters are now allowed to engage in the provision of labour legally, provided that they obtain a license. Consequently, the amendments made to the UK ER system have legalized their activity, making it conditional upon the awarding of a license. In turn, this shift from the informal to the formal economy has also changed the perception towards these labour providers, which are no longer seen as individuals carrying out illegal forms of intermediation, as they are now allowed to do so by the law.

Consequently, this legal change has led to a different sentiment towards gangmasters in the UK, which cannot be neglected in translation. In this sense, 'Given the reflexive role of language and culture in the construction of legal meaning, one might well ask how it could be otherwise. Legal evolution is unlikely to be a one-way street' (Ainsworth, 2016: 53). The legal, cultural and linguistic dimensions overlap, influencing one another, applying to ER, a discipline which is particularly susceptible to cultural changes and dynamics. The notion under discussion here nicely captures the interlinkage of culture, language, law, and translation. While before the entry into force of the Gangmasters (Licensing) Act the word gangmaster was a suitable one to translate *caporale* into English, the legal, and subsequently cultural, changes taking place in the UK had made this terminology unfit to convey the source-text meaning. 'Gangmaster' as a translation of *caporale* – and of course 'gangmaster system' for *caporalato* – is problematic in that in Italy, *caporali* still operate outside the law. Thus this wording might be misleading as it leads those who are not familiar with the Italian system of employee relations to assume that *caporali* carry out legal activities, which is far from the case.

'Gangmaster' then becomes a misnomer, as it expresses the opposite meaning to *caporali*. For this reason, its usage to render the Italian concept should be avoided. Perhaps, one might specify that *caporali* are gangmasters who are not licensed, although this statement is not entirely true. Arguing this will imply that *caporali* are given the opportunity to obtain a license, but this is not the case as they are considered as criminals exploiting labourers, especially migrants. It is precisely for this reason that one possibility to express

Table 5.3   *English translation of* caporalato *in EU documents (emphasis added)*

Italian version	English version
Oggetto: Emergenza *caporalato* nel Salento Risposta della Commissione (24 febbraio 2012)	Subject: *Illegal employment* in Salento Answer from the Commission (24 February 2012)

Source: List of titles of Written Questions by Members of the European Parliament indicating the number, original language, author, political group, institution addressed, date submitted and a subject of the question (2012/C 285 E/01).

the notion at hand, although in a less literal fashion, can be that of using 'illegal employment' (Table 5.3).

'Illegal employment' is undoubtedly a loose term, yet it seems to be more suitable than gangmaster because it stresses the illicit nature of work performed by *caporali*.

CONCLUSION

In this chapter, an attempt has been made to underline how culture and language are closely intertwined in the context of employee relations. In order to stress this link, the Italian and the British systems of employee relations have been examined, focusing on the practice of *caporalato*, that is, an illegal form of intermediation. It has been pointed out that, following the enactment of a piece of legislation in the UK – the Gangmasters (Licensing) Act – the terminology used in English to denote this activity (gangmaster) has undergone a cultural shift, as it no longer denotes illegal work but tasks falling within the law, provided that a license is obtained.

Emphasis has been placed on the fact that the legalization of gangmasters' activity in the UK has made this terminology unsuitable to translate the Italian concept of *caporalato*, as the latter is still seen as an illicit practice in the ER system where it is practiced. Yet, the examples provided of EU documents originally produced in Italian and then translated into English pointed to the fact that the newly-established linguistic divergence between *caporalato* and gangmasters is neglected, as the two terms are mostly employed as though they express the same meaning.

New, positive connotations acquired by gangmaster in the UK conflict with the negative ring attributed to the Italian word. It is here that translation should come into play. The way things stand now, the relevant difference between gangmaster and *caporalato*, which originated by major legislative and cultural shifts taking place in the UK, does not emerge at all. Failing to come to terms with these new developments might produce two, albeit related, implications. In linguistic terms, employing gangmaster to translate *caporalato* gives rise to misleading interpretations on behalf of those who are not familiar with the Italian ER system, leading one to presume that *caporalato* is a legal activity, which is far from the case. In cultural terms, the fact that *caporali* and gangmasters are placed on the same footing provides the latter with a positive – or at least more neutral – trait which is not there, as the work they perform is illegal.

One might also note that the suggested attempt to adjust terminology, for instance by adding words such as 'unlicensed' or 'unauthorized' to the English translation to point out the lawbreaking nature of the work of *caporali*, might also bewilder the English language reader. In the author's view, opting for this language might lend credence to the fact that, like gangmasters, *caporali* need a license to legalize their activity. Yet, the workings of the Italian and the UK systems of employee relations differ in this connection, and *caporali*'s activity is by definition an illegal one. So we are still stuck with this word and its possible English translation, which perhaps might benefit from a periphrasis rather than a word-for-word equivalent.

The example of *caporali* and its possible translation into English nicely accounts for the close linkages between language and culture in employee relations, which scholars and practitioners must take into account when engaging in cross-national comparative research. The example discussed above is also illustrative of the changing nature of national ER practices, which stem from cultural, economic, and historical factors.

These changes are reflected in language and, of course, translation. Interestingly enough, the terminology employed in the target text/ER system to refer to *caporali* no longer serves the purpose of adequately conveying the source-text meaning, as meanwhile the English word has been assigned new meanings. The English 'gangmaster' no longer applies because of the current cultural perception this terminology has been provided with following new legislation. The difficulty is to correctly render the Italian notion of *caporali*, which arises from this newly established divergence between the Italian term and its previously accepted translation – implying 'either conveying the cultural and social background of the source text in a meaningful way in the translation, or to translating cultural and social allusions into the equivalents in the culture of the target language' (Baker and Prys Jones, 1998: 238).

In conclusion, this study also offers the opportunity for two further considerations. The first one is that language and translation have a significant role in employee relations in comparative research. This statement might sound obvious, yet little research has been conducted into how language affects the understanding of employee relations practices, especially in TS. As pointed out by Frege and Kelly: 'In Continental Europe, and indeed in the rest of the world, research on work and employment has remained multi-disciplinary and thus a component of various social science discipline' (Frege and Kelly, 2013: 8). For this reason, comparative ER would greatly benefit from the perspective of TS scholars, especially at the time of examining the multitude of translation and language issues which frequently bewilder comparatists. The second consideration, which is related to the first one, is that the multidisciplinary character of comparative employee relations implies that scholars from different disciplines should work in harmony in order to jointly contribute to the full understanding of the practices under evaluation. As seen, culture, law, language, and translation are frequently intertwined, and a pigeonholed approach will fail to provide the 'big picture', frustrating the ultimate purpose of comparative research.

REFERENCES

Ainsworth, J 2016, 'Lost in translation? Linguistic diversity and the elusive quest for plain meaning in the law', in L Cheng, K Kui Sin and A Wagner (eds), *The Ashgate Handbook of Legal Translation*, London: Routledge, pp. 43–56.

Baker, C and Prys Jones, S 1998, *Encyclopaedia of Bilingualism and Bilingual Education*, Clevedon Hall: Multilingual Matters.

Bean, R 1999, *Comparative Industrial Relations*, London: Routledge.

Blanpain, R and Baker, J (eds) 2010, *Comparative Labour Law and Industrial*

Relations in Industrialized Market Economies, The Hague: Kluwer International.

Blum, A (ed.) 1981, *International Handbook of Industrial Relations*, London: Greenwood.

Bromwich, W 2006, 'Lessico negoziale, contesto culturale e processi comunicativi nello sciopero nei servizi essenziali a New York', *Diritto Delle Relazioni Industriali*, vol. 2, no. XVI, pp. 414–26.

Byrne, R and Smith, K 2016, 'Modern slavery in agriculture', in J F Donnemeyer (ed.), *The Routledge International Handbook of Rural Criminology*, Abingdon: Routledge, pp. 157–65.

Dundon, T and Collings, G D 2011, 'Employment relations in the United Kingdom and Republic of Ireland', in M Barry and A Wilkinson (eds), *Research Handbook of Comparative Employment Relations*, Cheltenham, UK and Northampton, MA, USA: Edward Elgar Publishing, pp. 214–39.

European Commission 2012, *List of titles of written questions by Members of the European Parliament indicating the number, original language, author, political group, institution addressed, date submitted and subject of the question (2012/C 285 E/01)*, https://eur-lex.europa.eu/legal-content/EN/ALL/?uri=CELEX%3AC2012%2F285E%2F01 (accessed 13 July 2018).

European Commission 2013, *Opinion of the European Economic and Social Committee on 'Abuse of the status of self-employed'* (own-initiative opinion) (2013/C 161/03), https://eur-lex.europa.eu/legal-content/SL/TXT/?uri=uriserv%3AOJ.C_.2013.161.01.0014.01.ENG&toc=OJ%3AC%3A2013%3A161%3ATOC (accessed 3 August 2018).

European Commission 2014, *Written questions by Members of the European Parliament and their answers given by a European Union institution (2014/C 357/01)*, https://eur-lex.europa.eu/legal-content/EN/TXT/?uri=OJ%3AJOC_2014_357_R_0001 (accessed 10 June 2018).

Frege, C and Kelly, J 2013, 'Theoretical perspectives in on comparative employment relations', in C Frege and J Kelly (eds), *Comparative Employment Relations in the Global Economy*, London: Routledge, pp. 8–27.

Gennard, J, Judge, G, Bennett, T and Saundry, R (eds) 2016, *Managing Employment Relations*, London: Chartered Institute of Personnel and Development.

Hofstede, G 1980, *Culture's Consequences: International Differences in Work-Related Values*, London: Sage Publications.

Howard, N 2016, 'Of coyotes and caporali. How anti-trafficking discourses of criminality depoliticise mobility and exploitation', in R Piotrowicz, C Rijken and B Heide Uhl (eds), *Routledge Handbook of Human Trafficking*, Abingdon: Routledge, pp. 250–71.

Hyman, R 1995, 'Industrial relations in Europe: theory and practice', *European Journal of Industrial Relations*, vol. 1, no. 1, pp. 17–46.

Hyman, R 2001, *Understanding European Trade Unions: Between Market, Class and Society*, London: Sage Publications.

Manzella, P 2017, 'Multilingual translation of industrial relations practices in official EU documents: the case of Italy's Cassa Integrazione

Guadagni', *Perspectives: Studies in Translation Theory and Practice*, vol. 26, no. 3, pp. 344–56.

Meardi, G. 2011, 'Understanding Trade Union Culture', *Industrielle Beziehungen*, vol. 18, no. 4, pp. 336–45.

Price, A 2010, *Human Resources Management*, Andover: Cengage.

Sarcevic, S 1998, *New Approaches to Legal Translation*, The Hague: Kluwer Law International.

Sargeant, M and Lewis, D 2008, *Employment Law*, Harlow: Prentice Hall.

Strauss, K 2014, 'Unfree labour and the regulation of temporary agency work in the UK', in J Fudge and K Strauss (eds), *Temporary Work, Agencies, and Unfree Labour: Insecurity in the New World of Work*, Abingdon: Routledge, pp. 164–80.

Verma, A, Kochan, T and Lansbury, R D (eds) 1999, *Employment Relations in the Growing Asian Economies*, London: Routledge.

Wilkinson, A, Wood, G and Deeg, R (eds) 2014, *The Oxford Handbook of Employment Relations*, Oxford: Oxford University Press.

6. Plant-Level Employee Representation in Germany: Is the German Works Council a Management Stooge or the Representative Voice of the Workforce?

Michael Whittall and Rainer Trinczek

INTRODUCTION – NEGATING THE CONTOURS OF GERMAN WORKS COUNCILS

Works councils are not the only form of worker participation and representation within the German model of industrial relations. Shop steward committees, management-sponsored structures (quality circles, group and teamwork), collective bargaining (both at a national and in-house level) as well as supervisory boards provide employees with other outlets to raise their voice. All the same, the works council is a body more than any other that has caught the imagination of academics, practitioners (on both sides of the employment divide) and legislators in the realm of German industrial relations.

What explains the burgeoning international interest in this German employee representative body since the 1980s? Although various factors can help answer this question, we contend two developments stand out. First, the neo-liberal frontal attack, especially in the USA and UK, on organized labour has helped raise the profile of other forms of non-union employee representation (Toscano, 1981; Addison et al., 1996; Gumbrell-McCormick and Hyman, 2006; Allen, 2007). In particular, institutions such as German works councils that are conceived as (1) bolstering the power of trade unions and (2) providing employees with an alternative medium of representation have seen their stock rise. Lest we should forget the works council is depicted as making a positive contribution to Germany's economic success, too (Hübler, 2015). Of course, the thought of sharing power with works councils has not always sat well with all union representatives, some have, and still do see the works council as a threat to their authority. If nothing else, though, the general focus on German industrial relations, in particular the works council, has helped introduce into English industrial relations vernacular terms such as social partnership and social dialogue.

The second factor relates to European legislation. In response to the twin prongs of globalization and European monetarism, a political climate has emerged which was susceptible to legislating in an area of law traditionally reserved for the Nation State, employment representation. Certainly, since the early 1990s ideas encompassed in the German works council have played a pivotal role in informing European legislation in this area. Although eventual company-based forms of representation outside of Germany made possible by European Works Council and the European Information and Consultation directives lack rights of co-determination, a key deficiency according to some commentators (Streeck, 1997), the German influence remains unmistakable.

In short, these factors help explain the existence of a German works council market, the fact that numerous articles, books, lectures and seminars attempt to understand and explain this very German institution. Anyone who has been tasked with such a chore, we include ourselves here, knows that it is far from without it perils, though. Although authors have done a sterling job in making German works councils accessible to the foreign eye, helping to explain the legislation underpinning works councils and how historically this body's relationship to trade unions has not always been trouble-free, a closer look at this German institution uncovers a complexity not always apparent at first sight (Whittall, 2015). As already outlined by the editors of this work, there exists a danger that the cultural setting that informs interactions between employee representative structures and management, we might term this 'real meaning', can literally 'get lost in translation'. As research on transnational employee relations demonstrates, a key challenge in the case of Germany often involves trying to explain to non-German employee representatives that the German works council is not the extended arm of the personnel department (Whittall, 2010; Whittall et al., 2017). That just because some managers hold this institution in high regard does not imply it is beholden to the company. As will be outlined in the following pages, the relationship is nuanced, works councillors are intermittently collaborators and adversaries.

How can we overcome this challenge? First, the obvious claim would be to contend the problem is a simple linguistic one, which we, a German schooled in England and Englishman living in Germany, should be able to address. Although we do not exclude the fact that knowledge of both languages may prove advantageous, we contend that the 'translation deficit' is ultimately not a linguistic problem, but rather involves acknowledging the cultural complexity of the institution under study. As Müller-Jentsch (2007) accurately notes, the German system is confusingly complex compared to other national industrial relations practices, a system riven with contradictions; contradictions which are not always easy to explain away.

We maintain therefore, that a starting point to unlocking such complexity, moving beyond a shallow description of works councils, has to involve a recognition that institutional bodies such as the works council do not represent an equilibria, they are not set in stone. Here, two academics renowned for their theoretical contribution to debates around the nature of institutions and research on works councils, Wolfgang Streeck and Kathleen Thelen, can help us provide a better understanding of the German works council. According to Streeck and Thelen (2005), it is useful to view institutions as 'regimes'. On the one hand, regimes are governed by "rules stipulating expected behavior and 'ruling out' behavior deemed to be undesirable" (Streeck and Thelen, 2015: 12–13). Interestingly, Trinczek's (2018) study of works councils appears to support such a notion. Trinczek (2018: 582) notes, that "over a period of time the history of a plant creates an internal understanding of what is acceptable behavior, a specific plant level interactive culture between capital and labour, which lays down a set of valid behavioral and interaction norms, which achieves for both sides a degree of predictability . . .".

That is not the full story, though. On the other hand, the regime concept accepts the existence of conflict, which implicitly means that we need to recognize how members of institutions fill such bodies with life. According to Streeck and Thelen (2005: 14), the "enactment of a social rule is never perfect and . . . there is always a gap between the ideal pattern of a rule and the real pattern of life under it". For this reason, although any description of the German works council needs to understand the role played by the State, the State representing what Streeck and Thelen (2005) would refer to as the 'rule maker', it has to be recognized that the State merely sets the rules of the game, the parameters within which actors can manoeuvre. Outcomes remain open, left to the key protagonists, management, works councils, workforce and trade unions to determine (Tietel, 2006).

Numerous researchers appear to confirm the applicability of such a theoretical approach to understanding the German works council (Kotthoff, 1994; Bosch et al., 1999; Tietel, 2006). Unfortunately, these leading works have only been published in German. Schmidt and Trinczek (1986), for example, argue this body is a living organism in which internal and external interest groups meet to 'discuss' and 'negotiate' employment conditions. In the follow-up study of his early work published in the 1980s, Kotthoff (1994: 13) catches aptly the complexity of this institution when comparing the works council to a river. He uses here the metaphor of a river to explain the organic nature of works councils. Although the river's "current and color remained to all intents and purposes the same" (Kotthoff, 1994: 13), some alteration had occurred. "The major change involved the fact that the river had developed new currents out of regions that had previously not been connected to it" (Kotthoff, 1994: 13).

This brings us to a second 'key' we believe to be essential to unlocking the complexity of the German works council. Like Streeck and Thelen (2005), Kotthoff (1994) too implies there exists a need to consider that institutions are embedded in a historical context. In short, something that will become apparent in the proceeding pages, the rules of the game as already discussed are contextual, societal factors, specifically economic, political, and technological developments, which enhance or impinge protagonists' ability to interpret and utilize the rules of the game to advance their particular interests. The focusing on context helps to bring to the surface power relations that have a bearing on interactions between works councils and management (Trinczek, 2018). Consequently, merely communicating the rights of works councils as laid down in the works constitution can prove a futile exercise if one forgets factors that influence the balance of power between works councillors and company representatives. Certainly, since the late 1970s and the era of free global-markets, works councils members and their negotiation partners have constantly had to consider how best to respond to increased global market competition so to sustain their firms' credibility.

In sum, a textbook account of the German works council, the process of setting up such a body, the process of electing the works council chair, the frequency of meetings, rights of information, consultation and co-determination, its working relations with other works councils within the same company as well as with shop stewards, that is, trade unions, can be beneficial. However, at best such an exercise offers a mere theoretical understanding of this institution, it fails to provide the reader with a topographical grasp of the contours of the works council. For this reason, the nature of the works council, a body that contests employment relationships on behalf of the workforce, a body which has to take account of historical circumstances, suggests to us it would be wrong to refer to *the* works council. For example, the above-mentioned researchers, Kotthoff (1981, 1994), Bosch et al. (1999) and Tietel (2006) have uncovered an array of works councils. These can include on the one side works councils that comply with the demands of management, rubber stamp managerial policy, but on the other side works councils that call for semi-illegal industrial action.[1] Consequently, as we shall see below, the classic German works council studies have rightly attempted to address this dilemma by reverting to typologies when describing works councils, typologies that unfortunately too often remain only accessible to German-speaking readers.

In what follows we will attempt to make the German works council more accessible. When at all necessary we will draw on existing typologies of works councils. Our first task involves providing an insight into the institution in question – specifically addressing the complexity of the works council regime. Such complexity is caught in the chapter's subtitle. How, for example, can a works council institutionalize, even neutralize conflict that arises in an employment relationship, but equally contest that very relationship? Considered another way, how can the notion of social partnership accommodate conflict? The chapter's ability to answer such questions will hopefully go some way in ensuring the readers understanding of this institution is not *lost in translation*. Of course, some textbook reference to the institution is required. For this reason, time is donated to explaining factors referred to above in connection with our earlier textbook comment. Next, we consider the question of historical context in light of developments affecting the character of works councils in recent years, in particular employers' push to modernize German industrial relations, modernize often a synonym that expresses a wish to undermine the representative rights of employees. We hope that this will provide the reader with an up-to-date cultural understanding of the German works council. Finally, the conclusion attempts to bring together the various discussion strands that have proceeded it.

MODELL DEUTSCHLAND – INSTITUTIONALIZING CONFLICT?

In offering a definition of industrial relations, and here his eye is firmly focused on the German model, aptly referred to as Modell Deutschland, Müller-Jentsch (1997) emphasizes how the system 'partly' involves the institutionalization of class conflict. Although "the underlying conflict between capital and labour today is not solved . . ." Modell Deutschland tries to ensure the "disarming and canalization of conflict between capital and labour" (Müller-Jentsch, 2008: 58). Furthermore, in the German industrial relations discourse it is considered naïve to conceptualize employer–employee relations only as antagonistic. Rather, the predominant pattern of interpretation suggests the need to speak of a relationship characterized by a peculiar mixture of common and conflicting interests between the actors: for example, both parties have a common interest in the existence of a prosperous company. Nevertheless, we need to acknowledge that different interests, specifically in relation to the distribution of profits, prevail. In short, 'Modell Deutschland' implies that unions and works councils regard the successful realization of common interests with 'capital' as the necessary precondition for the enforcement of labour's special interests. This seems to be the material basis for quite different characterizations of German employment relations, such as 'antagonistic cooperation', 'conflict partnership', 'Betriebsfamilie' (family unit)[2] or 'Leistungsgemeinschaft' (performance community).

This characterization of industrial relations represents a good starting point, it highlights what appears to represent an anomaly, one which some observers struggle to comprehend. Specifically, how can works councils retain their independence of management, that is, represent the interests of employees, but at the same time function as a body that neutralizes class conflict? Surely, its later task confirms the main criticism levelled at it by employee representatives outside of Germany, that works councillors are nothing more than management stooges empowered to undermine class opposition. Certainly, such works councils, what Kotthoff (1994) calls the organ of management type, can be observed. However, so can, also a term taken from Kotthoff (1994), the conflictual partnership type of works council. Furthermore, we would be ill-advised to believe these arrangements are fixed – a number of trajectories are possible. The German works council mosaic is complex, often imbued with a number of contradictory tendencies. Any attempt to decipher this complex mosaic requires an historical understanding of this body, an institution whose genesis can be traced back to the nineteenth century (Teutenberg, 1961). There seems to be a general agreement that the passing of the 1905 Mining Law, which followed numerous strikes for higher wages and better working conditions, signified the first move on the part of the State to empower employees at the plant level (Zachert, 1979). The next State intervention involved the *Vaterländischen Hilfsdienst* (1916), this secured trade union cooperation during the First World War (Trinczek, 2018). The law represented an important precedent that would later guide future legislators, a political attempt to accommodate and so pacify the labour movement. A strategy that would become the State's trademark in times of political instability. For example, according to Zachert (1979) the *Betriebsrätegesetz* (1920), which became a milestone for later works council legislation, was intended to nullify the Soviet style councils (*Räterbewegung*) that took hold of Germany after the First World War. The new law not only consigned the term worker committees to the history bin, the reference point now being councils, but the *Betriebsrätergesetz* set worker participation on a new path far removed from the revolutionary character of the *Räterbewegung* (Müller-Jentsch, 2008). A central aspect of the *Betriebsrätegesetz*, something that guides works councils until today, concerns the notion of social partnership, namely that they are compelled to act in a way that takes into consideration both the interests of capital and labour (Zachert, 1979). Referring to the 1952 *Betriebsverfassungsgesetz* (Works Constitution Act), which though amended in 1972 and 2001 still remains the legislative basis for todays' works councils, Müller-Jentsch (2008) applies the term double-loyalty to explain the partnership character of works councils.

As in the past, the political climate informed the eventual character of the 1952 *Betriebsverfassungsgesetz*. Following the end of the Second World War, the advent of the Cold War as well as a rejuvenated German trade union movement, whose 1949 Munich program was designated to overthrowing capitalism (Müller-Jentsch, 2008), saw the first post-war CDU government led by Konrad Adenauer commit itself to taming the revolutionary fervour of trade unions (Zachert, 1979). As in the 1920s, the government of the day went about drawing up a law, the *Betriebsverfassungsgesetz*, which was indebted to previous legislation. The new law offered employees a form of representation that was not only free and independent of their profession and position within a company's hierarchy, but moreover provided trade unions no formal access to such a body, the new works council law placing trade unions firmly outside the company (Markovits, 1986).[3] In short, it created a legally underpinned market for representing employees. Known widely as the dual-system today, such a market had the potential to drive a wedge between plant level and industrial level representation, a wedge that ultimately could undermine the power of German trade unions (Thelen, 1991; Whittall, 2001).

Again, the events of the early 1950s would seem to confirm the critical view that some protagonists have of works councils, that is, a management ploy to contain conflict and promote a managerial hegemony. From the employers' perspective, the 1952 *Betriebsverfassungsgesetz* had the benefit of not only sidelining unions, but also retaining the essence of social partnership, that is, the intermediary character of earlier legislation. Article 2 stipulating that representation is undertaken in a way that takes into account the company's interests. Seen from this perspective works councils delegates have two mandates, that of the constituents that elect them, that is, the workforce, but also the interests of shareholders and employers, the very people who employ them. Surely, though, the rules of the game as set by the State, rules developed to promote social partnership, cannot be realized if we accept that employers have the upper hand. Do not the employers possess superior resources? Does not the mere threat to close a plant, to introduce redundancy programmes make such a balanced approach nothing more than an illusion? Are not works councils ultimately beholden to employers, that is, they are members of a structure that exists to rein in the anger of employees? To function as the personnel department's mouthpiece in times of hardship? Undoubtedly, at the time this was the way the law was conceived and even led trade unions to argue the

1952 Act was sowing the seeds for 'yellow unions' (Limmer, 1996). The DGB even referred to the Act on the very day it was passed as a "dark day in the democratic development of the newly formed Federal Republic of Germany" (Müller-Jentsch, 2008: 163).

Aware of the danger posed by the Act, affiliated members of the DGB quickly adhered to a pragmatic approach. This was designed to try and alleviate the predicament works councils faced, that is, seek ways to release them from employers' shackles (Sorge, 1999; Kittner, 1997). To shift the balance of power away from employers in an attempt to ensure works councils retained the one important quality necessary of such an institution: independence (Rogers and Streeck, 1995). A key aspect of trade unions' approach entailed addressing the question of resources. Unions quickly began to offer works councils an important service, training, a service which it continues to provide until today (Bahnmüller et al., 1993; Schäfer, 2005; Whittall, 2005). In addition, works councils have benefitted from trade unions' lobbying power. Unions have helped to reform the *Betriebsverfassungsgesetz* on numerous occasions, most notably in 1972. Benefitting from the modernizing and reform spirit that had taken hold of the country in the late 1960s, for example, as well as the existence of a sympathetic SPD government (Müller-Jentsch, 2008), three major successes were recorded in the 1972 reform according to Zachert (1979: 28): First, trade union access to the workplace was made a lot easier. Second, the role of works councillors was improved, works councillors provided with greater protection against dismissal and more time to undertake their responsibilities (including training). Finally, their co-determination rights were improved.[4]

Training, a form of umbilical cord, as well as other factors such as trade unions' right to call for industrial action,[5] have helped to cement a lasting relationship between these two levels of employee representation. For their part, works council delegates, in particular chairs of works councils, have demonstrated their appreciation by (1) joining trade unions, (2) encouraging their constituents to do likewise and (3) ensuring that employers adhere to the parameters collectively negotiated by social partners. Combined, these factors have gone some way to nullifying the contradictions embedded in the *Betriebsverfassungsgesetz* as well as loosening management's hold over works councils. To return to Streeck and Thelen's (2005) theoretical proclamation that regimes demand its protagonist to adhere to certain expectations and behaviour, these laid down by the rules of the game, regimes also offer a certain space that allows respective parties to express their interests. Here, the presence of unions within the workplace has had the positive effect of reminding works councillors of their duty as independent employee representatives, that is, the need to constitute the works council in a way that provides it room to manoeuvre and express itself freely.

Seen from this perspective, works councils are not automatically management stooges. Arrangements exist whereby works councils can challenge management. According to Kotthoff (1994) these involve three types of works council, the conflict partnership, calculated conflictual and distant cooperative body. Certainly, where works councils have close working relations with trade unions, are well resourced, are of a size that allows delegates to be relieved of their normal duties (working solely for the works council) and have the backing of an organized workforce, then they are likely to remain independent of management's choke (Brinkmann and Nachtwey, 2017).

Nevertheless, we should not forget that until the late 1980s industrial relations in Germany, whereby employers generally demonstrated a rather cooperative attitude towards employee representatives, was widely viewed as a success story. Not only was Germany successful economically but also labour benefited from this hitherto unknown mass prosperity. Such prosperity had the effect of convincing labour that cooperation with capital was beneficial, which explains why some employee representatives continued to be convinced by the post-war arrangement even as conditions changed dramatically from the 1990s onwards.

As discussed in the introduction, this clearly suggests that understanding the nature of works councils requires us to consider contextual factors, factors that either enhance or restrict the ability of the works council to simultaneously serve the interests of labour and capital. For this reason, the proceeding section considers recent developments that have affected the ability of works councils to contest the world of employment – as will become apparent, the institutional gaps, the air they need to function, appear to have diminished somewhat.

WORKS COUNCILS – AND THE SHIFTING BALANCE OF POWER

Since the early 1990s, a vigorous debate concerning the state of German industrial relations has raged, with the focus very much on the role of works councils in this changing landscape. Although the first half of the 1990s, saw writers applaud the stability of this institution (Bosch, 1990; Thelen, 1991; Koch, 1992), some even suggesting its standing within society had improved now that management was convinced of its worth (Kotthoff, 1994), such optimism started to be questioned towards the late 1990s (Hassel, 1999; Whittall, 2005). As indicated in the opening section of this chapter, increased global competition, legally promoted changes in the labour market as well as the greater emphasis placed by management on flexibility in the post-Fordist era, specifically the decentralization of the decision-making process has, and continues to have, consequences for plant-level representation.

Of course, if we are to communicate the current cultural nature of works councils, that is, transmit beyond Germany's borders what terms such as social partnership and social dialogue represent today, according to Brinkmann and Nachtwey (2017) we need to consider how the democratic erosion of co-determination is affecting relations between capital and labour. This requires us to consider (1) the breadth of works councils, that is, their overall number and (2) the tasks they undertake. Concerning the first point, Figure 6.1 exemplifies how the actual percentage of employees represented by a works council fell by 11 percentage points in the western part of the country between 1993 and 2017. In what was once the German Democratic Republic, a mere 33 per cent of the workforce could rely on the support of a works council in 2015.

In terms of the number of firms complying with the *Betriebsverfassungsgesetz* this has fallen as low as 9 per cent. Of course, we need to recognize there exists considerable variation depending on the size of the company. In the case of large companies, those employing 500 and more employees, the density rate is a staggering 80 per cent (Ellguth and Kohaut, 2018: 304). This reflects the fact that in larger companies an important factor prevails that we have already discussed, that is, the close association between a well-resourced works council and the presence of a strong trade union. Hence, a mere 5 per cent of companies with a workforce between 5

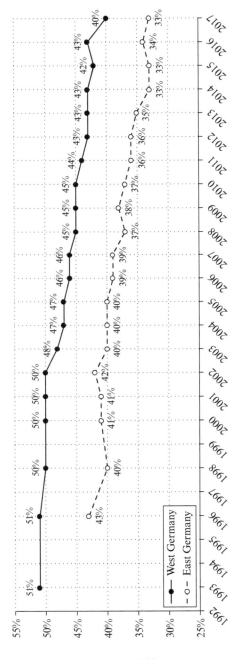

Source: Ellguth and Kohaut (2018: 303).

Figure 6.1   Percentage of employees represented by works councils in Germany

and 50 employees, traditionally difficult to organize, currently have a works council (Ellguth and Kohaut, 2018).

The coverage rate highlights an important and potentially dangerous quality associated with the *Betriebsverfassungsgesetz*, one that certain groups have critically addressed. This involves the fact that works council representation is a mere option, an option five or more employees can utilize. Although we cannot expend too much time on the so-called works council crisis in this chapter (Thannisch, 2015; Greifenstein, 2011), there is a growing call, especially on the part of trade unions and political parties such as the Greens and the Linke, for a reform of the current act. Specifically to make it compulsory to hold works council elections (Absenger and Priebe, 2016). Such a change in the law is conceived as necessary to halt the coverage rate crisis, especially amongst small- to medium-sized companies, these accounting for well over 90 per cent of all firms in Germany (Statista, 2018). As exemplified in Table 6.1, a mere 5 per cent of companies employing between 5 and 50 workers have a works council, whilst for larger firms employing 500 and more workers, the figure is 86 per cent.

The question of power, however, is not restricted to a decline in either the overall number of works councils or the strength of the

Table 6.1   *The spread of works councils according to plant size in 2017 (in %)*

Plant size	Plant with a works council	Employees with access to a works council
5–50 Employees	5	9
1–100 Employees	32	33
101–199 Employees	53	55
200–500 Employees	69	70
Over 500 Employees	80	86
Total	9	39
Further information:		
Plants as of 21	27	52
Employees	45	63
Plants as of 51		
Employees		

Source: Ellguth (2018: 5).

dual system. Another aspect needs to be considered, the issue of resources, a central factor that determines how resourceful works councils are in contesting employment conditions. For example, since the mid-1990s works councils have experienced an inflation in the number of issues they have been required to address, these increasingly overstretching their resources (Brinkmann and Nachtwey, 2017). A number of issues seem to have led to such an inflation. Ironically, one can be traced back to the institution's own success, certainly in the eyes of management. The works councils is seen as having achieved a degree of maturity that has astounded employers (Kotthoff, 1994). In a study into managements' view of works councils Whittall (2015: 91) notes, this body is considered "as competent and committed to resolving conflict". Such competence has come to good effect in recent years – works councils having been both encouraged to participate in redundancy and restructuring measures as well as oversee the introduction of new technical processes (Tietel, 2006).

Furthermore, a shift towards greater decentralized collective bargaining can be observed following the introduction of open-clauses from the early 1990s onwards (Whittall, 2005). A radical departure in German industrial relations, open clauses foresee a role for works councils in the collective bargaining process – the plant level actor increasingly empowered to adapt agreements to meet the demands of local circumstances (Whittall, 2005; Haipeter, 2010), or as Rehder (2003: 68) suggests, this development represents the advancement of US-style "concession bargaining". In contrast to this regulated, often referred to as re-regulated (Streeck and Thelen, 2005), form of collective bargaining, authors have also noticed a more sinister change in German industrial relations. This involves the forward march of wild and informal decentralization (Brinkmann and Nachtwey, 2017) or illegal deregulation (Whittall, 2005), a development which sees management not only unilaterally undermining collective agreements, that is, without the support of plant-level employee representatives, but also with the support of works councils (Tuckman and Whittall, 2002).

Added to this development is the emergence of a post-Fordist workplace. Characterized by the de-standardization of employment, post-Fordism possesses new challenges for works councils. On the one hand, this involves HRM policies that demand greater employee involvement, that is, the delegation of responsibility to the shop floor. On the other hand, employees have demands that take up the time of works councils, too. To name just a few, these include better work–life balance, access to training schemes, early retirement and temporary agency work issues (Lee and Whittall, 2019). Consequently, this requires employee representatives to become experts in a whole array of work-related issues. The last point in particular, the growth in temporary agency work, has proven a major drain on works councils' resources.

Combined, these developments highlight how works councils' tasks now greatly surpass those defined by the *Betriebsverfassungsgesetz* (Tietel, 2006). Where works councils exist, management appears to show them the utmost respect today, respect potentially never envisaged by either capital or labour. Works councils are the solution to the problem rather than its cause! However, Minssen and Riese (2006) argue, certain expectations are attached to such a managerial stance, that is, the need to toe the line. In fact, if we return to the cultural aspect of this chapter, the term 'management organ' is increasingly being applied to describe the current nature of relations between management and works councils, a term critically applied to question works councils' independence from management. In contrast to 'concession bargaining', works councils receiving something in return for yielding to management demands, the organ type of body appears to enter into a neo-liberal discourse with management. Consequently, not only does it comply with company policy potentially negligible to the workforce, but also plays an active role in the selling of such policies to the workforce.

CONCLUSION

How then to explain this German works council mosaic? In answering this question, we have been faced with a number of tasks. The first task involved acknowledging that the *Betriebsverfassungsgesetz* merely outlines certain parameters in which labour and capital can manoeuvre, the State restricts itself to that of referee, outcomes are left to management and works councils to determine. Second, although the State's role is one of arbitrator, one in which it uses the law to promote a culture marked by notions of social partnership and social dialogue, what Müller-Jentsch (2008) terms the institutionalization of conflict, what Streeck and Thelen (2005) refer to as mutual expectations, the cultural atmosphere at any given time is coloured by power resources. As discussed in the introduction, even though institutions, what Streeck and Thelen (2005) refer to as regimes, are underpinned by rules, historical circumstances throw shadows over such bodies as works councils. Regulatory expectations should not be perceived as all-encompassing, situations can arise whereby historical circumstances prove favourable to certain protagonists – their negotiation position enhanced to the detriment of their opposite number. As in the case of all institutions, any attempt to comprehend the culture of works councils involves acknowledging the importance of historical dependency, understanding the power relations that ultimately have a bearing on cultural settings. The interesting thing about the German works constitution is that even in times when there occurs a shift in power within the wider society it still allows for a high degree of state-guaranteed institutional stability.

Obviously, such a conclusion could be considered unsatisfactory for scholars interested in works councils – the suggestion even being that *the works council* does not exist. Certainly, that would appear to be the conclusion of key researchers of this German institution – studies of this body preferring to use a plural definition, that is, developing different works council typologies. Furthermore, this assertion becomes even more complex if we accept that typologies are not static, events might prevail whereby the body changes from being a co-manager, beholden to management, to a works council that confronts managerial decisions in a court of law. This last point highlights how determining whether the German works council is a management stooge or the representative voice of the workforce requires a deep methodological understanding of the institution at hand.

In sum, any discussion surrounding works councils needs to veer away from bland textbook definitions, which predominantly focus on the institution's co-determination, information and consultation rights as well as its social partnership-incorporating powers. Instead, we contend the focus should be on the regime character of the works council. Hence, such an approach requires the observer to recognize how historical circumstances currently prevail which raise questions about the works councils' ability to remain outside management's realm of control. A world marked by greater employment differentiation, something that overstretches works councils' resources, a weakened union movement that increasingly struggles to be the backbone of plant-level representation, that is, a key resource, as well as an emboldened management, suggests the term 'organ of management' appears best suited to describe the character of many German works councils today. Seen from this perspective, any understanding of the current German works councils landscape needs to take into consideration the possible need to add the term 'compliance' to the vocabulary to define this German institution.

NOTES

1. According to German law works councils are not allowed to organize industrial stoppages, this is reserved for trade unions. However, works councils are known to creatively apply the works constitution in such a way that results in industrial action, such as holding a 24-hour works meeting.
2. The term family unit should not be confused with the legal notion of a family owned company, which to date remains a unique aspect of German business enterprises. Instead, the term family unit can be applied to public limited companies; it describes a situation whereby management and works councils conceive each other as members of the same cohesive family.
3. This had the desired effect of externalizing conflict over wages and employment conditions outside of firms, negotiation over these issues left to actors within the realms of industrial-level collective bargaining.
4. The main benefits concerned an increase in the number of works councillors who could be relieved of their normal duties to undertake works council work, plus co-determination rights concerning working time, recruitment, dismissals and the right to negotiate a social plan regarding redundancies.
5. The social partnership character of the *Betriebsverfassungsgesetz*, specifically Article 74, clause 2, prohibits either the employer or works council from organizing industrial action. Hence, with its bargaining power reduced works councils' dependence on trade unions naturally becomes strengthened (Müller-Jentsch, 2007).

REFERENCES

Absenger, N. and Priebe, A. (2016): Das Betriebsverfassungsgesetz im Jahr 2016 – Mitbestimmungslücken und Reformbedarfe, *WSI Mitteilung*, (3): 192–200.

Addison, J., Schnabel, C. and Wagner, J. (1996): German Works Councils, Profits, and Innovation, *Kyklos*, 49 (4): 555–82.

Allen, M. C. (2007): *The Varieties of Capitalism Paradigm: Explaining Germany's Comparative Advantage?*, Basingstoke: Palgrave Macmillan.

Bahnmüller, R., Bispinck, R. and Schmidt, W. (1993): *Betriebliche Weiterbildung und Tarifvertrag*, München und Mering.

Bosch, A., Ellguth, P., Schmidt, R. and Trinczek, R. (1999): Betriebliches Interessenhandeln. Band 1. Opladen.

Bosch, G. (1990): From 40 to 35 Hours: Reduction and Flexibilisation of the Working Week in the Federal Republic of Germany, *International Labour Review*, 129 (5): 611–27.

Brinkmann, U. and Nachtwey, O. (2017): *Postdemokratie und Industrial Citizenship: Erosionsprozesse von Demokratie und Mitbestimmung*, Frankfurt: Beltz Juventa.

Ellguth, P. (2018): Die betriebliche Mitbestimmung verliert an Boden, IAB-FORUM. https://www.iab-forum.de/die-betriebliche-mitbestimmung-verliert-an-boden/?pdf=7871.

Ellguth, P. and Kohaut, S. (2018): Tarifbindung und betriebliche Interessenvertretung: Aktuell Ergebnisse aus dem IAB-Betriebspanel 2017, *WSI-Mitteilung*, 4 (71): 299–306.

Greifenstein, R. (2011): *Perspektiven der Unternehmensmitbestimmung in Deutschland: ungerechtfertigter Stillstand auf der politischen Baustelle?* WISO-Diskurs.

Gumbrell-McCormick, R. and Hyman, R. (2006): Embedded Collectivism? Workplace Representation in France and Germany, *Industrial Relations Journal*, 37 (5): 473–91.

Haipeter, T. (2010): Erneuerung aus der Defensive?: Gewerkschaftliche Perspektiven der Tarifabweichung, *WSI-Mitteilungen*, 63 (6): 283–90.

Hassel, A. (1999): The Erosion of the German System of Industrial Relations, *British Journal of Industrial Relations*, 37 (3): 483–505.

Hübler, O. (2015): Do Works Councils Raise or Lower Firm Productivity? Works Councils Can Have a Positive Impact on Firm Productivity, but only When Specific Conditions are in Place, *IZA World of Labor 2015*: 137.

Kittner, M. (1997): *Arbeits und Sozialordnung*, Köln: Bund Verlag.

Koch, K. (1992): Regulatory Reform in German industrial relations, in K. Dyson (ed.), *The Politics of German Regulations*, Aldershot: Darthmouth pp. 235–53.

Kotthoff, H. (1981): *Betriebsräte und betriebliche Herrschaft: eine Typologie von Partizipationsmustern im Industriebetrieb*, Frankfurt am Main: Campus Verlag.

Kotthoff, H. (1994): *Betriebsräter und Bürgerstatus*, München und Mering: Rainer Hampp Verlag.

Lee, H. and Whittall, M. (2019): *Mitbestimmung zum Lifelong and Lifewide Learning*, Düsseldorf: Hans-Böckler-Stiftung. Forthcoming.

Limmer, H. (1996): *Die Deutsche Gewerkshatsbewegung*, München: Olzog.

Markovits, A. (1986): *The Politics of the West German Trade Unions: Strategies of Class and Interest Representation in Growth and Crisis*, Cambridge: Cambridge University Press.

Minssen, H. and Riese, C. (2006): Qualifikation und Kommunikationsstrukturen des Co-Managers – Zur Typologie von Betriebsräten, *Arbeit*, 15 (1): 43–59.

Müller-Jentsch, W. (1997): *Soziologie der industriellen Beziehungen: eine Einführung*, Frankfurt am Main: Campus Verlag.

Müller-Jentsch, W. (2007): *Strukturwandel der industriellen Beziehungen -Industrial Citizenship zwischen Markt und Regulierung*, Wiesbaden: VS Verlag für Sozialwissenschaften.

Müller-Jentsch, W. (2008): *Arbeit und Bürgerstatus – Studien zur sozialen und industriellen Demokratie*, Wiesbaden. VS Verlag für Sozialwissenschaften.

Rehder, B. (2003): *Betriebliche Bündnisse für Arbeit in Deutschland. Mitbesti mmung und Flächentarif im Wandel*, Frankfurt am Main: Campus-Verlag.

Rogers, J. and Streeck, W. (1995): *Works Councils: Consultation, Representation, and Cooperation in Industrial Relations*, Chicago: Chicago: University of Chicago Press.

Schäfer, C. (2005): Die WSI-Befragung yon Betriebs- und Personalräiten 2004/2005 – Ein Uberblick, *WSI-Mitteilungen*, 58 (6): 291–300.

Schmidt, R. and Trinczek, R. (1986): Die Betriebliche Gestaltung tariflicher Arbeitszeitnormen in der Metallindustrie, *WSI Mitteilung*, (10): 641–61.

Sorge, A. (1999): Mittbestimung, Arbeitsorganisation und Technikanwedung, in W. Streeck and N. Kluge (eds), *Mitbestimmung in Deutschland*, Frankfurt: Campus Verlag, pp. 17–134.

Statista (2018): Anzahl der Unternehmen in Deutschland nach Beschäftigungsgrößenklassen im Jahr 2016.

Streeck, W. (1997): Neither European Nor Works Councils: A Reply, *Economic and Industrial Democracy*, 2 (18): 325–37.

Streeck, W. and Thelen, K. (2005): *Beyond Continuity: Institutional Change in Advanced Political Economies*, Oxford: Oxford University Press.

Teutenberg, J. (1961): *Geschichte der industriellen Mitbestimmung in Deutschland Ursprung u. Entwicklung ihrer Vorläufer im Denken u. in d. Wirklichkeit d. 19. Jahrhunderts*, Tübingen: Mohr.

Thannisch, R. (2015): Bedrohung für die Mitbestimmung, *Arbeitsrecht in Betrieb*, (36): 30–2.

Thelen, K. (1991): *Union of Parts, Labour Politics in Post-War Germany*, Ithaca, NY: Cornell University Press.

Tietel, E. (2006): *Konfrontation-Kooperation-Solidarität: Betriebsräte in der sozialen und emotionalen Zwickmühle*, Berlin: Edition Sigma.

Toscano, J. (1981): Labor–Management Cooperation and the West German System of Codetermination, *Industrial Relations Journal*, 12 (6): 57–67.

Trinczek, R. (2018): Betriebliche Regulierung von Arbeitsbeziehung, in F. Böhle, G. Voß and G. Wachtler (eds), *Handbuch Arbeitssoziologie*, Cham: Springer, pp. 579–617.

Tuckman, A. and Whittall, M. (2002): Affirmation, Games, and Insecurity: Cultivating Consent Within a New Workplace Regime, *Capital and Class*, 76 (1): 65–93.

Whittall, M. (2001): Modell Deutschland: Regulating the Future?, in S. Jefferys, F. Mispelblom Beyer and C. Thornqvist (eds), *European Working Lives*, Cheltenham, UK and Northampton, MA, USA: Edward Elgar Publishing, pp. 115–29.

Whittall, M. (2005): Modell Deutschland under Pressure: The Growing Tensions between Works Councils and Trade Unions, *Economic and Industrial Democracy*, 26 (4): 569–92.

Whittall, M. (2010): The Problem of National Industrial Relations Traditions in European Works Councils: The Example of BMW, *Economic and Industrial Democracy*, 4 (31): 70–85.

Whittall, M. (2015): Management's Perceptions of Social Dialogue at the Company in Germany, in M. Euwema, L. Munduate, P. Elgoibar, E. Pender and A. Garcia (eds), *Promoting Social Dialogue in European Organizations*, London: Springer, pp. 79–92.

Whittall, M., Martinz-Lucio, M., Rocha, F., Telljohann, V. and Mustchin, S. (2017): Workplace Trade Union Engagement with European Works Councils and Transnational Agreements: The Case of Volkswagen Europe, *European Journal of Industrial Relations*, 6 (1): 61–83.

Zachert, U. (1979): *Betriebliche Mitbestimmung: eine problemorientierte Einführung*, Köln: Bund Verlag.

7. Individualism, Democracy and Conflict in the USA

Peter Norlander

The United States has a highly diverse system of labor and employee relations (Katz and Wheeler, 2004). Although it would appear to be joined by a common language, legal system, and history, the employee relations system in the U.S. has a great need for translation, awareness of context, and comparative analysis. As a "human capital" consultant might discuss with the "people operations" leaders in Silicon Valley, the employment relations landscape today is experiencing new challenges requiring greater industry- and firm-specific knowledge, and awareness of context, local regulations, and cultural differences. As the National Labor Relations Board, the body that oversees labor law, has seen in a number of cases, "language matters" (Manzella and Koch, 2017).

Variety within U.S. employment relations is both a product of circumstance and design. The U.S. foreign-born population is at its highest level as a proportion of the population in a century, although the growth rate has been decelerating for some time (Norlander and Sørensen, 2018). The challenge of managing in a multicultural and multilingual environment aside, constitutional federalism is meant to bolster states as "laboratories of democracy," in which policy experimentation is the norm. From a legal standpoint, federal, state, and local governments each have authority to set employment policy, and local activism has been successful in increasing within country variations.

In the mid-1980s, scholars described the decline of stable U.S. employee relations (Kochan et al., 1986). The declining stability was due to changing human resources practices, growing employer resistance to unions, and changing economic circumstances due to intensified foreign competition. The promotion of teams and high performance HR practices, the decline of unions, and increased market competition continue to shape U.S. employee relations to this day. As this chapter will discuss, a growing divergence in employment policy within the country since 2000 is a major factor that is decreasing the stability of employee relations today.

Since 2000, stable, yet separate, systems of employee relations have emerged, driven by growing inequality, and political partisanship rooted in cultural divisions. Equity, efficiency and voice have been described as the core objectives at stake in employment relations (Budd, 2004). Today, one system in the U.S. emphasizes the rights of individual employers and employees to establish their own individual bargain over wages and working conditions. This system based on "egoism," or neoliberalism, prioritizes individual rights and efficiency in a free labour market (Budd and Bhave, 2008). The other system values equity and voice, emphasizing the imbalance of power inherent in the workplace, and advances the rights of a democratic majority to raise wages, set standards, and join unions. Where unified trends once dominated the discussion of employee relations, today, a growing divergence in policy, culture, and workplace relations between two systems is the trend.

Scholars have long written about diverging systems in U.S. employment relations in terms of a primary high-wage system and a secondary low-wage system (Piore, 1972), and more recently in terms of a fissured system between leading firms and their subcontractors (Weil, 2014). At the same time that many U.S. workers benefit from the high-wage system, where high returns to education predominate and global trade has led to greater benefits, nearly 20 percent in the U.S. work in a low-wage system that pays at or below the poverty level, and from which there are reduced opportunities for escape (Osterman, 2008).

While high-wage and low-wage systems co-exist throughout the country, this chapter argues that regional divisions in terms of legal individual rights and democratic rights have increased. Growing partisanship, and the growth of inequality, has led to increased local activism on employment policy, leading to a split between "equity and voice" states and "efficiency and individual rights" states.

Long before these recent developments, there were deep historical, cultural, and legal, tensions among American ideals. To many Americans, individual rights are not only protected by the Constitution, but are God-given freedoms: of speech, religion, and association that even democratic majorities cannot remove. In the last several years, voluntary and democratically elected workers' organizations – unions – have been a frequent target of lawsuits on the basis of individual rights to speech and religion. These courtroom conflicts grapple with the competing objectives of the employment relations system, as well as the competing rights of individuals and groups.

Democratic majorities in left-leaning states that support protecting the collective rights of workers have faced hostile federal courts, and democratic majorities in right-leaning states that oppose unions have passed "right to work" laws that create new individual rights to avoid paying union fees, or "free-ride." In both left- and right-leaning states, popular referendums raising the minimum wage or supporting unions have been overturned by elected officials, not only on the basis of individual rights protection, but in the interest of diminishing unions' influence on politics.

Conflict between individual rights and democratic majority rights is not new in the U.S., nor is instability in labor and employment relations. A long violent history of "industrial warfare," electoral, and legal contests over American liberties, precedes the present moment. The right to form democratic worker organizations, and the social compact that emerged from those battles was relatively recent in U.S. history, a post New Deal phenomena. Its gradual dissolution and the rise of the current period of instability and divergence are in some ways a return to the past. Fundamental rights, including the right to join unions without facing termination of employment, to assemble in protest of working conditions, and to picket and boycott are now once again in jeopardy. The historical precedent serves as a reminder that these objectives and conflicting values are not settled, but continually re-forged into a new social contract.

U.S. scholars advocated a post-Second World War U.S. system of labor relations as a model for other countries. Near the height of union representation in the U.S., the scholars foretold the arrival of "pluralistic industrialism" around the world due to the logic of industrialization (Kerr et al., 1960). Yet such pluralism, involving accepting the role of multiple stakeholders in the employment relationship, including unions and government regulation, never had a firm hold in certain states within the U.S. Pluralism never breached large swathes of the U.S. economy, including both anti-union employers as well as paternalistic and generous employers of the welfare capitalist mold (Jacoby, 1998).

Scholars need not travel beyond the U.S. to engage in comparative research, or to find cultural and linguistic factors that shape divergent outcomes. There is enough diversity in the United States' systems of employee relations and types of employment relationships to conduct extensive within-country comparisons, and to generate novel interpretive schemes.

The subject of employee relations includes the conflict among the stakeholders in the employment relationship. The contracts, the actors, and the specific context requires close attention to detail, as well as a broad understanding of the general themes and theories. This chapter will provide an analysis of growing divergence within U.S. employment and labor relations, and the tension between individual rights and democratic majorities.

AT-WILL EMPLOYMENT AND THE MARKET VIEW

In 2017, 137.9 million workers were employed in the U.S., according to the U.S. Bureau of Labor Statistics. For these workers, however, the conditions of their labor, and the rules under which they work, vary quite starkly when broken into separate areas of U.S. employee relations. While the governing doctrine in the U.S. gives employers wide latitude to set employment policy free of government intervention, exceptions to the laissez-faire norm in the U.S. seek to provide balance by protecting individual and collective rights at work.

The governing doctrine in U.S. employee relations is "employment at-will." Also called "at-will" employment, this term means that, in general, U.S. employees can be fired or laid off at any time, for no reason at all, or for any reason except an illegal one, including bad or arbitrary reasons. Likewise, employees have the right to quit at any time, for any reason, or for no reason at all. While each party has equal rights to terminate the relationship, many argue that the imbalance of bargaining power between employers and employees leads to a potential for abuse.

In general, the terms and conditions of employment agreed to by employee and employer are also at-will because each party has liberty of contract; an employer may revise terms and conditions of employment at any time, and a dissatisfied employee can quit. The doctrine of at-will employment is informed by a view of the employment relationship as a market. Under this laissez-faire view, workers freely exchange time and labor for wages. Thus, if wages or working conditions are not favorable, employees can quit their jobs. Under this view, the government should not regulate the labor market, leaving matters instead in the hands of individual employees and employers. This highly individualistic view emerged gradually after the civil war outlawed prevailing exploitative forms of labor. The 13th Amendment to the Constitution banned slavery and indentured servitude, and the 14th Amendment barred the state from depriving any person of "life, liberty, or property, without due process of law . . .".

While the emancipatory language of the post-Civil War amendments to the Constitution sought to end the most egregious forms of labor exploitation, new forms of exploitation emerged in the industrial era. Ultimately, these very amendments were used by the Supreme Court to restrict state efforts to improve working conditions. The Supreme Court of the United States ruled unconstitutional state employment regulations that sought to end appalling labor conditions. In the *Lochner v. New York* (1905) case, a New York law was passed to restrict workers' hours in the interest of health and safety, but the law was ruled unconstitutional under the 14th Amendment because it would limit a worker's liberty to labor for as many hours as the worker desired.

The at-will view of the employment relationship is a deeply held belief in the U.S. Although the Supreme Court eventually reversed the Lochner decision and accepted employment regulation as Constitutional (e.g., *West Coast Hotel Co. v. Parrish*, 1937) as part of a wave of New Deal legislation in the 1930s, and courts now accept many regulations of the workplace and exceptions to at-will employment, the overarching attitude and deeply ingrained belief in the market view continues to influence employment policy.

This doctrine of at-will employment is quite different from other countries, but as with every other rule in U.S. employee relations, there are large exceptions. Many states, under their own common law or court decisions, have recognized important caveats (Muhl, 2001). Further limits to employment at-will are included in "Labor Law" governing private sector unions and collective rights, and "Employment Law" that governs all workplaces and protects individual rights. Additional exceptions are created in individual employment contracts and employee handbooks. Further, most public sector workers are guaranteed the "due process of law" protected by the 14th Amendment. In addition to these routine exceptions, the political party in control of the executive branch regularly makes significant changes in direction and emphasis, destabilizing the system unlike other countries where basic questions tend to be more settled.

The following two sections will illustrate some of these notable exceptions to the at-will doctrine. A word of caution is in order. U.S. policy on labor and employee relations can be very difficult to follow because while there are rules, the rules are governed by a host of exceptions. As the illustrations of the litigiousness of U.S. employment relations below will demonstrate, a lawyer should always be consulted for specific issues. Much of this chapter, and a graduate level course, can discuss those exceptions in detail: the unionized workforce, the public sector civil service, employment discrimination law, and state-level common law.

EMPLOYMENT LAW EXCEPTIONS

Employment law is the phrase used to typically describe laws that regulate all U.S. employment relationships, including those involving individually signed employee contracts. Employment law includes anti-discrimination laws such as the *Civil Rights Act of 1964*, as well as other pieces of protective legislation that create exceptions to employment at-will and departures from laissez-faire.

One very active area, wage and hour law, sets minimum labor standards for wages and overtime. Recent activity in the wage and hour law area provides a good example of several phenomena: how exceptions to the laissez-faire doctrine have exceptions themselves, how changing political control leads to major policy changes, how litigious the U.S. system is, and how state-level policy is increasingly diverging within country and from federal policy.

Nearly all workers are covered by the primary wage and hour law in the U.S., the *Fair Labor Standards Act (FLSA)*. The FLSA stipulates that hourly wages must be higher than the federal minimum wage ($7.25), and that hours worked in excess of 40 hours in a week must be paid at 1.5 times the regular hourly rate of the worker. In 2016, 79.9 million workers were paid hourly wages, and by dictating to employers a minimum wage and overtime standards, the FLSA represents a major departure under U.S. law from laissez-faire. However, this exception to the rule has major exceptions.

Exceptions to Exceptions

The terms "exempt" and "non-exempt" are common in reference to wage and hour laws. Many workers are classified "exempt" from overtime requirements, for example, because they are highly paid, earn a salary, and work in a specific occupation that qualifies for an exemption. While the FLSA sets baseline wage and hour standards for the country, large numbers of workers are exempted from both of the central requirements of the law.

For example, some farm and seasonal workers are exempt from minimum wages, and disabled workers, and young workers all carry exceptions. Below the federal minimum wage, there is a legal "sub-minimum" wage for tipped workers ($2.13). The federal minimum wage has eroded significantly in terms of purchasing power, and has not been changed since June of 2009, but states have been active in eliminating or reducing some of these exceptions. Many states and cities have passed higher minimum wages, and several have eliminated the tipped wage discrepancy.

In addition, many workers are exempt from both requirements of the law because they are considered independent contractors and not employees. When workers are incorrectly classified by employers as independent contractors instead of employees, lawsuits are brought seeking damages, a feature of the U.S. system discussed further in the below discussion of litigation and arbitration.

Reversals of Reversals

A proposed overtime regulation brought forward toward the end of the Obama administration would have significantly increased the number of workers eligible for overtime. Under the proposed regulation, an additional 4.2 million workers would have been automatically eligible for overtime because they earned less than $47,476 a year (Department of Labor, 2016). The policy proposal achieved this by increasing the amount of money a worker must be paid to be considered exempt. The goal was to reverse a decline in the number of workers eligible for overtime, which was initially intended to apply to all but a few narrowly drawn exempt workers.

The policy was set to take effect in December 2016. However, because of a court challenge brought by the State of Texas, implementation was delayed into 2017. When the new Trump administration arrived, they decided to reverse the regulation, and the regulatory change was never implemented.

As an illustration of the consequences of the instability of U.S. employee relations, consider that, in late 2016, companies had communicated to many workers that they would be newly eligible for overtime pay. A month later, companies either faced the choice of rescinding their decision or going forward with a policy that was never implemented. Many workers were left with a promised raise rescinded.

Litigation and Arbitration

Enforcement of wage and hour laws is generally weak in the U.S. There are far fewer inspectors than needed to investigate all complaints, and so enforcement, when it occurs, is often done via civil litigation (i.e., lawsuits) brought by employees or through settlements between the employer and the Department of Labor. The widespread problem of "wage theft" involves the non-payment of wages owed to workers as required by the FLSA and other statutes. Noncompliance with employment and labor laws in the largest U.S. cities is a substantial problem (Bernhardt et al., 2013), and some states and cities have sought to increase criminal enforcement of these laws. Research suggests 2.2 million workers in the U.S. were paid the minimum wage or less, which does not necessarily violate the law given the exceptions noted above (Bureau of Labor Statistics, 2016).

The FLSA applies only to "employees" who an employer "suffers or permits to work." Yet many workers in the U.S. are not employees. Rather, they are independent contractors who run their own business and thus are exempt from the law. Workers can be correctly classified as independent contractors instead of employees if they are running their own business, and possess freedom from employer control. Recent litigation has emphasized the importance of correctly classifying workers as employees.

Consider two workers involved in parcel delivery. The worker who delivers parcels for the U.S. Postal Service is an employee with benefits, a union, and a federal civil service job protecting them from arbitrary termination. If the U.S. Postal Service worker falls sick or is injured, they have insurance that can provide support for them. For much of the last decade, however, a person who delivered parcels through the private company, FedEx Ground, was likely an independent contractor, who did not receive benefits, or pay into the unemployment insurance system. This was the case until a lawsuit challenging the independent contractor status of FedEx Ground drivers was settled for $228 million in California in 2016, and $240 million in 20 other states.[1]

There are significant consequences for employees in the case of a misclassification of an employee as an independent contractor. An employer must pay an employee the minimum wage, and overtime, and also contribute to fund the state unemployment insurance and workers' compensation funds (thus making the employee eligible for these benefits), as well as contribute to federal social security retirement and disability funds (approximately 7.5 percent of the wage cost, which again, gives a worker eligibility for these benefits), and provide health insurance under the Affordable Care Act. For independent contractors, none of this is true. Experts suggest large losses to social welfare systems in tax revenue and unemployment and workers' compensation insurance funds due to employees being misclassified as independent contractors.

Employment disputes, as seen in the FedEx case, have long found an outlet in the courtrooms. While individual lawsuits are brought by a single person in cases where they experience wrongdoing, class action lawsuits are typically brought by a small number of employees, yet represent the collective interests of many employees affected by an employer's decision. Such class action lawsuits may be less common in the future, however, due to a recent Supreme Court decision in *NLRB v. Murphy Oil USA* (2018) that permits employers to force collective issues into individual arbitration.

The traditional litigiousness of U.S. employment relations has been undermined in recent years by the steady rise of a private system of arbitration for individual employment disputes. Arbitration agreements typically require cases to be heard by a private-sector arbitrator, often a retired judge or expert in the employment relations area, who hears the case and renders a final and binding verdict. Such decisions typically cannot be appealed.

Scholars argue that this emerging system is part of a changing social compact in the U.S. (Lipsky et al., 2003). Estimates by Alexander Colvin (2017) suggest that 53.9 percent of workers are covered by mandatory arbitration clauses. This number is likely to rise. The Murphy Oil case cited above means that employers may now require employees as a condition of continued or new employment to sign a mandatory arbitration agreement that prevents the employee from ever bringing an individual or collective lawsuit before a federal court. Many scholars, and the dissent to this decision written by Justice Ruth Bader Ginsburg, suggest that this increases the imbalance of power toward employers and harkens back to an earlier labor relations era prior to the passage of the National Labor Relations Act.

LABOR RELATIONS AND PUBLIC EMPLOYEE EXCEPTIONS

Labor relations is the sphere related to the collective rights of workers, especially pertaining to the unionized workforce as well as the rights of unorganized workers to organize labor unions. In Section 7 of the National Labor Relations Act (NLRA), all workers are provided protection from employer retaliation when taking action as a collective to shape their terms and conditions of work. The NLRA further endorses a role for unions and collective bargaining, and requires employers to negotiate in good faith with unions. U.S. labor unions are democratic organizations in which workers elect leaders to negotiate collective bargaining agreements with their employers on their behalf.

The terms and conditions of work for the 14.7 million employed American workers who were union members in 2018, and the 16.4 million who were covered by union contracts, are governed by clauses contained within negotiated collective bargaining agreements (CBAs) between employers and unions that represent workers (Bureau of Labor Statistics, 2019). These CBAs are legal contracts that are negotiated between workers and individual employers, and unlike many countries, typically cannot be negotiated at the industry or more central level.

At-will employment almost never applies to workers covered by union contracts. Among the most common union contract clauses are specific provisions protecting workers against arbitrary termination. Language in contracts, including *just cause* clauses, requires employers to have *bona fide* or legitimate reason for terminating a worker (Dau-Schmidt and Haley, 2006). Thus, a separate body of contract law covers union members' rights. Similarly, a separate area of law applies to the 20.7 million American workers in the public sector at the local, state, and federal government, and an additional separate body of law covers 7 million public sector workers in unions. Union and non-union workers employed by the government in civil service positions typically must be given *due process of law* under the 14th Amendment. This often translates into a requirement that employees have an opportunity to hear reasons for their termination or adverse employment actions, hire an attorney, and to appeal determinations.

Recent years illustrate several patterns in U.S. labor relations: the instability of labor relations policy as political partisanship over labor issues has grown, the rise of individual rights as a courtroom weapon to counter democratic union organization, and the growing divergence within the country.

Instability of Labor Relations

As in many other countries, unionization has declined significantly in the U.S., falling from 14.9 percent in 2000 to 10.5 percent in 2018 (Bureau of Labor Statistics, 2019). In the private sector in 2018, unionization is at 6.4 percent. Public sector employees are now the majority of union members, a troubling sign for the union move-ment, and are also increasingly under attack.

Unions face very diverse constituencies and have diverse world-views. Some unions, typically industrial unions, promote broad pro-workers campaigns and advocate social justice. Other unions, typically craft and trade unions, are dedicated to "pure and simple" delivery of services to their members. The schisms among unions have led at times to divisions within the union movement. Most sig-nificantly, in 2005, several of the largest unions in the U.S. split from the prevailing federation of U.S. unions, the American Federation of Labor – Congress of Industrial Organizations (AFL-CIO) to form a new coalition "Change to Win."

The Change to Win coalition believed it was necessary to invest more funds in organizing unorganized workers and to lead broad campaigns on behalf of unorganized workers. The *Fight for $15*, a campaign for a $15 minimum wage, for example, has been one of the most visible products of these efforts. Beyond organizing workers, the advocacy campaigns and social movements such as the *Fight for $15* have played a critical role in putting employee relations policy such as minimum wage increases before voters in local referenda.

Alternative forms of labor organization have also increased in the last two decades. Workers centers advocate for workers' rights without organizing workers into unions. They serve the non-union workforce through organizing and advocacy activities that emphasize social justice, workers' rights, and immigrant rights. From 5 workers centers in 1993 to over 200 in 2010, workers centers have joined into national networks to achieve scale, spread knowledge, and build consistent organizing models (Fine, 2011).

The NLRA's Section 7 also protects non-union workers, and despite the decline of unions in the U.S., there has been a variety of worker resistance in unlikely places. Individual forms of protest against employers, including absenteeism, shirking, sabotage, and quitting remain popular among U.S. employees. These individualistic protest activities, interestingly, are likely to be more present in locations where union representation or a history of collective worker action is absent (Roscigno and Hodson, 2004).

Unorganized workers have also engaged in collective action. Walkouts and wildcat strikes demonstrate the fundamentally unpredictable nature of labor relations in the U.S. The teacher strike wave that spread across "red states" in the summer of 2018 in response to low wages transformed state level discussion of public education and led to significant wage increases in several states. The Google employee walkout in the fall of 2018 in response to the company's handling of sexual harassment claims brought against senior executives came with demands for employee representation on the board, and policy changes.

Individual Rights Against Collective Rights

In the last two decades, one of the most dramatic changes has been in terms of "right to work" legislation. These laws give individuals covered by union contracts the right to opt-out of paying union dues. Advocates, in proposing such legislation, state that such right to work laws advance individual freedom. The preamble to a proposed national version of the law states that right to work laws: "Preserve and protect the free choice of individual employees to form, join, or assist labor organizations, or to refrain from such activities." Such laws make the "agency shop," in which workers must pay toward the cost of bargaining and enforcing collective contracts, unlawful. Right to work laws effectively make all unions "open shops," in which workers represented by the union need not pay at all toward the cost of the union.

Critics, however, argue that the "right-to-work" label is misleading. Closed shops that require union membership as a condition of employment are already outlawed under federal law, the Taft-Hartley Act of 1947. The gap between union membership and union coverage suggests that 9.7 per cent of workers covered by a union contract are not members of their unions. These "free-riders" may, however, be required to pay union dues that cover the cost of bargaining their contract if they are not in a right to work state. Advocates of unions criticize right to work laws as undermining unions' ability to exist, and point to the advantages of unions. For example, in comparative research, workers in states with greater union representation tend to have fewer workers at the poverty level, without negative effects on employment (Brady et al., 2013).

Right-to-work advocates view the open shop as a fundamental issue of individual rights against the collective rights of a majority of workers. Under right to work, while a majority may wish to be represented by a union, that majority should have no right to require any worker who opposes the union to pay for the union's costs. In addition to state-level legislative victories, right-to-work advocates have successfully pursued their case in the federal court system.

Lawsuits brought by public employees, culminating in the recent Supreme Court decision in the *Janus v. American Federation of State, County, and Municipal Employees*, Council 31 (2018) case, argue that individual workers' right to free speech is impeded by the requirement that government workers spend money on union activities that an individual worker opposes. In Janus, the court ruled against the unions and in favor of workers who oppose unions.

The Janus decision applies today and effectively makes all public sector collective bargaining agreements open shops. The ramifications of this decision are yet to be seen, but it may lead to a further decline in union representation, as fewer workers choose to pay for the cost of union representation. Research has found that states that passed right to work laws experienced a significant increase in voting for conservative elected officials, indicating that the political implications may also be significant (Feigenbaum et al., 2018).

LOCAL DEMOCRACY AND DIVERGENCE IN U.S. EMPLOYEE RELATIONS: 2000–2016

While the above description outlines the contours of the U.S. employment relations system, changes over the last twenty years have led to significant departures from the national norm at the state level. Political polarization has increased in the U.S., and this has been occurring at the state level since 1970 (Grumbach, 2018). Labor and employment policy have been no exception. Conservative states and donor-networks have advocated at the state level for new right to work laws, eliminating prevailing wage laws, and preventing localities from passing or enforcing minimum wage laws (Lafer, 2017). Liberal states and localities have passed minimum wage laws, as advocated by the Fight for $15 movement, added resources for wage and hour enforcement, and enacted additional protective measures for workers.

The U.S. employee relations system is ultimately governed by democratic choices, in both federal, state, and local government elections, under a *federal* constitutional system. Federal statutes set a minimum for labor and employment standards, and states and localities may often set higher standards. At each level, power is balanced between the typically unelected judges who must balance rights in each case, the elected legislators who decide upon the correct laws within the limits of the constitution, and the elected executive branch, which enforces and administers the law through regulatory rule-making and enforcement activity.

In an attempt to measure the change in state-level employment policy since the turn of the century, Table 7.1 and Figure 7.1 summarize recent changes within the U.S. to examine whether the description of growing divergence is accurate. In Table 7.1, the policies used to construct a measure of state-level employment ideology are listed.

Figure 7.1 presents the change in policy from 2000 to 2016 on a single left–right ideological scale. Each "right" leaning policy enacted in a state is scored "+1" and each "left" leaning policy "-1" to create the ideological scale. Such a single scale can be useful to reduce the complexity of individual policies and understand broad trends in the direction of employment policy. For the purpose of visualization in Figure 7.1, the values for each state are mean centered at zero. States are sorted from top to bottom from the most "right" leaning to the most "left" leaning in 2016, to better visualize how consistently states have diverged since 2000. Figure 7.1 demonstrates that divergence

Table 7.1   State-level employment policy ideology items

"Left"-leaning state-level legislation	"Right"-leaning state-level legislation
Has a state-wide minimum wage law Number of common law exceptions to at-will employment Bans on asking for salary history Paid sick leave Paid family leave Sexual orientation anti-discrimination laws Unemployment compensation system modernization	Pre-empts local minimum wage laws Pre-empts local benefits laws Pre-empts "fair scheduling" laws Pre-empts prevailing wage and project labor agreements Right to work laws

has increased within U.S. employment policy since the turn of the century. State-level actors have become increasingly active in pushing their local jurisdictions to the left or the right. The following section will discuss the increasing divergence in several key areas.

Anti-Discrimination Law Divergence

An example of growing state level differentiation emerges in another exception to employment-at-will: protections against discrimination. The Civil Rights Act of 1964 was landmark legislation that provided employees protection against discrimination on the basis of an employees' membership in a protected class. Since the passage of the Civil Rights Act, an employer may not alter the terms or conditions of the employment relationship because an employee is a member of a protected class, including race, color, religion, sex, national origin, veteran status, age (over 40), and disability. The federal laws against discrimination have evolved through court rulings to protect workers against sexual harassment, including *quid pro quo* and *hostile work environment* harassment. The Equal Employment Opportunity Commission exists to enforce the anti-discrimination laws.

Federal law does not, however, currently prevent employers from discriminating against workers on the basis of sexual orientation or gender identity. Increasingly, states have added protections. State level protections against sexual orientation and gender identity now exist in twenty states (Movement Advancement Project, 2018). As

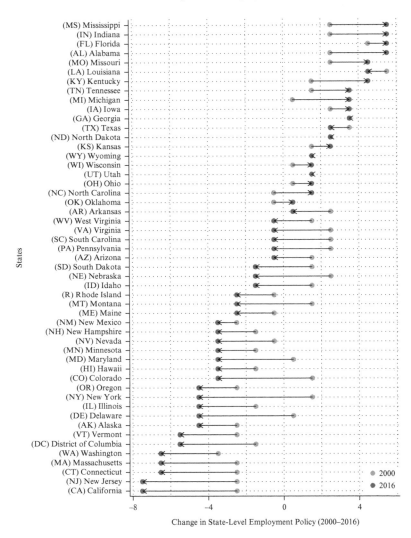

Figure 7.1   Change in state-level employment policy (2000–2016)

a counter-initiative, several states have also passed laws permitting business owners with deeply held religious beliefs to discriminate against customers (and in Mississippi, workers) if the sexual orientation or identity of the customer/worker is disfavored by the business owner (Human Rights Watch, 2018). Non-governmental organizations including civil liberties groups, religious organizations, and advocates for gay and lesbian workers have tracked, lobbied, and vocally sought to shape these employment policies.

Benefits Divergence

The United States is unique among developed nations for not guaranteeing workers any paid leave under federal laws, yet it is not the case that all U.S. workers do not have the right to paid leave. In addition to minimum wage legislation, states and localities have enacted paid sick days, and paid maternity and paternity leave benefits for workers. The first state-level paid sick leave law was enacted in 2011; ten states and the District of Columbia now require employers to provide workers paid sick leave. Three states now provide paid family leave through state disability insurance programs.

While some states have been moving toward greater regulation of the labor market, others have taken steps to prevent municipalities within the state from enacting protective labor legislation. For example, since 1997, 26 states have passed laws that pre-empt (or prevent) a city within the state from enacting a higher minimum wage than state law. St. Louis, Missouri, for example, passed a city ordinance in 2015 to raise the minimum wage to $10 per hour in 2017, and $11 per hour in 2018. A state law passed in 2017, however, overturned the city ordinance and denied cities within the state the authority to set minimum wages. Since 2011, 21 states have enacted laws that prevent municipalities from enacting benefits legislation such as paid sick days.

Wage and Hour Law Divergence

Since 2000, protective laws, passed both by elected local and state representatives and through ballot initiatives (a form of direct democracy in which voters vote directly on laws), have increased minimum wages, reduced the sub-minimum wage for tipped workers, created paid sick leave and family leave programs, paid maternity and paternity leave, and placed new emphasis upon the enforcement of wage and hour law and prevention of wage theft.

The federal minimum wage of $7.25 for non-farm and non-tipped workers has not increased since 2009. But where the federal government has not acted, states increasingly have. According to the Bureau of Labor Statistics, in 1988, only 2 states had a minimum wage higher than the federal minimum wage; in 1998, only 6 states required a higher minimum wage; by 2017, 29 states had a higher minimum wage. Eighteen states now automatically increase minimum wages with inflation each year (Economic Policy Institute, 2018). In addition, 42 localities across the U.S. have adopted local minimum wages that are higher than their state minimum wage. The effect of these within-country variations in minimum wages increases has created many "natural experiments," which have been studied extensively (Dube et al., 2010, 2016).

Under authorities created during the Great Depression, but not used for many years, New York State recently established a wage board to examine labor conditions in the fast food industry, and set a minimum wage of $15 for that industry in New York City by December 31, 2018, with lower rates for surrounding counties and for fast food workers outside of the city. Such industry-wide wage setting is not anomalous in U.S. history, but had not been attempted recently until New York's action. States and localities have thus begun to promote different minimum wages for different industries, and localities, and these proposals have attracted national attention as well as the potential to serve as a model at the federal level (Madland, 2018).

Labor Law Divergence

Twenty-one states enacted right-to-work legislation between 1944 and 1985 (seventeen between 1944 and 1955). There was no further RTW state law until Oklahoma enacted right-to-work in 2001. Since 2012, six more states, including Michigan, Wisconsin, and Missouri have enacted RTW legislation.

Despite these laws passing in the legislature, they have not all been popular. In Wisconsin in 2011, the passage of the law was met with massive protests in the state capitol. A ballot initiative passed by voters repealed Missouri's 2017 right-to-work law in August 2018. Efforts to pass a right to work law in Ohio in 2011 also failed when put before voters in a referendum.

CONCLUSION

This chapter illustrates the continued importance of context and regional culture within the U.S. While the market individualism that predominates in the U.S. has been ascendant for some time, some state level actors have increasingly pushed back against this trend through protective employment legislation.

The data presented here demonstrates a growing divergence within U.S. employment policy, as the federal government is increasingly perceived as ineffective at providing desired change. The deeply rooted contests between individualism and democracy, efficiency and equity and voice, have produced repeated conflicts in the courts, and at the ballot box. These trends illustrate the important subnational and regional cultures and the conflict between adherents of individualism and those who favor the collective rights of majorities to democratically set employment policy.

The chapter further sheds light on the critical importance of terminology, as doctrines have exceptions, which have exemptions, which lead to multiple classifications (and misclassifications) of workers. The instability of U.S. employee relations, and the reversals of policy that come with changing political control, emphasize the need for professionals to be aware of the specific context of situations in which conflict arises.

NOTE

1. Two separate circuit courts found that FedEx misclassified employees. When lower courts agree, parties often settle, but when lower courts disagree, conflict often rises up to higher courts. For the circuit court decisions, see, e.g., *Alexander v. FedEx Ground Package System, Inc.*, 765 F.3d 981 (9th Cir. 2014), and *In re FedEx Ground Package System, Inc.*, 792 F.3d 818 (7th Cir. 2015).

REFERENCES

Bernhardt, A., Spiller, M. W. and Polson, D. 2013. All Work and No Pay: Violations of Employment and Labor Laws in Chicago, Los Angeles and New York City. *Social Forces, 91*(3), pp. 725–46.

Brady, D., Baker, R. S. and Finnigan, R. 2013. When Unionization Disappears: State-Level Unionization and Working Poverty in the United States. *American Sociological Review, 78*(5), pp. 872–96.

Budd, J. W. 2004. *Employment with a Human Face: Balancing Efficiency, Equity, and Voice*. Ithaca, NY: ILR Press.

Budd, J. W. and Bhave, D. 2008. Values, Ideologies, and Frames of Reference in Industrial Relations. *The Sage Handbook of Industrial Relations*. London: Sage, pp. 92–112.

Bureau of Labor Statistics 2016. Characteristics of Minimum Wage Workers, Report, 2016. Bureau of Labor Statistics. Published April 2017. https://www.bls.gov/opub/reports/minimum-wage/2016/home.htm. Accessed February 13, 2019.

Bureau of Labor Statistics 2019. Current Population Survey: Union Members – 2018. Published January 2019. https://www.bls.gov/news.release/union2.nr0.htm. Accessed October 1, 2019.

Colvin, A. J. S. 2017. *The Growing Use of Mandatory Arbitration*. Economic Policy Institute, September 27, 2017.

Dau-Schmidt, K. G. and Haley, T. A. 2006. Governance of the Workplace: The Contemporary Regime of Individual Contract. *Comparative Labour Law and Policy Journal*, *28*, pp. 313–50.

Department of Labor 2016. Overview and Summary of Final Rule: Overtime for White Collar Workers. May 18, 2016. https://www.dol.gov/sites/default/files/overtime-overview.pdf. Accessed February 13, 2019.

Dube, A., Lester, T. W. and Reich, M. 2010. Minimum Wage Effects Across State Borders: Estimates Using Contiguous Counties. *The Review of Economics and Statistics*, *92*(4), pp. 945–64.

Dube, A., Lester, T. W. and Reich, M. 2016. Minimum Wage Shocks, Employment Flows, and Labor Market Frictions. *Journal of Labor Economics*, *34*(3), pp. 663–704.

Economic Policy Institute 2018. Minimum Wage Tracker. Economic Policy Institute. https://www.epi.org/minimum-wage-tracker/. Accessed February 13, 2019.

Feigenbaum, J., Hertel-Fernandez, A. and Williamson, V. (2018). From the Bargaining Table to the Ballot Box: Political Effects of Right to Work Laws (No. w24259). National Bureau of Economic Research.

Fine, J. 2011. New Forms to Settle Old Scores: Updating the Worker Centre Story in the United States. *Relations Industrielles/Industrial Relations*, *66*(4), pp. 604–30.

Grumbach, J. M. 2018. From Backwaters to Major Policymakers: Policy Polarization in the States, 1970–2014. *Perspectives on Politics*, *16*(2), pp. 416–35.

Human Rights Watch 2018. Religious Exemptions and Discrimination against LGBT People in the United States. February 19, 2018. See https://www.hrw.org/report/2018/02/19/all-we-want-equality/religious-exemptions-and-discrimination-against-lgbt-people. Accessed February 13, 2019.

Jacoby, S. M. 1998. *Modern Manors: Welfare Capitalism Since the New Deal*. Princeton, NJ: Princeton University Press.

Katz, H. C. and Wheeler, H. N. 2004. Employment Relations in the United States. In Bamber, G. J., Lansbury, R. D. and Wailes, N. (eds), *International and Comparative Employment Relations*. London: Sage Publications, pp. 67–90.

Kerr, C., Harbison, F. H., Dunlop, J. T. and Myers, C. A. 1960. Industrialism and Industrial Man. *International Labor Review*, 82, pp. 236–50.

Kochan, T. A., Katz, H. C. and McKersie, R. B. 1986. *The Transformation of American Industrial Relations*. Cornell University Press.

Lafer, G. 2017. *The One Percent Solution: How Corporations are Remaking America One State at a Time*. Ithaca, NY: Cornell University Press.

Lipsky, D. B., Seeber, R. L. and Fincher, R. D. 2003. *Emerging Systems for Managing Workplace Conflict: Lessons from American Corporations for Managers and Dispute Resolution Professionals* (Vol. 18). San Francisco, CA: Jossey-Bass.

Madland, D. 2018. Wage Boards for American Workers: Industry-Level Collective Bargaining for All Workers. Center for American Progress. https://www.americanprogress.org/issues/economy/reports/2018/04/09/448515/wage-boards-american-workers/. Accessed February 13, 2019.

Manzella, P. and Koch, K. 2017. Legal and Cultural Implications Inherent in Managing Multilingual and Multicultural Labor: Selected Translation Issues from the US National Labor Relations Board. *Lebende Sprachen*, *62*(1), pp. 59–78.

Movement Advancement Project 2018. Non-Discrimination Laws. See http://www.lgbtmap.org/equality-maps/non_discrimination_laws. Accessed February 13, 2019.

Muhl, C. J. 2001. The Employment-at-Will Doctrine: Three Major Exceptions. *Monthly Labour Review*, *124*(3), pp. 3–11.

Norlander, P. and Sørensen, T. A. 2018. 21st Century Slowdown: The Historic Nature of Recent Declines in the Growth of the Immigrant Population in the United States. *Migration Letters*, *15*(3), pp. 409–22.

Osterman, P. 2008. Improving the Quality of Low-Wage Work: The Current American Experience. *International Labour Review*, *147*(2–3), pp. 115–34.

Piore, M. J. 1972. Notes for a Theory of Labor Market Stratification. Working Paper No. 95. Department of Economics, Massachusetts Institute of Technology.

Roscigno, V. J. and Hodson, R. 2004. The Organizational and Social Foundations of Worker Resistance. *American Sociological Review*, *69*(1), pp. 14–39.

Weil, D. (2014). *The Fissured Workplace*. Cambridge, MA: Harvard University Press.

8. Fragmented Democracy and Employee Participation in Nigeria

John Opute

INTRODUCTION

Many developing economies lack 'consistent democracy' leading to several infrastructural and societal challenges in business management. Their controversial evolution towards viable democratic structures has a considerable consequence for the wider world. On the other hand, the promotion of employee participation through such structures as collective bargaining has created a new contour in the process of trade union development, which if properly harnessed, will lead to business efficacy and generate the so much heralded wealth for sustaining these economies (Xhafa, 2014). Commentators reviewing developments in management and labour relations in Africa have sought to treat the continent as a homogenous cultural entity, which is an assumption to be challenged (Adeleye, 2011). The chapter focuses on the changes to work and the notion of participation and democracy in Nigeria as an example of a developing nation in Africa. It also examines the emerging forms of labour relations such as employee participation, collective bargaining as well as the role of the state, the trade groups and employer associations – a view which is shared by some authors (Koçer and Hayter, 2011). Furthermore, it captures historical perspectives on democracy which underpins much of African affairs today. This is covered in the accompanying subsections of the chapter. The intention is to address key and emerging issues that contribute to the robustness of the discussions on the evolving democratic settings of Nigeria and the interface with culture and labour relations.

The starting point is the discussion on the role of colonisation in

Africa. The scramble for Africa was the occupation, division and colonisation of African territory by European powers during the period between 1881 and 1914 and this lasted until the late 1950s and early 1960s when independence was gradually being achieved by the respective states. Labour relations took the central place in all the struggles for democracy and so the initial outcome of democratic process was extended to the labour relations in many developing economies albeit this faced different contours (Ayittey, 1992; Nkomo, 2011). Some of these are related to imperialism that took a prominent place in several African countries and robbed the continent of some key cultural underpinnings (Hack-Polay, 2018). Colonialism, imperialism and neocolonialism have given rise to modern organisations in Nigeria which mirrors the organisation of work in the former colonial powers, mainly Britain, France, Portugal and Spain. Contemporary organisations in Africa are therefore a legacy of domination. These were likely to cause disruptions to the societal and organisational arrangements, including labour relations and the sourcing and management of people. The chapter draws attention to the need for management and labour processes which are congruent with Nigerian cultural values but at the same time can respond to the constraints of globalisation as a way of enhancing the sustainability of contemporary African organisations.

DEMOCRACY AND EMPLOYEE PARTICIPATION

With several countries in Africa now independent, it should be recognised that these states were previously under colonial rules and it is worth investigating if the effect of the colonial rule remains prevalent (Ayittey, 1992) and whether these can be examined from a comparative narration and to investigate the similarities, differences and the extent to which these past experiences influence labour relations in Nigeria. Labour relations is a significant area on which these recent developments have had a dramatic impact and redefining relationships between institutional structures, decision-making processes and the key actors in the employee relations system is essential in this new global environment. Concomitant with this understanding is the recognition that an effective employee relations system is an important determinant of economic performance.

The field of employee relations and human resource management in many developing economies, particularly Africa, lacks significant contributions in terms of depth of studies and empirical findings. HRM practices are often labelled administrative and clerical as opposed to more strategic endeavours (Kamoche et al., 2004; Okpara and Wynn, 2008) to help organisational performance. Most publications have dealt with the development of human resources management but there are limited publications on the narrow focus of comparative labour and employment relations, particularly from the perspective of colonial imperialism across the region on the one hand and the nature of these interconnectivity across the regions (Adeleye, 2011). As a result, the ailments of African organisations is in part due to the failure of HRM and labour relations in addition to political mismanagement (Kamoche, 2002). Apart from the paucity of publications in this area, there appears to be limited publications from African authors with the required exposure and working experiences in many of these economies. This may not be because of lack of interest or availability but in several cases, funding has remained a great limitation.

Thus, this chapter captures the evolving developments of freedom of association in the workplace from a different perspective. The practice of 'labour democracy' varies from industry to industry, from trade group to trade group and from region to region. The first are those with freedom of association and collective bargaining, the second have some restrictions but allow independent trade unions, the third have stringent restrictions, and the final group have practically no freedom of association. Therefore, the provocative nature of the chapter (linking employee participation, management practices as well as current political dispensation) highlights the central role of collective bargaining in modern-day Nigeria.

Interestingly, the chapter reveals that employees are not necessarily searching for freedom of association (which is traditionally pursued by trade unions) but for recognition, which comes from understanding their orientation. Therefore, they wish their minds and hearts to be won by their employers, which is beyond 'filling their pockets' and sometimes beyond the roles of trade unions and collective agreements. Additionally, there has been significant literature on employee voice but understanding employer voice provides an even better platform for effective workplace participation (Kaufman, 2014).

The framework of employee relations in Nigeria is centred on a tripartite arrangement of government and its agencies, workers and their organisations and employees and their associations. This partnership can be illustrated and summarised as follows:

The State

With the inception of a democratically elected government in 1999, the government's focus was directed towards the process of developing and institutionalising democracy and true federalism in the country. This approach brought about a new dispensation in labour policy with a view to pursuing voluntarism, and thus democratising the trade union. Accordingly, the Federal Government of Nigeria passed the Trade Union (Amendment) Act 2005 "to provide amongst other things, the democratisation of the labour movement through the expansion of opportunities for the registration of Federation of Trade Unions as well as the granting of freedom to employees to decide which unions they wish to belong" (Opute, 2010: 155). Some of the significant clauses are:

- Withdrawal of one central labour union in Nigeria;
  - o This implies that employees can only contract into their respective unions for deductions to be made from their wages. Union membership thus becomes voluntary;
- Conditions for strike action/lock out;
  - o There are several 'hurdles' to go through before a strike action or lock out can be carried out. This implies some procedural restriction.

The Employers

The employers have formed associations along industry lines, primarily for the purposes of presenting a united front with respect to collective bargaining, they have built on this by maintaining close contact with the Nigeria Employers' Consultative Association (NECA). As a federation of employers, as well as a parliament of employers, NECA's role among its members is purely consultative, since it does not enforce its advice on its members. Amongst its key role is, advising members on negotiations on wages, conditions of work, dispute handling and representation to government (on behalf of employers) on specific labour matters.

Trade Unions

The labour unions have been structured along industrial lines by the state for better coordination of all employee/employer activities, such as collective bargaining. Accordingly, the NLC serves as the central negotiating body for workers, albeit with now a rival central body. The role of the NLC is political. It represents workers' interests at the national level and in recent times has continuously engaged the government on matters of national interest. It resolves inter-union and intra-union disputes and takes the lead in providing education and counselling to members. However, the Trades Union Congress (TUC), which is now a rival/optional central trade union has been given legal backing with the democratisation of the unions. It is intended to operate in a similar fashion as the NLC. However, a most recent development suggests there is an emerging United Labour Congress (ULC, a break away from the NLC) suggesting that the labour movement is facing a new challenge from within (Adedigba, 2019).

The state continues to be involved in trade union matters, essentially to encourage industrial peace and promote economic development. Such interferences come through regulated incomes and productivity policies to inhibit inflations; encouraging freedom of association through legislations to permit national and plant negotiations through the machinery of collective bargaining process; setting up Arbitration Panels and the National Industrial Court for the settling of industrial relations disputes. On the part of employers, the NECA provides a forum for encouraging the setting up of employers' associations for industry-wide collective bargaining processes, advice and consultations amongst members and as a liaison body with the state on behalf of employers. The framework for collective bargaining is completed by the centralised trade unions with some issues left at company/plant level. The Trade Union Act 2005 emphasised the importance of freedom of association and increased relevance of collective bargaining at both national and plant levels. There have been several efforts to review and amend the act by the machinery of government to address the reality of modern labour relations but this has not progressed.

BACKGROUND: NIGERIA

The Historical Context

The history of Nigeria dates to its amalgamation into a single nation by the military forces of the British Empire in 1914. Prior to this period, Nigeria was a loose collection of autonomous states, villages, and over 250 ethnic communities, largely classified as northern and southern Nigeria. The modern Hausa and Fulani societies in northern Nigeria are the cultural successors of the Sokoto Caliphate, a theocratic state founded by Muslim reformer Uthman dan Fodio in 1817. They were geographically isolated in the north and governed by Islamic laws and maintained greater commercial and cultural links to North Africa and the Arab states than to West Africa. By contrast, the Yoruba and Igbo in the south maintained contacts with the Europeans since the 1500s. A minority of southerners converted to Christianity and the majority followed traditional indigenous religions, although the reverse is the situation today. Coastal Nigerians established thriving trade fashioning the coast into a hub for products like palm oil (a product sought after by industrialising Europe) and serving as a key source for the slave trade, prior to its abolition in 1807 by the British parliament.

The Niger Delta province (which is also referred to as the Niger Delta region) is the contemporary heart of the petroleum industry and a region of dense cultural diversity, inhabited by about forty ethnic groups. Most of the communities of the Niger Delta region during the medieval times lived in small fishing villages within the inlets of the delta. But as the slave trade grew in importance in the sixteenth century, coastal port cities like Bonny and Brass developed into major trading points and served as exporters of fish. The historical developments and arrangements that have shaped the Nigerian state are influenced by the major ethnic groups of the Hausas/Fulanis, Igbos and Yorubas. These ethnic groups are the most populous and politically influential and have, thus, maintained historical pre-eminence in Nigerian politics.

Language and Culture

Language and culture have mutual impact and can be viewed as a mirror of each other in Nigeria. Therefore, the death of one is the death of the other (Obiegbu, 2016). Whilst the number of languages in Nigeria is currently estimated in excess of 400, the English language was chosen as the official language to facilitate the cultural and linguistic unity of the country post colonialisation by the British. The major national languages spoken in Nigeria represent three key regions – the North is Hausa, the West is Yoruba, and the East is Igbo languages. Nevertheless, most ethnic groups prefer to communicate in their languages, but the English language remains the official language and is widely used for education, business transactions and for official matters.

In Nigeria, language empowers self-expression and cultural heritage and due to the ethnic make-up, communication styles vary. As an example, the Yoruba tribe in the South West of the country employs proverbs, sayings/quotations and even songs to enrich the meaning of what they say and consequently improve communication. Additionally, humours are sometimes used to prevent boredom during long meetings such as Town Hall or company briefings and during collective bargaining sessions – between management and trade unions. Proverbs and humours are also used to calm down tensions during collective bargaining sessions. From a cultural perspective, it is believed that embedding humour in messages guarantee that what is being said is not easily forgotten.

Since the English language is the national language, 'Nigerian English' has been adapted for home use to enhance employee participation. Many scholars (Adetugbo, 1998; Banjo, 2007; Adegbija, 2008) assert that 'Nigerian English' exists and stress that it has gone a long way to link culture to language successfully. Although it deviates from standard English, the immediate translation attracts some uniqueness in communication. For example, the Nigerian English expression of: Let us conclude this negotiation 'quick, quick' is a direct translation of the Yoruba word 'kia, kia' and the Igbo word 'ozugbo, ozugbo'. Therefore, the development of language can lead to cultural enhancement and efficacy of employee participation.

The Political and Economic Context

The political structure of Nigeria transformed from a British protectorate in 1914, through regions in 1954, independence in 1960 and republic in 1963, to a twelve-state structure in 1967. Today, the country operates a three-tier federal structure, comprising a central government, 36 states and a federal capital territory, Abuja and 774 local government areas.

Four years after independence, the first Nigerian national election to usher in a democratic government took place. Unfortunately, boycotts, malpractice and widespread violence (especially in the old Western Nigeria) marred the elections. This development instigated a military coup, which ensued in 1966. In 1979, Nigerians voted for a new national Assembly (The Senate, and the House of Representatives) but this experience only lasted for around four years as a result of another military intervention in government. Thereafter, there were several intrigues and fragmented democracy by subsequent military governments for a democratically elected government, but this did not happen until 29 May 1999 when a democratically elected government was established. This return to democracy is the longest so far and has brought some stability to the country.

After over 30 years of military governments, Nigeria is now undergoing a democratic experience, but this takes a while to settle in. The political environment is a gradual settling and points to an encouraging future but there are still bumps on the way. Corruption, for instance, is widely established as one of the most serious obstacles to economic growth in Nigeria despite the current government's continued effort to tackle this head-on on many fronts.

From the perspective of its regional influence, Nigeria's role in the

Table 8.1   Economic indices/status

No	Factor	Amount/percentage		
		2015	2016	2017
1	Population (million)	179	184	189
2	GDP per capita (USD)	2,766	2,206	1,995
3	GDP (USD bn)	494	405	376
4	Economic growth (GDP, annual variation in %)	2.8	−1.6	0.8
5	Unemployment rate	4.3	7.1	7.0
6	Inflation rate (CPI, annual variation in %)	9.0	15.7	16.5
7	Exchange rate (vs USD)	196.5	304.5	305.5

Source: http://www.focus-economics.com/countries/nigeria.

Economic Community of West African States (ECOWAS) is significant. On 28 May 1975 fifteen West African countries (later joined by Cape Verde) signed in Lagos, Nigeria, a treaty creating ECOWAS. According to Ojo (1980), Nigeria played a key role in the intensive diplomatic initiatives culminating in the formation of ECOWAS; an organ for promoting co-operation and integration in economic, social and cultural activities in West African states. Apart from the vast size of Nigeria, its ability to operate as a driving force for development in West Africa is as a result of its economic influence in the region. In affirming this position, Soule and Obi (2001) explain that Nigeria represents around 60 per cent of its consumers, 47 per cent of the regional GDP, and 50 per cent of its industrial potential. Nigeria has thus been ready to play an important development role in West Africa.

Last collated as 166.2 million in 2012, the Nigeria Bureau of Statistics (NBS) has estimated the population to be around 178.5 in 2016, although the United Nations estimate has placed it at 186 million. Apart from being the most populous country in Africa, it also means that about 1 out of 43 people in the world call Nigeria their home (Population Review, 2017). The Nigerian economy depends largely on oil and export earnings from oil production accounts for over 90 per cent of export earnings. The rest of the economy demonstrates a typical developing African model; around 30 per cent of GDP comes from agriculture and the manufacturing sector is limited and developing slowly (Afangideh, 2012). However, Nigeria offers an example as a country with increasing business opportunities. With the drastic fall in oil prices, the government could not execute several projects neither could foreign exchange be made available to pay for raw materials imports. There has been severe rationalisation of foreign reserves and this has had tremendous impact on SMEs and business in general.

The continuous attack on oil pipelines in the Delta region of the country has also reduced the production of crude oil, making a tough situation even worse (Afinotan and Ojakorotu, 2009; Njoku, 2016). The Niger Delta region has long constituted a threat to crude oil production in Nigeria. According to the International Crisis Group (2015), the reason for the incessant oil pipeline vandalism in Nigeria includes the pervasive poverty and frustration in the Niger delta. There was also severe unemployment among the educated youths, which has led to anti-social actions such as pipeline vandalism, oil theft and kidnapping for ransom. Two agencies established to drive development, the Niger Delta Development Commission (NDDC) and the Ministry of Niger Delta Affairs (MNDA) established in 2000 and 2008 respectively, have floundered, according to the International Crisis Group (2015). In a broad sense, the federal government continues to initiate dialogue with all stakeholders in the region, including state governments, with support for entrepreneurial and job creation activities. For example, educational programmes were embarked upon and targeted at youths to enhance skills acquisition and position them for meaningful employment in the oil companies within the region (Njoku, 2016).

As the Nigerian economy continues to grow and remains attractive for foreign investment, the management of human resources and the appropriateness of employee participation becomes a strategic tool for business efficacy. Understanding the petroleum industry therefore is of essence because of its strategic contribution and influence in management of the wealth of the nation.

Petroleum and Gas in Nigeria

The petroleum industry is the largest and main generator of GDP in Nigeria. Since the British discovered oil in the Niger Delta region in the late 1950s, the oil industry has been marred by political and economic strife largely due to a long history of corrupt military regimes and complicity of multinational corporations, notably Royal Dutch Shell. The Nigerian government and oil corporations have been criticised as slow in implementing reforms aimed at assisting the environmental degradation that petroleum extraction has wrought. Natural gas reserves are well over 100 trillion ft (2,800 km), thus the gas reserves are three times as substantial as the crude oil reserves. With the building of two new liquefied gas (LNG) plants with a combined capacity of about 32 metric tonnes yearly, Nigeria is on track to be the second largest growing LNG capacity in the world, second only to Qatar. According to Budhwar and Debrah (2001), Nigeria's population and potential resources makes it one of the most attractive countries for foreign investment in Africa.

The Oil Industry and Nigerian Economy

Oil holds a key place in the Nigerian economy. Oil companies continue to struggle with continuous community unrest and vandalism of oil infrastructure because the communities see that the extraction of crude oil has adversely affected their economic and cultural life. For example, cases of oil spillage are common within the communities and this destroys fish farming. However, on their own part, major multinational oil companies (like ExxonMobil, Agip and Shell) have launched their own community development programmes in their communities of operations to improve the standard of living of the residents. Examples of such programmes are rural electrification, provision of schools, roads, water, clinics, and television viewing centres.

Management of Oil Wealth

In examining the place of the petroleum industry in Nigeria, Da Costa (2009) explains that oil has generated an estimated $600 billion since the 1960s. Unfortunately, most inhabitants of the country's main oil-producing areas have seen few benefits from over four decades of oil extraction that has damaged their environment. On the other hand, oil theft, according to Walker (2009), with the connivance of officials from international oil companies, national oil parastatal officials and captains of vessels costs Nigeria an estimated $5 billion every year. A tighter regulatory framework is therefore required, according to several commentators.

The Nigerian constitution from 1960 to date affirms that the federal government has exclusive control over the oil and mineral wealth of the nation. Omoruyi (2000) explains that the Nigerian constitution makes no provision for either shared power between the federal government and the state governments or between federal government and oil-producing communities. Accordingly, coping with the neglect of the areas that produce the oil is assumed to be the responsibility of the federal government acting with the oil companies. He explains that, "the quest for ownership by the oil producing states should and ought to be sought through the interplay of politics and not through the constitution" (Omoruyi, 2000: 8).

The government has adopted a carrot-and-stick approach to addressing the unrest in the Niger Delta region by offering an amnesty to militants after launching what is considered its biggest military offensive in years, but few expect the strategy to lead to rapid restoration of security (Burgis, 2009; Green and Burgis, 2009). According to Iwuagwu (2009), the decision by Shell Petroleum Development Company to settle its once lingering case with the Ogonis (one of the communities in the Niger Delta region) out of court, and its agreement to pay $15.5 million in settlement, signifies a new beginning in the relationship between oil companies and their host communities. It also provides the basis for a significant change of direction by the Nigerian government towards the oil-producing communities of the Niger Delta region. In support of this proposition, Green (2009) explains that many indigenes of the delta region believe that the only way to end the violence will be to stimulate the kind of broader economic revival that could provide alternatives for thousands of unemployed youths.

Earnings from oil have propelled most economic activities and thus industrialisation. Payments for imports of raw materials and various government spending and developmental projects arise from foreign exchange. The stability in the oil industry is not only necessary for sustaining the foreign reserves of the nation but also provides a basis for increased economic activities and the stability in the prices of goods and services. This will in return provide for enhanced budgetary management and the sustenance of appropriate monetary and non-monetary compensation for effective management of human resources in the Nigerian economy. This stability will promote competitiveness and business efficacy in the country.

CULTURAL FRAMEWORK OF EMPLOYEE PARTICIPATION

With respect to the developing economies, there has been discussions on alternative approaches to examining development and participation such as classic accounts of development and participation, contemporary institutional approaches, cultural accounts and dominant models but it is still recognised that allowing for the periodic emergence and diffusions of alternative models cannot be ignored (Hollingsworth, 2006; Wood, 2010). In their study of a 10-country comparison on the impact of culture on human resources management practices, Aycan et al. (2006) alluded to the fact that the model of culture fit suggests that organisational culture is shaped by multiple forces external and internal to the organisation which are unrelated to societal culture, albeit paying attention to selection of organisation (and by implication, country) is paramount.

Although Project Globe (a network of social scientists and management scholars from several cultures working in a coordinated long-term effort to examine the interrelationship between societal culture, organisational culture and leadership) identifies the Human-Oriented approach as a management orientation based on cultural studies, this perspective identifies this leadership style as supportive and includes compassion and generosity towards subordinates (Javidan et al., 2006). However, Project Globe does not provide factor(s) that drive this perspective, other than culture in a wider perspective. Furthermore, the work of some scholars (Besamusca and Tijdens, 2015), in comparing contents of collective bargaining agreements for developing countries (mainly Africa) is quite revealing but it does not elucidate the appropriateness of the contents in the challenging environments of many developing countries, neither does it anticipate any emerging scenarios and the required pragmatism. However, the findings of Hayter et al. (2011) – alluding to innovative practices in respect of the applications of collective bargaining and the role of stakeholders, provides an interesting trajectory for the chapter.

Accordingly, the socio-economic and cultural underpinnings have significant bearing on all forms of employee participation. For example, the majority of HR practitioners interviewed confirm that addressing employee demands outside of the collective agreements is a normal occurrence. The study of Black (2005) alluding to the fact that countries with high individualistic tendencies will have relatively low collective bargaining coordination is relevant to this chapter. It highlights the importance of collective bargaining in a collectivist environment because this is the channel for making collective demands either as a result of collective bargaining or as an avenue to seek additional support.

Most collective agreements (from the primary sources) cover various employee benefits. The intention is to demonstrate the commitment of the company in addressing various issues that are relevant to employment relationships. For example, it is common to indicate items such as utility, education support, housing loan, meal subsidy and vehicle loans (to name a few) in conditions of employment. This

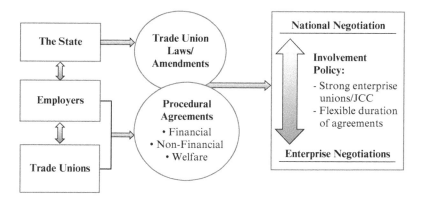

Figure 8.1   Employee participation model

strong paternalistic approach to management helps to explain the reason the employee views the employer as an extension of family (Opute, 2010). Building on this assertion, a significant percentage of HR practitioners (out of 227 participants) who attended the HR Expo Africa Summits (2016, 2017 and 2018) support welfare needs and the applicable cultural factors as captured in Figure 8.2. This has provided the basis for the employee participation model as depicted in Figure 8.1. This model is based on the tripartite relations of employee participation in Nigeria, which is made up of the state, employer and the trade union. This tripartite relationship is governed by the respective labour laws and procedural agreements which form the basis of applicable negotiations. The latter is influenced by the existing involvement policy of the respective national trade unions or enterprise unions.

Accordingly, the discussions of the chapter extend beyond the broad connotation and juxtaposing of culture, theories, models and contents of collective agreements (which in themselves are instructive) but rather provides appropriate conceptualisation of collective bargaining in Nigeria as well as highlighting the associated employee orientation and the underlying expectations as sacrosanct. The framework of this finding is based on an earlier research (Opute, 2010) which captured employee attitude (Table 8.2) of some selected Nigerian companies with over 400 participants. This has been supported with a focused group questionnaire of HR practitioners during the HR Expo Africa Summits (2016, 2017 and 2018). The

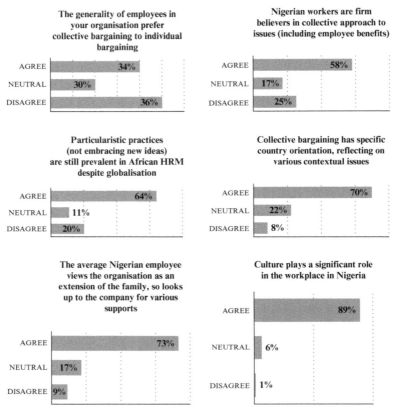

Source: Author's compilation, 2018.

Figure 8.2   HR survey: data analysis of participation

HR Expo Summit is a broad-based human resource platform that attracts a wide spectrum of HR practitioners and other professionals from the private, public and third-party sectors of the Nigerian economy to its annual vibrant and exciting hub of ideas, to shape the conversation on human capital development and organisational performance with special focus on new trends and dynamics. The survey findings illustrate the contextual variables that are paramount in the Nigerian workplace and highlights the importance of a symbiotic relationship which thus calls for a pragmatic approach to employee participation and the ensuing collective bargaining strategy.

Table 8.2   *Distribution of employee attitude – workforce participation*

Variables	N	Minimum	Maximum	Mean	Std deviation
Collective approach	415	1.00	5.00	3.9470	0.89393
Teamwork and solidarity	415	1.00	5.00	4.2265	0.76882
Dependence on employers	415	1.00	5.00	3.9446	0.96775
Assistance from employers	415	1.00	5.00	3.8482	1.04654
Relevance of employee representation	415	1.00	5.00	4.3952	0.71423
Teamwork cultural attribute	415	1.00	5.00	3.8361	0.95409
Self-negotiation	415	1.00	5.00	2.9253	1.29350
Valid N (list wise)	415				

Source: Author's compilation, 2018.

INSTITUTION OF COLLECTIVE BARGAINING: THE EVOLUTION

The institutional settings should aim to advance pro-labour policies and lower the threshold of national collective bargaining. Finally, collective bargaining should aim at the strengthening of the link between individual needs and the individual organisational relationship as a scenario, which once investigated thoroughly, becomes a pragmatic approach for the improvement of workforce participation and thus the sustenance of collective bargaining whether at the national or local level. Nevertheless, if the workforce 'understands the destination', they can 'endure the duration' of the journey and a win-win situation will emerge. The popular opinion of many HR practitioners is that the company is viewed as an extension of the family. This development unfortunately distracts the average business organisation from focusing on its core business.

This notion therefore reveals that whilst paternalism contributes to a co-operative atmosphere in the workplace, it is being encouraged by the failure of the state to provide adequate welfare and social services. Furthermore, the institutional setting requires 'consistent democracy' from the part of the state since the continued slow pace of regulatory posture of the state will inhibit the maturing of the relationship between the employers and trade unions. This apart, the continued 'flirting' of the state with trade unions (whether registered and/or unregistered) needs urgent addressing if indeed a partnership posture is to be established in the existing tripartite posture of labour relations in Nigeria. From the perspective of the employers, every effort to engage employees will enhance employee participation and ultimately a boost to collective bargaining or any other existing employee participation structures. An involvement policy does not obliterate formal collective bargaining mechanisms but could instead improve flexibility/symbiotic agreements particularly at the enterprise levels.

The sustenance of collective bargaining or any other participatory machineries in the workplace is driven by the broader Nigerian framework. The chapter therefore highlights significant contextual factors (collectivism, paternalism, welfare and evolving economy) and how they impact the system (culture and employee relations) in establishing a participation strategy which is the consequence of employee voice. It also highlights the challenges of the institutional settings as well as employee engagement as important 'ingredients' in the sustenance of collective bargaining.

Finally, apart from providing an enabling environment, which requires the institutional and employee engagement initiatives (from the state on the one hand, and the employer on the other hand), the sustenance of collective bargaining whether at the national or local level will require the pragmatic approach of all the actors in the employee relations system. In other words, we should end the search for the one 'right' collective bargaining strategy, but rather understand what in the context matters.

DISCUSSION AND CONCLUSION

Trade unions will continue to fight for relevance and the indications are that many governments will continue to prefer a formal voice for employees because labour market through laws and regulations can be better enforced to ensure economic growth and stability

Table 8.3 Evolution of collective bargaining/new scenarios and challenges

Focus	Pre-1970 era	Post 1970/early 2000	Post 2000/early 2010 era	Post 2010/early 2018 era
Procedural Agreement	Enterprise levels only	National levels only	National levels only	National levels/enterprise levels
Contents of collective bargaining	Enterprise levels Financial/non-financial benefits: – Salary ranges – Allowances – Benefits – Vehicle loans – Other welfare issues Discretionary matters: – Meal subsidy – Long service awards	National levels Financial: – Basic salary – Housing allowance – Transport allowance – Leave days/allowance – End of service benefits Non-financial: – Leave days/benefits – End of service terms Enterprise levels Financial: – Heat allowance – Inconvenience allowance – Vehicle loan – Death benefits Discretionary: – Laundry supplies – Meal subsidy – Long service awards	National levels Financial: – Like previous era Non-financial: – Like previous era Enterprise levels Additions: – Relocation allowance – Acting allowance Discretionary matters: – Laundry supplies – Meal subsidy – Long service awards	Developing scenarios: enterprise levels Involvement policies: – Welfare issues – Duration of agreement – Consultations – Non-direct financial issues Challenges: – Review of contents of procedural agreement – Strong JCCs

Table 8.3 (continued)

Focus	Pre-1970 era	Post 1970/early 2000	Post 2000/early 2010 era	Post 2010/early 2018 era
Duration of Agreements	Staggered/varied: – Tied down to various concluded agreements – Extenuating circumstance	National: – 2 years Enterprise: – Varied but not less than 1 year	National: – 2 years Enterprise: – Varied but not less than 1 year	Flexible/symbiotic
Re-Opener Clause	Mutual understanding: – Flexible	National/enterprise: – Extenuating circumstances	National/enterprise: – Extenuating circumstances	Flexible/symbiotic

Source: Author's compilation, 2018.

(Koçer and Hayter, 2011). The chapter supports this view albeit highlights the fact that workforce participation is embracing new scenarios.

Although numerous studies (Wood, 2010; Besamusca and Tijdens, 2015; Lamarche, 2015) highlight the importance of collective bargaining in the HR literature, there are limited literature and empirical studies that identify workforce cultural orientation as concomitant to workforce expectations in many developing economies. Neither do Western employment frames of reference represent appropriate theoretical paradigms for analysis of the socio-economic context inherent in employment relations in many developing economies (Khan and Ackers, 2004; Wood, 2010). The chapter also highlights the challenges of the institutional settings (such as lack of pro-labour policies, law providing social protection, expanding collective bargaining converges and lowering the threshold for collective agreements) as important 'ingredients' in the sustenance of collective bargaining (Koçer and Hayter, 2011).

The result of the empirical study reveals that a cultural characteristic, such as collectivism is significant in determining any participation structures. Although collective bargaining appears to be the most common means of participation in developing economies, there appears to be some new scenarios emerging. A significant conclusion of the chapter is that the cultural characteristics of collectivism and paternalism are very prominent in the workplace. First, teamwork and solidarity are highly valued across all job groups. Second, the collective approach is highly valued amongst the entire workforce, inclusive of trade union and non-union members. This cultural orientation therefore is deep-rooted in the belief and value systems of the employees (Opute, 2010).

In contrast, individualism is hardly practised by the average employee. The study has revealed that employees tend to maintain cohesion with their work groups. The recently amended Trade Unions Act 2005 that cancelled the automatic check-off system is a significant example. There are no records of individuals who have ceased to be financial members of trade unions in the workplace though they consider themselves non-members. Even when employees were required to contract out during the era of the automatic check-off system, there was also no record of employees contracting out of trade union membership. It is believed that the society frowns at individualism from every perspective.

One unique result of the study is that collectivism does not imply representation by the trade unions only. The even distribution of membership/non-membership of trade unions across the case study companies confirms this (Opute, 2010). However, the study, on the other hand, confirms relevance of employee representation in the workplace. This is not in any way a contradiction to non-union membership but does confirm the resilience of employee representation in the workplace. What therefore remains to be addressed is whether the trade unions will retain the central position in future collective bargaining efforts or processes.

One scenario could be a gradual reversion to strong house unions within the framework of the national trade unions but with increased listing of items for local collective bargaining. This approach, which can be termed an 'involvement policy', will improve creativity in the way in which organisations agree terms of collective bargaining. It will recognise the varying economic issues that each organisation faces together with any pertinent peculiarities. The play out of other cultural norms such as paternalism can be a tool for a co-operative existence in various organisations. The challenge will be a radical review of the procedural agreements (the document which identifies the matter for national and in-house negotiations at the respective trade groups) at the national levels – a move that may diminish the hold of the national unions in the short run but could be the required catalyst for change as captured in the emerging collective bargaining model.

Finally, this model highlights a strengthening of the link between individual needs and the individual organisational relationship as a scenario, which once investigated thoroughly, becomes a pragmatic approach for the improvement of workforce participation and thus the sustenance of collective bargaining whether at the national or local level.

REFERENCES

Adedigba, A. (2019) Nigerian government warns rival labour union, ULC, against strike. https://www.premiumtimesng.com/news/top-news/243317-ni gerian-govt-warns-rival-labour-union-ulc-strike.html (accessed 11 February 2019).

Adegbija, A. (2008) Features of language use in Yoruba tradition. PhD Thesis (University of Ibadan, Oyo Sate, Nigeria).

Adeleye, I. (2011) Theorising human resource management in Africa:

beyond cultural relativism, *African Journal of Business Management*, 5(6), pp. 2028–39.

Adetugbo, B. S. (1998) *Transformations: Thinking through Language*. London: Routledge.

Afangideh, U. (2012) Economic dualism: understanding monetary policy, *Central Bank of Nigeria Report*, Series 23.

Afinotan, L. A. and Ojakorotu, V. (2009) The Niger Delta crisis: issues, challenges and prospects, *African Journal of Political Science and International Relations*, 3(5), pp. 191–98.

Aycan, Z., Kanugo, R., Mendonca, M. M., Yu, K., Deller, J., Stahl, G. and Kurshid, A. (2006) Impact of cultural on human resource practices: a ten country study, *Applied Psychology; An International Review*, 49(1), pp. 192–21.

Ayittey, G. B. N. (1992) *Africa Betrayed*. New York: St. Martin's Press.

Banjo, A. (2007) An endonormative model for the teaching of English language in Nigeria, *International Journal of Applied Linguistics*, 3(2), pp. 22–43.

Besamusca, J. and Tijdens, K. (2015) Comparing collective bargaining agreements for developing countries, *International Journal of Manpower*, 36(1), pp. 86–102.

Black, B. (2005) Comparative industrial relations theory: the role of national culture, *The International Journal of Human Resource Management*, 16(7), pp. 1137–58.

Budhwar, P. S. and Debrah, Y. A. (2001) *Human Resource Management in Developing Countries*, 1st edn. London: Routledge.

Burgis, T. (2009) Legal bid to create a national champion, *Financial Times* (London 1st edn), 21 July 2009, p. 4.

Da Costa, G. (2009) *Nigeria's Oil Communities Blame Oil Industry for Misery*. https://www.voanews.com/english/2009-07-05voa18.cfm (accessed 6 July 2009).

Green, M. (2009) Grievances fuel region's sense of marginalisation, *Financial Times* (London 1st edn), 21 July 2009, p. 4.

Green, M. and Burgis, T. (2009) Vested interests block reform, *Financial Times* (London 1st edn), 21 July 2009, p. 1.

Hack-Polay, D. (2018) Compassionate investment? Diaspora contribution to poverty alleviation in Francophone West Africa, in D. Hack-Polay and J. Siwale (eds), *African Diaspora Direct Investment Establishing the Economic and Socio-cultural Rationale*. London: Palgrave Macmillan, pp. 87–109.

Hayter, S., Fashoyin, T. and Kochan, T. A. (2011) Review essay: collective bargaining for the 21st century, *Journal of Industrial Relations*, 53(2), pp. 225–47.

Hollingsworth, J. R. (2006) Advancing our understanding of capitalism with Niels Bohr's thinking about complementarity, in G. Wood and P. James (eds), *Institutions, Production and Working Life*. Oxford: Oxford University Press, pp. 62–82.

HR Expo Africa Summits (2016, 2017, and 2018) Available from https://hrexpoafrica.com/conferences/ (accessed 10 February 2019).

International Crisis Group (2015) Available from https://www.crisisgroup.
org/africa/west-africa/nigeria/curbing-violence-nigeria-iii-revisiting-niger-
delta (accessed 29 August 2017).

Iwuagwu, O. (2009) Import of Shell's agreement with the Ogoni, *Nigeria
Business Day* (Comment & Analysis), 21 June 2009, p. 11.

Javidan, M., Dorfman, P. W., de Laque, S. and House, R. J. (2006) In the eye
of the beholder: cross cultural lessons in leadership from Project Globe,
Academy of Management Perspectives, 20(1), pp. 67–91.

Kamoche, K. (2002) Human resource management in West Africa: practices and perceptions, *The International Journal of Human Resources
Management*, 13(7), pp. 993–7.

Kamoche, K. N., Debrah, Y. A., Horwitz, F. and Muuka, G. N. (2004)
Managing Human Resources in Africa. London: Routledge.

Kaufman, B. E. (2014) Explaining breadth and depth of employee voice
across firms: a voice factor demand model, *Journal of Labour Resources*,
35, pp. 296–319.

Khan, A. and Ackers, P. (2004) Neo-pluralism as a theoretical framework
for understanding HRM in sub-Saharan Africa, *International Journal of
Human Resources Management*, 15(7), 1330–53.

Koçer, R. G. and Hayter, S. (2011) Comparative study of labour relations
in African countries, AIAS Working Paper WP 116, University of
Amsterdam, Amsterdam.

Lamarche, C. (2015) Collective bargaining in developing countries, IZA
World of Labour 2015: 183.

Njoku, O. (2016) Oil pipeline vandalism and its effects on the socio -economic
development in Nigerian society, *International Journal of Multidisciplinary
Academic Research*, 4(4), pp. 47–60.

Nkomo, S. M. (2011) A postcolonial and anti-colonial reading of 'African'
leadership and management in organization studies: tensions, contradictions and possibilities, *Organization*, 18(3), pp. 365–86. DOI: https://doi.
org/10.1177/1350508411398731.

Obiegbu, I. (2016) Language and culture: Nigerian perspective, *African
Research Review*, 10(4) Serial No. 43, pp. 69–82.

Ojo, O. J. (1980) Nigeria and the formation of ECOWAS, *International
Organization*, 34(4), pp. 571–604.

Okpara, J. O. and Wynn, P. (2008) Human resource management practices
in a transition economy: challenges and prospects, *Management Research
News*, 31(1), pp. 57–76.

Omoruyi, O. (2000) *The Politics of Oil: Who Owns Oil, Nigeria, States or Communities?* https://www.nigerdeltacongress.com/particles/politics_of_oil.htm
(accessed 15 May 2009).

Opute, J. E. (2010) Compensation strategies and competitive advantages in
the globalised economy: Nigerian based study, PhD Thesis, January 2010
(London South Bank University, London, UK).

Population Review (2017) https://www.worldpopulationreview.com/countries/
Nigeria-population/ (accessed 29 August 2017).

Soule, B. G. and Obi, C. (2001) Prospects for trade between Nigeria and its neighbours, Paris: Organisation for Economic Co-operation and Development (OECD) Publications.

Walker, A. (2009) 'Blood oil' dripping from Nigeria. https://news.bbc. co.uk/1/hi/world/africa/7519302.stm (accessed 6 July 2009).

Wood, G. (2010) Employee participation in developing and emerging countries, in A. Wilkinson, P. J. Gollan, M. Marchington and D. Lewin (eds), *The Oxford Handbook of Participation in Organisations*. Oxford: Oxford University Press, pp. 552–69.

Xhafa, E. (2014) Trade unions and economic inequality: perspectives, policies and strategies, *International Journal of Labour Research*, 6(1), pp. 35–55.

9. Exploring 'Bundles' of Employment Practices: Culture, Language and Translation Perspectives

Susanne Tietze

The purpose of this edited book is to provide deep explanations and analysis of international comparative employee relations as they have been subject to enormous changes in a global epoch. While there is 'increased integration between countries' (see Chapter 1 in this volume) which is driven primarily by the liberalization of international trade, there are also cross-country variations of employee relations, which continue to exist. The existence of such different forces for either integration or for continued variation and difference makes for a dynamic and multifaceted field of inquiry. Brewster in Chapter 2 predicts a radically changed world of employment relations; a world which contemporary academics would find difficult to explore, capture, describe and analyse as it lacks the terminology to investigate crucial issues of work, for example in global value chains which fall outside the traditional (conceptual) territory of employment relations research. Likewise work gets 'moved around the world, and as it gets done by "the machines", employee relations will become a restrictive terminology' (Chapter 2: 54). Such considerations raise the question of what the future may bring in terms of useful approaches and ways of thinking about such radical and deep-reaching changes and how to understand and research them.

Comparative approaches to understanding ER are mainly based on national differences and develop awareness about how different systems of ER operate; however, they may not provide the depth of insights required to understand the intricacies of how and why employee relations change at micro levels of practice, nor are they able to capture the nuances of interactions that result at localities where such changes become enacted.

CULTURAL APPROACHES

In the past comparative cultural approaches, that is, etic approaches, looked at variances and co-variances of variables between (national) cultures, enabling some 'law-like' principles governing large numbers of people. Its main assumption is that there is something to compare as there must be similarities between (national) cultures and these are expressed as 'cultural dimensions'. Once these are established they provide a measurement tool to compare the relative importance of national cultural traits and their respective constellations. The most famous example is perhaps the school of thought initiated by Geert Hofstede (1980), where cultural dimensions are used to explain similarities and differences between different national systems. In this way of thinking, employee relations are part of national systems and subject to the same cultural difference and similarities as other institutional systems. In Chapters 7 and 8 it is shown how strong individualist (US) and strong collectivist (Nigeria) societal cultures both impact and reflect the constitution, laws and processes of employee relations and employee participation in them. Opute in Chapter 8 shows that employees in Nigeria have a strong collectivist orientation, which means that they are not always searching for freedom of association, but for recognition of their role not just as employees, but as having minds and hearts – one could say a quite 'holistic orientation' to how they wish to be viewed and treated. Yet, in Chapter 4 located in China and its different traditions of understanding and framing employee relations, employee relations and general workplace relations demonstrate that applying a label such as 'collectivist orientation' does not reach all possible interpretations and practices that can be associated with a collectivist mindset. Indeed, Chapter 4 serves as a good example where the semantic distance between meanings deriving from other localities and traditions is far removed from Chinese meanings, traditions and practices. Thus many Chinese words are left visible (i.e. untranslated) as there is simply not 'sufficiently good' equivalent expression in English to express the particular origin and meanings of the Chinese words and practices. In sum, the application of the cultural dimensions individualist and collectivist orientation are useful, but only if discussed in contexts rather than treated as 'absolute measurements'. Thus, what having a collectivist orientation means is contingent on a host of other influences, history and socio-political contexts being some of them. It could be argued that the dynamics and influences that shape enacted relationships situated in specific contexts would be better understood by embracing an emic approach. This means an approach focusing on the unique constellations at specific micro-settings, which shape ER workplace practices.

The comparative approach is a useful starting point, though it could be argued that it does not capture the dynamic nature of how contexts, agents, ideas and systems interact in multifaceted ways. In order to understand such dynamics, it is possible to turn to language and translation as phenomena as well as concepts to parse in particular the micro processes through which change unfolds. While the influence of national culture is by now an established and accepted aspect of international comparative research, there are two further approaches which could usefully be incorporated into a research agenda for the future. These are 'languages' and 'translation'. I provide now a brief overview about their reception by different academic communities, which are engaging with international research in a global world.

LANGUAGES AND TRANSLATION

Languages (as in the English language, the Italian language etc.) have been discovered as an interesting phenomenon within international business and management research, where situations and developments in 'typical' international business contexts such as cross-border mergers and acquisitions were investigated from a languages perspective. Conceptually, these researchers in this field decoupled language from culture (Brannen et al., 2014) and focused on the use of language in situated contexts. Here, it was shown, for example, that language diversity and how it is managed impacts strongly not only on the flow of communications and the sharing of knowledge, but equally on the exercise of control and coordination in particular in multinational corporations (Marschan-Piekkari et al., 1999), on the enactment of HRM functions (Marschan-Piekkari et al., 1999), on the group coherence and trust relationships in dispersed global teams

(Hinds et al., 2014; Tenzer et al., 2014) and on contemporary identity constructions in different sections of the MNC (Vaara et al., 2005), which included the evocation of past political–historical relationships. For this school of inquiry, a focus on language and language diversity also included a critical engagement with the role of English as a lingua franca of management knowledge (Steyaert and Janssens, 2013; Tietze, 2018) and its limitations to express knowledge and meaning that is coded in different language systems. In this regard, this group of scholars has made the English language itself subject to its enquiry. As quoted in the introductory chapter: '. . . linguistic standardisation due to the universal use of English is not always matched by a similarity of structure and functions' (Tiraboschi, 2003: 192). Chapter 4 is a prime example of this statement as cultural heritage, communist ideologies and the influx of ideas and practices from market economies contribute to a multifaceted understanding and practice of industrial relations. To understand such a multitude of different labels and practices is described by Xi as a 'quite complicated thing'. A complication which led him to choose a strategy of foreignization, that is, leaving visible 'difference' in the form of Chinese words as a means to document the existence of difference in employee and industrial relations concepts and regimes.

The term 'translation' became more widely spread within organizational research in the 1990s with a significant contribution being made by Scandinavian institutional scholars (Boxenbaum and Strandgaard Pedersen, 2009; Czarniawska and Joerges, 1996; Czarniawska and Sevón, 1996, 2005; Sahlin-Andersson and Engwall, 2002). The notion of translation which has been adopted captures processes of change and transformation. Boxenbaum and Strandgaard Pedersen (2009: 190–91) state that translation refers to the 'modification that a practice or an idea undergoes when it is implemented in a new organizational context'. Thus, a translation lens could be used to understand how and why ideas and practices change when they are adopted in a local context. This adoption is done by local actors, who remain embedded in the local context, its systems, traditions and values, and frequently these agents are assumed to be managers, though they could equally be trade union officials, workplace representatives or members of the local workforce. Yet, the role of these actors, that is, trade unionists or trade union members, is less well explored or understood (Cassell and Lee, 2016) in how they relate to new and incoming ideas and make them happen through translation. Cassell and Lee (2016) provide a longitudinal narrative analysis of the travel of a trade union idea (here: learning representative initiative) and how it required distinctive trade union translation work. Questions that this kind of approach – in contrast to a more comparative approach – can answer are: 'How do the relationships between different stakeholder groups and translators influence how the idea is edited? How do different translators negotiate the meaning and purpose of the idea? And how does the nature of these idea change through translation? (Cassell and Lee, 2016: 1087). In other words, adopting this metaphorical approach to translation unearths the nature of a dynamic process that is relational and changes the very idea (or practice) itself.

It is interesting to note that Whittall and Trinczek, in leaning on Streeck and Thelen (2005) in Chapter 6, describe the German work council as a 'regime', which is governed by rules that are locally enacted as the history of a plant creates 'an internal understanding of what is acceptable behavior … and interaction norms'. The notion of the work councils as regime is built, amongst other, on the existence of conflict, as members of institutions fill such bodies with life. This take on work councils as regimes of organically evolving local practices is as much an outcome of historical factors as of local enactments. Thus, a conceptual take on comparative employee relations based on regimes of 'practice' is advocated as a means to un-lock the complexities of work council's operations and to move beyond mere description. As an intriguing point Whittall and Trinczek state that the leading works using and developing this particular conceptual take have been published in German and have not been translated into English. A clear case, where translation is needed in order to share knowledge more effectively.

There are two take-aways from this chapter and these observations: in order to research bundles of practices, it is necessary to focus investigative effort on the micro processes at organizational and institutional levels. Once particular practices have been identified and vocabulary to describe them has been coined, it becomes possible to 'compare' then with either comparative elements of the same study or with available other sources and their findings.

The approach used by Cassell and Lee is quite similar to the approach advocated by Scandinavian Institutional scholars, as they are too concerned with exploring what happens when a 'practice' (or a regime of practices) begins to travel around the globe, rather than adopting a comparative approach. It is reasonable to assume, that such travel of ideas and practices needs to entail considerations of interlingual translation – as if it does not happen, knowledge is not shared. The employed definition of translation as a descriptor for change does not engage with the linguistic character of translation from a source text/context to a target text/context; that is, it uses translation in a metaphorical sense, rather than an interlingual one. It has been argued and shown that interlingual translation is, in particular in contexts of incoming change, a useful focus for research projects as acceptance, resistance and adoption of the incoming new idea/practice can be traced through focusing on the interlingual translation work undertaken by local agents. For example, a recent study by Ciuk et al. (2018) focuses on the interlingual translation work of a group of managers in the context of an incoming idea/practice (from US Headquarters) to a Polish subsidiary, where the new change programme needs to be literally and metaphorically translated. They show that struggles, exchanges, meaning-making and discussion over how to translate particular words and texts from US English into Polish is a situated, political–historical micro practice, through which cultural adoption and domestication is achieved. Thus, they take interlingual translation as their conceptual point of departure to generate insight into the micro negotiations.

Likewise, investigations into the change and reception of ideas from international employee relations could equally be investigated through a language and translation lens. An example provided in Chapter 3 relates to Hyman (2005) and that translating *shop steward* (a union representative appointed by members in the workplace) into French is complicated as no equivalent exists in how employee relations are practiced in France. Similarly, in Chapter 3 it was also discussed how three employee participation models and their respective vocabulary and technical terms, reveals complex historical genesis, reflection of social-political differences, and an underlying deeper significance for each of the three countries (Germany, UK, USA). It was also demonstrated how legal changes (the example given was *gangmaster* and the Italian *caporali*) make a difference in how a role and practices are either embedded in the law or remain illegal – pointing to a potential for misunderstandings and irritations if such difference in meaning becomes hidden in the translation process. Manzella (Chapter 5 in this volume) offers a detailed analysis of the genesis and use of the words *gangmaster* (English) and *caporali* (Italian); he provides the historical background on how these terms came to be interpreted in different ways and are now either considered to be illegal activity, punishable by law in Italy or have become integrated into the legal structures as in the UK. By leaving translation decisions of these two terms visible in the text, he follows what is called a 'foreignization strategy' of writing, whereby one leaves visible the 'foreign' aspects of one's thoughts and themes.

In the example selected by Manzella, a comparative approach between the different meanings of the terms *gangmaster* and *caporali* works well as it enables this author to reveal the historical dimensions of how these terms were integrated into different legal systems; which in turn could lead to misinterpretations as *gangmaster* has become a misnomer, expressing the opposite meaning to *caporali*. Thus, detailed translation work, including providing historical details as relevant to the employment practices of *gangsters/caporalis*, are used in this chapter to make a case for combining language/translation work to parse this employment practice and to explain where the differences in meaning and cultural connotations come from.

This is a useful approach to develop as it reveals that some key vocabulary does not translate easily from one language to another and, for example, in classrooms the reasons for this could be established and debated. Likewise, research projects relating to how workforces from these three different institutional systems enact their understanding of 'voice' when in collaborative contexts, for example, will provide additional depth in how pre-understandings are enacted and potentially re-negotiated.

CONCLUSION: FROM COMPARISON OF SYSTEMS TO THE TRAVEL OF PRACTICES

In a global epoch difference and similarities between ER systems have been explored from a comparative perspective. This is a useful point of departure to understand the diversity of practices, perspectives and underpinning ideologies that exist and likewise this approach enables the establishment of differences between systems and practices. However, these approaches could usefully be supplemented by a focus on the dynamics of what happens when ideas and practices travel around the globe and how localities, traditions and different meanings inform the existence of variance and differences between them. Therefore, it is advocated that a useful focus for future inquiry could be on the 'travel of bundles of ER practices', how and why they change, under whose agency and how vocabularies (in translation) are used to achieve this. Taking a dynamic, relational approach instead of a strongly comparative one, this approach enables investigations into the complexities that occur in local contexts. Translation and language work form part of interactions and relationships through which bundles of employment relational practices are understood and performed.

A useful focus of research into global employment relations could be developed by drawing more attention to the language- and translation-related aspects of practice. This has been successfully done in some chapters of this book. Such approaches, however, can only be developed if 'language' (or language diversity) is no longer taken for granted and integrated as a topic into research projects. Likewise, translation needs to be seen not as a mechanistic, automatic act, but inextricably linked to data analysis and interpretation (Xian, 2008).

In Chapter 2 some possible future scenarios and contexts are described for which the contemporary IR or ER scholarship has not yet developed the conceptual tools to engage with; situations and scenarios of employment relations that escape the scholarly gaze as they fall outside the conceptual scope of how ER/IR scholarship frames. Brewster in Chapter 2 points out that 'Words cannot always be translated directly or exactly into other languages' and words always come with a background and meaning and have implications. One wonders, for example, how English is used by people living outside their home country, 250 million according to the United Nations in 2017, and only a small percentage is the global elite, able to access English to gain information, share knowledge and create opportunity for themselves. The majority of people will be economic migrants, or people displaced by natural disaster, climate change, political oppression or war, as Brewster points out. These people come with less 'access to English', but equipped with local languages and some equipped with the ability to translate between different worlds. Understanding what their 'bundle of practices and experiences' are remains a challenge for all social science fields.

Some academic fields, for example, accounting, international business, organization studies scholars have begun to turn to translation and language to come to terms with the multifaceted nature of practices and meanings as they are generated and change in an ongoing and interrelated dynamic. These include situations where dominant logics are challenged, for example as documented in Chapter 1, where Ryanair was forced to recognize trade unions or where Google's 'benign individualism' is disputed by staff walkouts. One wonders, how English as the language used by pilots was part of expressing active solidarity across language borders and how perhaps translation was also drawn upon to achieved shared visions and goals. Here, a focus on the micro setting and understanding language and translation as situated practices is useful to understand how the tensions of globalization are enacted in sometimes surprising ways.

Some approaches provided in this book, some themes provided in this book, some observations and insights provided in this book may well be part of the process through which new conceptual impetus is achieved. For example, the deliberate choice of leaving translation visible (Chapter 3) is a 'foreignization strategy' in terms of text and knowledge production. Most of the chapters in this book are informed by this approach, rather than by 'domestication strategies' of writing whereby difference is hidden and becomes subsumed within the English language. In Chapter 3 it is stated that contemporary knowledge about the 'bundles of regimes and practices' is not yet translated and that important insights that may assist the advancement of employment and industrial relations cannot be shared.

Ironically, this points to the importance of English as a shared language of knowledge, while simultaneously evoking the notion of translation as an always precarious and incomplete project. This is so, as 'bundles of practices' are historically grounded and situated in traditions as well as experiences – all of which do not translate all that easily.

From both a pedagogic and research perspective, it could be argued that comparative approaches could include comparing specific vocabulary, for example, the word *Betriebsrat* (English: work council) and how it translates, if at all, into other languages. Students and researchers could take this exercise as a point of departure to become sensitized to differences in meaning and practice, and also where they originate from. From thereon, comparison leads to discussions and explorations of uniqueness, which fold back into shared understanding through publications and exchanges facilitated through the two main global communicative sources we have got at our disposal: English and Translation. The pressures to publish in English-speaking journals almost exclusively have set undue constraints to the generation and exchange of knowledge (Tietze, 2018), leading to erroneous assumptions of attributing the English language with universal powers of expression, an assumption that is as much misguided as it is wrong (Wierzbicka, 2014).

REFERENCES

Boxenbaum, E. and Strandgaard Pedersen, J. (2009). Scandinavian institutionalism: a case of institutional work. In T. B. Lawrence, R. Suddaby and B. Leca (eds), *Institutional Work: Actors and Agency in Institutional Studies of Organization*. Cambridge: Cambridge University Press, 178–204.

Brannen, M. Y., Piekkari, P. and Tietze, S. (2014). The multifaceted role of language in international business: unpacking the forms, functions and features of a critical challenge to MNC theory and performance, *Journal of International Business Studies*, 45(5), 495–508.

Cassell, C. and Lee, B. (2016). Understanding translation work: the evolving interpretation of a trade union idea, *Organization Studies*, 38, 1085–106.

Ciuk, S., James, P. and Sliwa, M. (2018). Micropolitical dynamics of interlingual translation processes in an MNC subsidiary, *British Journal of Management*, doi 10.1111/1467-8551.12323.

Czarniawska, B. and Joerges, B. (1996). Travels of ideas. In B. Czarniawska and G. Sevón (eds), *Translating Organizational Change*. Berlin: de Gruyter, 1–17.

Czarniawska, B. and Sevón, G. (1996). *Translating Organizational Change*. Berlin: de Gruyter.

Czarniawska, B. and Sevón, G. (2005). *Global Ideas. How Ideas, Objects and Practices Travel in the Global Economy*. Copenhagen: Liber & Copenhagen Business School Press.

Hinds, P. J., Neeley, T. B. and Cramton, C. D. (2014). Language as a lightning rod: power contests, emotion regulation, and subgroup dynamics in global teams, *Journal of International Business Studies*, 45(5), 536–61.

Hofstede, G. (1980). *Culture's Consequences*. London: Sage.

Hyman, R. (2005). Words and things: the problem of particularistic universalism, in J-C. Barbier and M. Letablier (eds), *Comparaisons internationales des politques sociales, enjeux epistemologiques et methodologiques/Cross-National Comparison of Social Policies: Epistemological and Methodological Issues*. Brussels: Peter Lang, 191–208.

Marschan-Piekkari, R., Welch, D. and Welch, L. (1999). In the shadow: the impact of language on structure, power and communication in the multinational, *International Business Review*, 8, 421–40.

Sahlin-Andersson, K. and Engwall, L. (2002). *The Expansion of Management Knowledge: Carriers, Flows and Sources*. Stanford, CA: Stanford University Press.

Steyaert, C. and Janssens, M. (2013). Multilingual scholarship and the paradox of translation and language in management and organization studies, *Organization*, 20, 131–42.

Streeck, W. and Thelen, K. (2005). *Beyond Continuity: Institutional Change in Advanced Political Economies*. Oxford: Oxford University Press.

Tenzer, H., Pudelko, M. and Harzing, A.-W. (2014). The impact of language barriers on trust formation in multinational teams, *Journal of International Business Studies*, 45(5), 508–35.

Tietze, S. (2018). Multilingual research, monolingual publications: management scholarship in English only? *European Journal of International Management*, 12(1–2), 28–45.

Tiraboschi, M. (ed.) (2003). *Marco Biagi: Selected Writings*. The Netherlands: Kluwer Law International.

Vaara, E., Tienari, T. J., Piekkari, R. and Säntti, R. (2005). Language and the circuits of power in a merging multinational corporation, *Journal of Management Studies*, 42(3), 595–623.

Wierzbicka, A. (2014). *Imprisoned in English. The Hazards of English as a Default Language*. Oxford: Oxford University Press.

Xian, H. (2008). Lost in translation? Language, culture and the roles of translator in cross-cultural management research, *Qualitative Research in Organizations and Management: An International Journal*, 3(3), 231–45.

Index